020603

8.99

DISCOVERING SUICIDE

DISCOVERING SUICIDE

Studies in the Social Organization of Sudden Death

J. Maxwell Atkinson

© J. Maxwell Atkinson 1978

First published 1978 by
THE MACMILLAN PRESS LTD
London and Basingstoke
Associated companies in Delhi
Dublin Hong Kong Johannesburg Lagos
Melbourne New York Singapore Tokyo

Printed in Great Britain by
UNWIN BROTHERS LTD
Woking and London

British Library Cataloguing in Publication Data

Atkinson, J Maxwell
  Discovering suicide
  1. Suicide
  I. Title
  364.1'522   HV6545

  ISBN 0-333-21915-5

'Being unable to find an example of suicide that cannot be explained by Durkheim's theories, I cannot but be convinced of their validity.'

'Durkheim's analysis is extremely convincing. After reading his book, one tends to think of various situations in which suicide could occur, and always it will fit in with his theory.'

Extracts from essays by first-year sociology students

Contents

Tables and Figures

Preface

The research reported in this book was originally written up as a thesis for a Ph.D. in Sociology at the University of Essex. Other research and teaching committments meant that it always had to be done as part-time venture, which is one reason why it took about seven years to complete. Another is that the work was started in the late 1960s at a time when the theoretical and methodological turmoils which have characterized the last decade of sociology were beginning to have widespread influence in Britain. The emergent debates posed new and difficult challenges for empirically oriented researchers so that, having begun with an almost total lack of awareness that there might be serious problems with traditional positivist research procedures, I developed during the present work a commitment first to symbolic interactionism and second to ethnomethodology. While such changes in orientation clearly involve taking theoretical writings seriously, I started with and retained a certain scepticism about the kind of abstract sociological theorizing which abounds with criticisms and suggestions about empirical research without showing any sign of being based on attempts to resolve the problems at first hand. I like to think, therefore, that the transition from positivism through interactionism to ethnomethodology described in this book was influenced at least as much by the attempts to explore theoretical ideas in empirical settings as by reading about the competing theories themselves. To this extent, then, it can be read as a chronicle of one empirical researcher's attempts to come to terms with the theoretical developments which were taking place in the discipline while the research was being done.

There is another sense in which the book may be seen as a reflection of (or perhaps a reaction against) contemporary developments in professional sociology. For it is arguable that the dominant British response to the availability of competing paradigms has been to talk *about* them rather than to try working *within* them. Such a trend was probably inevitable given the way academic life in Britain is structured and the rapid growth of sociology during the late 1960s. Compared with, for example, the situation in American universities, there is much less scope for British academics to get the amount of time away from teaching that is needed to engage in extensive empirical work. This may not matter too much as far as survey research is concerned, as the time-consuming work of data collection and analysis can be conveniently passed on to assistants and other agencies, but the kinds of unstructured observational studies called for by some perspectives are much less amenable to such delegation. In selecting examples of empirical studies to illustrate different approaches for their students, therefore, teachers have to rely heavily on the work of others, so that the ever-present and sometimes only option as far as their own research output is concerned is to tidy up lecture notes for publication as synthesizing texts. This temptation, furthermore, was added to greatly by the demand for textbooks that was created by the massive expansion of sociology in British higher education.

The point of these remarks is to prepare the way for a confession that the present book was originally conceived of as two separate studies. The first was to have been a literature review/personal essay on the sociology of suicide, and the second an empirical thesis/monograph. The beginnings of the former project have survived in Chapter 2 of the present volume, which was intended to provide a version of what it is about suicide that sociologists have found interesting. Having got that far, however, I found I could no longer distinguish satisfactorily between the two enterprises, as my views on the suicide literature were so closely bound up with a very particular empirical problem which underpinned so much of the research on suicide by sociologists and others, namely the status of the data used in testing hypotheses. Indeed, it was not until I had redefined the project as a single and more limited one that I was able to continue writing beyond Chapter 2 and, while it was originally prepared with the literature review project in mind, it has nevertheless been retained more or less intact. For one thing, it provides some kind of a warrant for not giving too much attention to the issues which sociological researchers into suicide are normally expected to attend to (e.g. anomie; the dispute between sociological and psychological modes of explanation; etc.). And more generally my hope is that the discussion of 'The Suicide Problem in Sociology' will give student and non-sociological readers some clarification of the character of sociologists' interest in suicide.

My main regret about the book is that the journey through the perspectives does not extend further than it does into the final one, so that it may be open to the complaint that it is no more than yet another programmatic statement on behalf of ethnomethodology. Against this, however, I would note first that some of the analyses, which were done even before the final transition, were carried out (albeit unwittingly) in a style which is just about recognizable as ethnomethodology of the pre-conversational analysis era. Second, I would like to think that it both differs from and complements more abstract programmatic writings by describing an empirical route to ethnomethodology which has not previously been documented in detail. Thus, I have tried to elaborate as clearly as I am able how the empirical research not only was guided by interpretations of the competing perspectives, but also prompted reassessments and new commitments. And a possible lesson in all this may be that attempts to work naïvely within a particular paradigm can be just as convincing and satisfying a way of discovering strengths and weaknesses as purely theoretical exegesis. Finally, to the extent that the research was heavily influenced by the interactionist literature on the sociology of deviance, the direction taken as a way forward from labelling theory contrasts markedly with the dominant post-interactionist tendencies, particularly in Britain, which have been quick to dismiss ethnomethodology in favour of a variety of macro-structural-radical alternatives. In this particular area, then, there is arguably a special case even for abstracted programmatics which give voice to a dissenting view, and this work will hopefully make a small contribution towards redressing the balance away from the new conventional wisdoms about deviance.

The slow pace of the work, coupled with the fact that it was done in three universities, has meant that I have discussed various parts of it with more people than is perhaps usual in ventures of this sort. Those who have encouraged me will mostly know who they are and if they are not aware of my gratitude to them, I thank them now. Of those deserving special mention, Terence Morris did me a great service by sparking off the initial interest in official statistics in a seminar at the London School of Economics. Alasdair MacIntyre, my supervisor for the first couple of years or so, then gave me the opportunity to pursue it by hiring me as his research assistant and, had he not taken my ill-formulated ideas seriously, the research would almost certainly never have got off the ground. For this and the ongoing stimulation which is a feature of regular encounters with him I shall always be grateful. During the transition to interactionism, Dorothy Smith was a constant source of help and encouragement and, after her departure from Essex to North America, similar sub-cultural support was provided by the regular contact with friends at meetings of the National Deviancy Conference, and particularly with Phil Strong, Mike Hepworth and Margaret Voysey. The transition to ethnomethodology was greatly eased by Rod Watson, to whom my debts of gratitude cannot readily be documented. The final stage of writing up the research coincided with Harold Garfinkel's stay at Manchester as Simon Visiting Professor and, without his sympathetic encouragement, I might well have scrapped the whole project on the grounds that the kind of work I was doing had been superseded by the emergence of conversational analysis within ethnomethodology. Of those who read and commented on the book when it was still a thesis, I am particularly grateful to Colin Bell, Stan Cohen, Gordon Horobin, Jeff Coulter and John Heritage for being encouraging about publication, even though not all of them agreed with the general thrust of the argument.

The empirical materials could not have been gathered without the help and co-operation of coroners, policemen and others who must remain anonymous. My gratitude to them and my high regard for their competence as theorizers will hopefully be evident in what follows. One who can be mentioned is Dr Charles Clark who, as Essex County Coroner, played an important part in initiating suicide research at his local university by offering to make his records available for researchers there. I took advantage of his offer and also of his willingness to talk more generally about his work, and for this I am very grateful.

I must also record my thanks to the University of Lancaster for granting me a term's study leave which enabled me to get on with some of the fieldwork and writing. Parts of my research were also made possible by the award of Social Science Research Council Grant HR 1496/1 'Community Reactions to Deviance'. I am also grateful to Penny Anson and Margaret Whittall for surviving the task of typing so morbid a manuscript. Without the constant support and encouragement of my wife the project would certainly never have been completed and, in addition to the things wives are normally commended for in prefaces, I am particularly thankful to mine for not being a sociologist. Her lay member's scepticism about the discipline has continually kept me on my toes.

MAXWELL ATKINSON

Acknowledgements

Some of the material in Chapter 3 was originally published in 'Status Integration, Suicide and Pseudo-Science', in *Sociology*, 7 (1973) pp. 251–64. Some of that in Chapter 4 first appeared in 'On the Sociology of Suicide', in *Sociological Review*, 16 (1968) pp. 83–92, and was also reprinted in A. Giddens (Ed.), *The Sociology of Suicide* (London, Frank Cass, 1971). Parts of Chapters 5 and 6 were previously included in 'Societal Reactions to Deviance: The Role of Coroners' Definitions', in S. Cohen (Ed.), *Images of Deviance* (Harmondsworth, Penguin Books, 1971) pp. 165–91. Some of the interview data quoted in Chapter 5, 6 and 7 were derived from a programme prepared for the Open University's course 'Sociological Perspectives' (BBC. Radio 3).

I am indebted to all these sources for permission to reprint the materials in question.

PART I

Suicide and Sociology

Chapter 1
Background and Introduction to the Research

Although a concern with the nature and validity of data derived from official sources is now part of the conventional wisdom of the sociology of deviance, it was still possible in the late 1960s to be asked in a graduate course on the subject to prepare an essay on 'How Much Deviance is There?'[1] The question was designed to set the scene for an introductory seminar by providing a generalized summary of the relative numerical importance of various different types of deviance. After volunteering to do the paper, I was instructed to consult various official statistical publications as well as textbooks on deviance and to report on the 'size and shape' of problems such as crime, mental illness, suicide, alcoholism, drug addiction, etc. On turning to the recommended sources, it struck me as obvious that, to varying degrees, they only told part of the story. It was also obvious that, apart from the occasional reference to the 'dark number problem', sociologists seemed singularly unconcerned by the problematic nature of the figures and were not at all inhibited about making far-reaching generalizations on the basis of crime rates, suicide rates and the like. I therefore prepared a paper which outlined the kinds of reportage problems that seemed to be present with respect to each of the types of deviance I had been asked to consider, in an attempt to provide a reasoned case to the effect that the question could not be answered given the present state of knowledge about the inclusiveness or otherwise of the various statistics. Had my efforts met with even a moderately interested or favourable reception, my interest in the matter would probably have ended there and then. It was, however, received with considerable displeasure, and I was accused of not answering the question and of discussing mundane problems which were well enough known to sociologists anyway.

The nature of that response, coupled with the kind of research I was engaged in at that time, served only to confirm me in the view that there was something strange about the willingness of sociologists and criminologists to proceed to make generalizations in spite of known difficulties.[2] On the one hand research methods courses and textbooks urged methodological rigour via careful sampling procedures and the

like, and on the other such exhortations could, it seemed, be conveniently ignored when it came to the examination of substantive subject areas. At about the same time as this 'discovery', I had the chance
to prepare a research proposal on some subject which interested me.[3] I
had already realized that the scope of any study designed to explore the
accuracy of the official statistics would have to be limited at least to one
subject area and, for a variety of reasons, I proposed a study aimed at
an assessment of suicide statistics. Not only had all the sociological
research into suicide that I knew about been concerned with the
analysis of suicide rates, but it was also attractive because initially it
seemed to raise less complications than other possibilities. With crime,
for example, there were special difficulties peculiar to different crimes,
whereas suicide, I thought, was much more 'clear cut' and hence more
amenable to analysis. That assumption was not my only mistake at
that early stage, for I also thought that suicide would be an easier topic
for research because less seemed to have been written about it than
other sorts of deviance, and hence that a comprehensive survey of the
literature could be incorporated in the research.[4] Another reason for
choosing suicide was that someone I knew had recently attempted
suicide, and the concern and interest provoked by that had already led
to some preliminary reading on the subject. Finally, suicide had the attraction of having been a central interest to sociologists since
Durkheim's *Le Suicide* (1897) and Durkheim, of course, had relied
heavily on official statistics. This is not to say that my original intention
was to disprove or invalidate Durkheim's theory, but it was rather to
find a way of calculating 'more accurate' rates so that his hypotheses
could be retested with reference to 'better' data.[5]

1.2 CHANGES IN DIRECTION AND PROBLEMS OF PRESENTATION

As will be apparent from the above, the initial interest which led to this
research was naïvely 'positivist' in character. My concern was almost
exclusively with the problem of the *accuracy* of the statistics, which, with
the accompanying assumption that there is some *real* suicide rate to
which the official rate approximates, meant that the problem at issue
was the closeness of that approximation. That suicide was in principle
explainable and that there was nothing wrong with the Durkheimian
model other than the possible errors in the data he used were similarly
not seriously questioned at that early stage. The research began, then,
with a survey of the literature on suicide, which involved noting any
reference to possible errors and the nature of those errors with a view to
designing some empirical study which would enable their seriousness
to be assessed. At the same time, I began reading in the sociology of
deviance more generally with a view to noting any similar clues from
studies of other kinds of deviance. Very soon I encountered the writing

of Becker (1963; 1964), Lemert (1951) and other protagonists of the interactionist approach to deviance, and it became clear that their focus
on the labelling process, societal reactions and so on was crucially relevant to my interest. In addition, their work provided a more clearly
defined theoretical base for what had to that point seemed something of
an eccentric obsession with an obsure empirical issue.[6] The transition
to interactionism came fairly easily, for the approach had not only involved an explicit concern with and critique of traditional sociological
interpretations of official statistics, but also their conclusions seemed to
point to more interesting research than the rather narrow technical
focus involved in the original formulation of the problem.

With the discovery of an article, and subsequently a thesis by Jack D.
Douglas (1966; 1965), it seemed that the research I was proposing was
no longer necessary, for not only had he presented a detailed critique of
Durkheim by reference to ideas very close to those of the interactionists,
but he had also done an extended examination of the way in which
official statistics on suicide were constructed. Fortunately, there was an
alternative to my initial view that the research could be immediately
discontinued now that someone else had covered the same ground,
which was to be encouraged by the fact that one was not alone in one's
interest. After reading his thesis, then, I attempted to formulate a
model of the suicide process which was based on the different materials
I had encountered to that point, and which would provide for some empirical research to be done which might throw additional light on the
problems raised by Douglas and others (Atkinson, 1968). The subsequent publication of that and later papers (Atkinson, 1969; 1971;
1973), however, was partly responsible for the problems of presentation
referred to below.

After attempting a variety of research strategies, some of which are
reported in Part II of the book, problems began to emerge which raised
doubts about Douglas's work on suicide and the varieties of interactionist approaches to deviance more generally. Not only did it seem
that there were errors in Douglas's treatment of the way definitions of
suicide are done, but his recommendations as to how social meanings
should be studied proved increasingly less useful as the research
proceeded. It was, furthermore, not clear from the interactionist or
other sociological literature what one should do next in the light of the
kinds of findings the research produced. There followed (just prior
to the final preparation of the book) a new look at the
ethnomethodological writings I had already known about, and further
reading of later and unpublished ethnomethodological materials.[7] As a
result of this, it was realized that ethnomethodology was not just
another type of 'labelling theory', but had apparently irreconcilable
differences with symbolic interactionism as well as with other sociology
of which the interactionists were also critical. In the way that this
difference was elaborated, it clarified the kinds of findings which had

been encountered and the troubles they had presented in a manner which seemed incompatible with other sociological writings. And, in addition to clarifying those difficulties, they seemed to have developed ways of doing sociology which could provide an answer to the otherwise unanswerable question posed by the research, namely that of 'what to do next'. A further discovery was that some of the work I had already done was closely concerned with interests central to ethnomethodology and might even have been represented as such with a slight change in terminology and in the works referred to in the footnotes (e.g. Atkinson, 1971).

The research reported in this book, then, followed a somewhat turbulent course which was very far from the normatively prescribed process of 'reading-research-writing up'. A closer approximation would be something like 'reading-writing-research-writing-research-writing-reading-research-writing', where some of the writings were published, some presented at conferences and some filed away, all of them ultimately being intended for inclusion in one volume. This kind of deviation in the idealized way in which research is supposed to happen is, at least according to Galtung (1969), not unusual, but from the point of view of completing a report on work done it poses serious problems of presentation which were made all the more difficult by the movement from positivism to interactionism to ethnomethodology which occurred during the research. Thus it emerged that what I had written during the research could not simply be joined together to provide the nucleus of a thesis or book, for not only did the papers tend towards repetition, but the fact that they were written at different times meant that they were also not consistent with one another in terms of the methodological presuppositions on which they were based. The alternative to this was to rewrite the research completely and, although this is what was done, it was not without its complications. The first danger was that the work might be reformulated and reassessed in the light of the position finally reached at the time of writing, so that much of the research that had been done would have to be excluded on the grounds that it could now be seen to have been misguided. I have reported on it nonetheless, and in so doing have attempted to preserve the logic of the research as I understood it at different stages in its development, even though I may now regard some of it as having been oversimplified or mistaken. Thus I have included parts of some published papers and have greatly extended one of them (Atkinson, 1971), which was distinctly lacking in empirical support when originally published. I have also criticized some of my earlier published formulations where this has seemed appropriate.

Although this approach may go some way to resolving the problems posed by having published papers on the research at different times over a period of years, it does pose a further problem, which is that the research may be portrayed as having developed in a more orderly and logical progression than was actually the case at the time. Here I can only hope that reference may be made to the published papers which, in so far as they can be seen as progress reports from different periods in the research, will provide a means of ascertaining how far any claims to a logical progression are justified. And the book as it now stands does involve such a claim by depicting the work as having developed steadily towards the ethnomethodological position elaborated in the final chapter. That this is so may appear to be yet another instance of reconstructed logic, but I hope it will emerge that there was an important sense in which the research did develop in stages towards this final resolution. Thus the topic originally chosen turned out to be one which had been already examined at some length from an interactionist perspective. In examining the various responses to the problem, those of Kitsuse and Cicourel (1963), Cicourel (1968) and Sudnow (1965) had seemed the most useful from the point of view of designing empirical research (see Chapter 3) and these writers, it emerged later, were ethnomethodologists and not the simple interactionists they are often presented as being. There were also serious empirical difficulties in the way of doing research along the lines suggested by those who advocated the use of a 'sequential model' (e.g. Becker, 1963) or an exclusive focus on social meanings (see Chapter 4). The initial search for an official definition of suicide, coupled with problems which arose out of early encounters with coroners, subsequently suggested that the question 'How do deaths get categorized as suicides?' was the most appropriate way of formulating the research question (see Chapter 5). And that question, it was to emerge later, was not unlike the kind of question an ethnomethodologist might have asked (see Chapter 8). Perhaps not surprisingly in view of that, the kinds of results obtained in trying to find an answer (Chapters 6–7) were later found to be consistent with some of the more important contentions of ethnomethodology.

Hopefully, then, the progression depicted in the following pages does reflect something other than the retrospective imposition of order on the research in the light of a current fad. This 'something other' could be that the continued efforts to design and do empirical research uncovered problems which were either not alluded to or which were inadequately solved in the more conventional responses to the phenomena of labelling and categorization. The attempt to overcome these may then have led to the formulation of a research question in quasi-ethnomethodological terms and to results consistent with that particular perspective. Implicit in this is a more general claim that obsessive empiricism can point to the need for a paradigm shift by generating findings which cannot be made sense of in any other way. In the present context, therefore, I have to hope that the ethnomethodological solution outlined in Chapter 8 does indeed follow on logically from the earlier discussion and analysis. Otherwise I am left in the curious position of having to hope that my findings were mistaken, given the gloomy implications they seem to have for further research in this area and possibly for sociology more generally.

Chapter 2
The Suicide Problem in Sociology

2.1 INTRODUCTION

Although it was noted in the previous chapter that sociological studies of suicide represent only a very small proportion of the mass of available literature on the subject, no attempt is made in the present work to provide a complete survey even of this small number of studies by sociologists. One reason for not doing this is that several such reviews are already available (e.g. in Douglas, 1967; Gibbs, 1966; Porterfield, 1968; Labowitz, 1968; Martin, 1968; Rushing, 1968; Maris, 1969), and there would seem little point in trying to add to or to compete with the extended treatments to which they have already been subjected. A further reason for avoiding the total literature review is that they tend to give the impression that researching the subject of suicide has been an important activity for sociology and that reports on such work that has been done are of interest to sociologists in some general way. The main theme of this chapter, however, is that such impressions are false and that sociological interest in suicide is best characterized as 'fascination from a distance'. The paradox is that it has been discussed by most major theorists, methodologists and text-book writers, it has to be confronted at one time or another (and often many times more than once) by almost all sociology students, and yet very few sociologists since Durkheim have become actively involved in suicide research. In Britain, for example, the only research monographs which are even remotely sociological have been written by non-sociologists (Sainsbury, 1955; Stengel, Cook and Kreeger, 1958; West, 1965), while professional sociological contributions have been almost totally confined to discussions of conceptual problems posed by the *prospect* of doing research (e.g. Giddens, 1966; Atkinson, 1968).

By concentrating on the ways in which suicide, and particularly Durkheim's *Suicide*, has been a problem in sociology, the discussion in this chapter is intended to clarify two related features of the remainder of the book. The first is the subsequent focus on an apparently narrow set of methodological concerns, and the second is the absence of any attempt to clarify, develop or direct research towards two of the general issues typically discussed by reference to suicide, namely the debate

between psychologism and sociologism (outlined in Section 2.4 below)
and functionalism and anomie theory (outlined in Section 2.5 below).
These omissions are justified, as I hope will become clear, on the
grounds that any serious interest in them is premature given the fundamental nature of the methodological problems posed by the debate
about positivism (outlined in Section 2.3 below).

2.2 DEFERENCE TO DURKHEIM

The most obvious and trite reason why Durkheim's *Suicide* 'seems to
have been an unfailing source of wonder to most sociologists' (Douglas,
1967, p. 13) is simply that it was written by Durkheim. For in the
development of a science, the substantive areas of enquiry studied by
those who later come to be regarded as 'founding fathers', or in Kuhnian terminology 'paradigm innovators' (Kuhn, 1962), are almost certain to attract the deferential attention of subsequent practitioners. But
this is hardly adequate in accounting for how *Suicide* came to occupy a
special place in sociology, and its special place in the development of
Durkheim's thought was probably much more important. Thus the essence of his conception of society and his approach to sociology had
been worked out earlier in *The Division of Labour in Society* (1954) and
The Rules of Sociological Method (1938), so that in *Suicide* and later in *The
Elementary Forms of Religious Life* (1954) Durkheim was seeking to
demonstrate the appropriateness of his ideas for the analysis of particular social phenomena. As the first of these attempts and as the one
chronologically closest to his earlier formulations, *Suicide* represents the
clearest and most explicit synthesis of his previous conclusions about
the nature of society and the nature of sociology. In other words, most
of what has been considered important about Durkheim's work is to be
found in *Suicide*, and Gibbs (1968, p. 7) is no doubt right to conclude
that 'had Durkheim investigated stuttering instead of suicide,
sociologists would have followed his lead no less diligently'. And in
making this observation, Gibbs draws attention to one of the main
reasons for the curious position of the suicide problem in sociology
referred to above, for it is the theoretical and methodological content of
Suicide which has fascinated generations of sociologists and *not* that
phenomenon which members of a society call 'suicide'.

We should not, however, be surprised that there has been more interest in the ideas expounded in Durkheim's classic monograph than in
the study of suicidal behaviour, for there are strong grounds for believing that this was precisely what Durkheim intended and hence that he
shared such an order of priorities. Thus the studies of pre-Durkheimian
works on suicide by Giddens (1965) and Douglas (1967) clearly show
that most of the 'facts' about suicide, which subsequent English-speaking sociologists have tended to regard as discoveries made by

Durkheim, were well known to him long before he came to write *Suicide*. The studies of suicide which had already been published by the moral statisticians (see the summary in Douglas, 1967, pp. 3–20) 'provided an abundant source of data which could be used to develop a systematic sociological analysis of suicide' (Giddens, 1965, p. 10). And quite apart from the convenience of applying his craft to easily accessible data, Durkheim's intellectual case against his contemporary psychologists was to benefit greatly from the apparent demonstration that even such a seemingly individual act such as suicide could be analysed sociologically. That Durkheim himself was concerned more with using suicide as a peg on which to hang pre-conceived ideas about society and sociology than with the phenomenon of suicide (Douglas, 1967, Chapter 2) finds support in his preface to *Suicide*, where he says:

> by such concentration [on suicide], real laws are discoverable which demonstrate the possibility of sociology better than any dialectical argument . . . by thus restricting the research, one is by no means deprived of broad views and general insights. On the contrary, we think we have established a certain number of propositions concerning marriage, widowhood, family life, religious society, etc., which, if we are not mistaken, are more instructive than the common theories of moralists as to the nature of these conditions or institutions [Durkheim, 1952, p. 37].

That his main interest is in broader social issues than suicide is further intimated in the passage immediately following this, where his choice of language implies a particular value position which will be referred to again later:

> There will even emerge from our study some suggestions concerning the causes of the general contemporary maladjustment being undergone by European societies and concerning remedies which may relieve it [ibid.].

And finally, Durkheim is quite explicit about his bid to show how *The Rules of Sociological Method* can be applied:

> in the course of this work, but in a concrete and specific form, will appear the chief methodological problems elsewhere stated and examined by us in greater detail [ibid.].

But to claim that suicide has been a problem for sociologists only in so far as one of the discipline's founding fathers presented an important statement of his central ideas in a book on the subject is to say very little about why so relatively few sociologists have engaged in suicide

research. Before suggesting why this might be, however, a brief statement of Durkheim's central theoretical propositions is in order.

Of the many available summaries of the logical structure of
Durkheim's theory of suicide, one of the clearest and most concise is the
schematic presentation in *Social Forces in Urban Suicide* by Ronald Marris
(1969), who writes on pp. 32–3:

> Having disposed of the extra social factors to his satisfaction,
> Durkheim proceeds to compound lower level generalizations of the
> 'greater than', or ordinal scale variety from his statistics. Some of the
> more important first level generalizations are listed below, roughly
> in the order of the appearance in *Suicide* (for the sake of brevity the
> symbol > is employed to mean 'tend to have a higher suicide rate
> than').
>
> h1. City dwellers > rural dwellers
> h2. The sane > the insane
> h3. Adults > children
> h4. Older adults > younger adults
> h5. In March through August people > in September through
>   February
> h6. In daytime people > in the night
> h7. Protestants > Catholics > Jews
> h8. Majority groups > minority groups
> h9. Upper social classes > lower social classes
> h10. The learned > the unlearned
> h11. Males > females
> h12. The unmarried > the married
> h13. The married without children > the married with children
> h14. Those in smaller families > those in larger families
> h15. Bachelors > widows
> h16. Those living in time of peace > those living in time of war
> h17. Soldiers > civilians
> h18. Elite troops > non-elite troops
> h19. Those whose society is experiencing an economic crisis >
>   those whose society is not experiencing an economic crisis
> h20. Those living in a period of rapid social change > those liv-
>   ing in a period of slow social change
> h21. The rich > the poor
> h22. The morally undisciplined > the morally disciplined
> h23. Divorcees > non divorcees.

Maris goes on to quote direct from *Suicide* (Durkheim, 1952, p. 208)
what he refers to as Durkheim's second-level hypotheses from which all
those listed above can be deduced:

> H1. Suicide varies inversely with the degree of integration of
>   religious society.

H2. Suicide varies inversely with the degree of integration of domestic society.

H3. Suicide varies inversely with the degree of integration of political society.

Finally, on the third level, Durkheim posits a grand hypothesis intended to subsume all previously mentioned hypotheses. This hypothesis (which is also a grand empirical generalization if we can assume that the previous hypotheses were true and that the determination of the common denominator of them were accurate) states that:

H. Suicide varies inversely with the degree of integration of social groups of which the individual forms a part [Maris, 1969, pp. 32–3].

Now although it might be argued that Maris has endowed Durkheim's theory with an even greater degree of logical consistency than Durkheim himself intended, his summary makes it easy to understand why generations of sociologists have returned to *Suicide* for proof that the social sciences really *are* capable of producing laws which are similar in form to those generated by natural scientists. Thus works on theory construction seldom fail to cite Durkheim's theory of suicide as an example of how it is to be done,[1] while methodological studies regularly go back to Durkheim for their illustrative material.[2] And, at another level, teachers of sociology still use *Suicide* in precisely the way Durkheim intended it, namely to demonstrate the social nature of even this seemingly psychological phenomenon and the appropriateness of attempting to explain it by reference to social factors.[3]

Post-Durkheimian studies of suicide by sociologists have on the whole been supportive of this view of *Suicide* as some sort of definitive sociological statement which has never been surpassed. In the first place it is noticeable how infrequently subsequent analyses are referred to in sociological studies not directly concerned with the subject of suicide, a situation which further supports the view that it was features of *Suicide* other than its substantive subject matter which has been the major focus of sociological fascination. Second, most of the subsequent research on suicide has taken Durkheim as the starting point before proceeding to use almost identical methods to generate more or less minor modifications to the central tenets of the master's original thesis. Thus one of the more recent examples of this sort of study is Maris's large-scale statistical survey of suicides in Chicago, at the beginning of which he notes that 'after 70 years . . . *Suicide* is still *the* sociological treatise on suicide' (Maris, 1969, p. 3). With one or two exceptions, his findings largely replicate those of Durkheim and his predecessors, and he ends up by arguing that the 'degree of external constraint' is a preferable conceptualization to Durkheim's 'degree of social integration' (ibid., pp. 183–9). This, together with the many other statistical studies which confirm most of the earlier findings, can also be seen in Kuhnian terms, with Durkheim cast as the 'paradigm innovator' and researchers like Maris being those who get down to the business of doing studies within the dominant paradigm in the ensuing period of 'normal science'. As had already been noted, however, this phase of sociological suicidology has lasted rather a long time.

Two studies of suicide by sociologists which have aroused rather more interest among professional colleagues not directly concerned with suicide research than is usual with post-Durkheimian analyses are those by Henry and Short (1954) and Gibbs and Martin (1964). The first of these was an attempt to incorporate the social psychological theory of frustration-aggression in the Durkheimian model, which tends towards a somewhat mechanistic model of aggression-venting according to class position, the working class being more likely to direct it towards others (homicide) and the middle class towards themselves (suicide). As will be seen later, this view of homicide and suicide as opposite sides of the same coin has parallels in English law, where suicide has been defined in the same terms as homicide with the victim as the self (see Chapter 5 below). As far as sociology is concerned, it can hardly be claimed that Henry and Short's work aroused a great deal of interest beyond the relatively restricted bounds of social psychology and the sociology of deviance, and even in these areas there appears to have been only limited interest. Similarly Gibbs and Martin's contribution, as far as the broader theoretical concerns of the discipline are concerned, has apparently had no more than a limited response, their notion of 'status integration' being of marginal interest to some writers on stratification[4] Gibbs and Martin criticize Durkheim for his sloppy operationalization of the concept of social integration, and then seek to improve on it by introducing the concept of 'status integration' which they claim is more readily operationalizable for the purposes of empirical testing. They begin by noting that people occupy many statuses. If the roles attached to these statuses do not conflict, then the statuses can be said to be integrated, but if they are in conflict with one another (i.e. not integrated), then a person may be expected to have problems and hence is more likely to commit suicide. Having elaborated this theory, Gibbs and Martin produce a vast number of rank order correlations in support of hypotheses derived from the theory. Not only do they use their data in a remarkably uncritical way, but, as is usual with almost all post-Durkheimian studies of suicide, it is nowhere spelled out precisely how the independent variable (be it social integration, status integration, lack of external restraint, or whatever) is linked with the dependent variable (suicide rates). In other words, a characteristic feature of such works and indeed of *Suicide* itself is the failure to explain why suicide in particular, rather than some other course of action, is a likely consequence of the particular structural condition posited as the independent variable. Indeed, even though Gibbs and Martin singularly fail to provide for how suicide rather than something else results from the lack of status integration, Gibbs himself has nevertheless criticized Durkheim for the same kind of failure: 'Note, however, that Durkheim's argument may apply to practically all forms of deviant behaviour' (Gibbs, 1966, p. 285).

Although the studies of suicides by English-speaking sociologists referred to so far may have had little impact on mainstream sociology compared with *Suicide,* an important paper by Giddens (1965) would seem to suggest that the suicide problem *per se* had greater prominence in French sociology. On careful reading, however, it emerges that the way in which the 'suicide problem' was handled by French sociologists was not very different from the approach that I have suggested has predominated among English-speaking sociologists. Thus the debate centered on the appropriate ways of attempting to explain suicide and, in particular, on the conflict between sociology and psychology. Of the authors involved in the intellectual exchanges described by Giddens, for example, only Durkheim (1897) and Halbwachs (1930) were unequivocal in their claim to be in the sociologists' camp, while the other main combatants like Esquirol (1838), de Fleury (1924) and Achille-Delmas (1932) were explicitly forwarding psychological, or, to be more precise, psychiatric versions of suicide. And, as the major post-Durkheimian French sociologist to have entered the lists, Halbwachs (1930) falls clearly into the category of modifier rather than serious critic of Durkheim's paradigm, focusing as he does on the way in which social isolation is likely to provide people with motives for committing suicide. Thus the controversy described by Giddens as ''The Suicide Problem in French Sociology' was debated not so much *within* sociology, as *between* sociologists on the one hand and psychologists on the other. To the extent that the debate was concerned more with general issues about the relative merits of what were and still are considered to be competing approaches to the study of human behaviour, rather than with studying suicide *per se,* the situation in French sociology seems to have been a fairly accurate reflection of the way in which I have suggested it has been handled elsewhere in Western sociology. Before going on to look at what these issues were, however, I want to consider briefly why general *issues* rather than *research into suicide* have provided the main focus of sociological attention.

To say simply that one of the founding fathers gave a masterful demonstration of his most important ideas in a book on the subject rather begs the question, for he might never have achieved this posthumous status had he not published *Suicide.* More probably the answer lies partly in the necessity which confronts even theorists, textbook writers and teachers of sociology to find a substantive example to support whatever case they are presenting, and partly in the reluctance of researchers (in spite of textbook pleas for replicative research) to do research which comes up with 'nothing new'. With regard to the first of these, suicide has a number of advantages which commend it to sociologists in search of an example. In addition to the fact that it so often strikes the uninitiated as a straightforward and uncomplicated case of a 'social act' or a 'social fact', suicide has the further attraction of being a topic of more general fascination in Western culture, so that the interest of an audience can be held however abstract or complex the argument being presented. At the same time, of course, it provides a convenient way of introducing the ideas of one of the founding fathers. But perhaps most important of all is the amazing degree of logical consistency of the structure of the theoretical propositions. For if one is going to use an example to illustrate the explanatory potential of sociology – how to relate theory and research findings, the essentially social nature of human behaviour, or whatever – one might as well select a good one. And as I implied earlier, Durkheim's achievement is almost too good to be true.[5]

But if sociologists have turned to *Suicide* so regularly to exemplify a point in the absence of obviously better alternatives, the problem of why so few subsequent sociologists have actually become involved in suicide research still remains. Here the impressiveness of Durkheim's contribution is also important, for as has been suggested earlier, it has proved very difficult for those who have embarked on such projects to come up with anything very different from the original. Thus analyses of suicide rates invariably reveal that most of the same old findings still hold good, while attempts at reformulating Durkheim's theoretical position never achieve the same degree of consistency or comprehensiveness of the original. As will be argued in later chapters, there are good reasons for expecting that studies which take the official statistics at their face value will come up with similar 'findings' repeatedly, but for the present it is enough to note that such findings may prove depressing to the student of suicide working within the Durkheimian paradigm. For he will almost certainly find that any hopes he may have had for going down in sociological history as the man who showed Durkheim's findings to be wrong will be dashed by the similarity of his findings. And if he thinks that such findings will impress those social scientists who see replication as one of the marks of a 'real' science, he is also likely to be disappointed, for assertions that this is an important activity for the sociologist are to be found a good deal more regularly than actual examples of research explicitly designed to replicate earlier work. What I am suggesting here, then, is that the diligent practitioner of Kuhnian 'normal science' is most unlikely to achieve fame within professional sociology. Add to this the fact that many potential students of suicide may be put off by the prospect of having to 'compete' with someone as eminent as Durkheim, and the internal structural pressures within sociology against embarking on suicide research come to look fairly substantial.

The discussion so far has centered on the way in which the suicide problem has been regarded as a problem by sociologists, and I have argued that it has been the general issues posed by Durkheim rather than an empirical interest in doing research into the subject which has been the major focus of interest. The remaining sections of this chapter, then, involve a brief consideration of those issues, which are characterized as the three 'isms': 'positivism,' 'sociologism' and 'functionalism'. The first of these involves an ongoing debate about the appropriateness of viewing social phenomena as 'facts' and about how these should be studied, the second with the sorts of causes appropriate for explaining behaviour and the third with the nature of the societies in which these causes should be sought.

2.3 POSITIVISM

Durkheim was writing during a period of intellectual history which has been described by H. Stuart Hughes (1967) as having been dominated by a revolt against positivism. It can therefore be regarded as a major achievement that a work so explicitly positivist in orientation as *Suicide* not only achieved such great prominence in the development of sociology, but was also very influential in stemming the tide against the revolt described by Hughes. Thus post-Durkheimian sociology came to be largerly dominated by the sorts of positivist assumptions so clearly presented in *Suicide*, and it is only relatively recently that sociologists in any numbers have come to express serious doubts about them. Yet in spite of the increased interest in reinterpretations of Weber, symbolic interactionism and more recently in the more phenomenological writings of Schutz (1962), Berger and Luckmann (1966) and Garfinkel (1967a), explicitly positivist sociology continues to thrive as if such works had never been written. At one level are those who work on ever more sophisticated mathematical techniques for application in sociology (e.g. Coleman, 1964; Blalock and Blalock, 1968), while at another level, the majority of British university sociology departments still demand some mathematical qualifications as a necessary condition for admission. Other evidence of the persistence of positivism can be found in the research-grant awarding policy of the Social Science Research Council, which still seems to give high preference to quantitatively oriented survey research.[7]

As far as the growth of a positivistic sociology was concerned, one of Durkheim's major contributions in suicide was to provide an apparently clear example of what he meant by his earlier exhortation that sociology was concerned with the study of social facts and that social facts were to be regarded as things. Thus, in the abstract, what precise-

ly a social fact is supposed to be, or what is meant by saying that social
facts are to be analysed 'as if they were things',[8] may seem obscure. By
pointing to the constancy of suicide rates over time, however, and to the
variations by social groupings revealed in the statistics, the sense in
which suicide can be regarded as both a *social* and a *fact-like* entity can
be clarified. Furthermore, the manipulation of the statistics in order to
test hypotheses involves procedures which appear to be identical to
those used by natural scientists in measuring and analysing the *things* of
the natural world. And by this demonstration, of course, Durkheim was
able to give the impression of a high degree of 'scientific objectivity',
problems of value and meaning being conveniently left on one side by
the assertion that it was simply 'facts' which were being studied.

It is always tempting to conclude that Durkheim was successful in
propagating the idea of a rigorously objective sociology simply by his
demonstration of the way in which statistical techniques could be used
for testing sociological hypotheses. But as was noted earlier, there had
already been several extensive analyses of suicide statistics prior to
Durkheim, which suggests that this was only part of the story. Probably
more important, however, was his success in constructing a series of
law-like propositions to account for the statistical differences he found,
for, in addition to the view that natural science methods can be used to
study social facts, another key characteristic of positivism is its *deter-
minism*, which involves the belief that just as natural scientists have uncovered natural laws, so also are there social laws which can be uncovered by the sociologist. This belief that it is possible to isolate a
series of propositions which will provide some sort of ultimate explanation of human conduct is of course one which has dominated all schools
of sociology to a greater or lesser extent, even including those which
claim to have found an alternative to positivism. But, as has already
been suggested, Durkheim was more successful than most in producing
a set of interrelated law-like propositions.

It is of special interest, however, that Durkheim was not the first
sociologist to have attempted to explain variations in suicide rates by
reference to a series of related theoretical propositions. Sixteen years
before the publication of *Suicide*, Thomas Masaryk, founder and first
president of Czechoslovakia, had published his *Der Selbstmord als sociale
Massenerscheinung der modernen Civilisation* (1881), a study of which
Durkheim was certainly aware when he came to write his own
monograph (see Durkheim, 1952, p. 53). In Masaryk's preface are
strong indicators of a positivism which reflects almost verbatim some of
the more widely quoted statements on the subject by Durkheim.
Notable examples are the following:

No one, however, has yet undertaken a definitive explanation of
suicide from the sociological point of view. It is precisely this kind of
explanation that most concerns us here ... [Masaryk, 1970, p. 3].

I have attempted, therefore, to present a sociological monograph that follows the example of natural science [ibid., p. 4].

To psychologists and sociologists, social phenomena are simply facts, just as stellar phenomena are simply facts to the astronomer [ibid., p. 5].

Masaryk's view of social facts and his desire to arrive at a sociological explanation of suicide, then, were remarkably similar to those of Durkheim, though he was less obviously waging a polemical war against psychology. The book itself contains an examination of a great deal of the same statistical data as that used by Durkheim as well as an attempt to make sense of the figures in an analysis of the 'nature of the sickness' of the century. Masaryk argues that the variations in suicide rates can all be explained by reference to a loosening of 'moral restraints', which also seems remarkably close to Durkheim's theory. It is arguable, however, that his analysis fails to achieve as impressive an appearance of scientific objectivity as *Suicide* because of the interpretation of the origins of this weakening of the moral order, in which Masaryk's own value position is much more explicitly stated than is the case with Durkheim's later analysis. For not only is Masaryk convinced that high suicide rates can all be explained by a high degree of 'irreligiosity', but he is also sure that the solution to the problem lies in a return to traditional Christian values (ibid., Chapters 5–6). Though in essence their general theories of suicide may not have been very different, Masaryk's choice of terminology was less convincingly 'scientific' than Durkheim's, 'moral restraints' and 'religiosity' being much less easy to pass off as objective value-neutral terms than is the case with 'norms' and 'social integration'. To this extent, Masaryk's work was a less effective demonstration of the potential of the orientation he shared with Durkheim than was *Suicide*, but it is doubtful whether that is the main or only reason why it remained in obscurity for so long. Probably more important were features of Masaryk's biography, for, unlike Durkheim, he became less and less involved in academic sociology as his political career developed, so that he was never able to establish a comparable reputation as a sociologist. Furthermore, his academic career took place away from the centres where the significant advances in nineteenth-century social thought were taking place, and, although he wrote in German, his work was very different from the predominant concerns of his contemporary German social theorists. Thus Masaryk was to remain in obscurity as far as the development of sociology was concerned, and it was Durkheim's version of the sociology of suicide which was to become the idealized paradigm of positivist research methodology.

The precise extent to which Durkheim's *Suicide* had a direct influence on the ever-increasing attention later sociologists were to give to statistical data, problems of measurement and operationalization of theoretical concepts, and the construction of explanations based on such techniques, is difficult to ascertain. Indeed it may well be that Durkheim tends to be attributed a more important role in this than is due. It is noticeable, for example, that the English translation of *Suicide* did not appear until 1951. Furthermore, it has been argued that a serious interest in Durkheim's work did not develop in the United States until the 1930s (Hinkle, 1960) which, if Durkheim were the dominant influence on the growth of positivism, might suggest that such an orientation in American sociology would not have become firmly established until after that time. Yet not only had the more positivistic brand of Chicago ecology already emerged in the 1920s,[9] but there had also been a number of sociological studies of suicide based on official statistics published by American sociologists before the mid-1930s (e.g. Cavan, 1928; Schmid, 1928, 1933). Whatever the exact role of Durkheim's treatment of the suicide problem was on the growth of a sociology which came to take the positivist paradigm largely for granted, it was to become, as was noted above, the most frequently cited example of the appropriateness of such an approach to the study of social phenomena. And in so far as this was precisely what Durkheim had intended, his work can only be described as a resounding success.

The logic of positivism, as was noted above, has increasingly been called into question so that it has become one of the most controversial issues in contemporary sociology. As the later chapters of this book deal in more detail with particular aspects of that debate, only a brief characterization is provided here. A schematic summary of what I take to be the central differences between positivism and its critics is presented in Table 2.3.1. The central issue turns on the validity or otherwise of viewing social phenomena as *facts* and on the related question of the extent to which sociologists can adapt a natural science perspective for the study of subject matter which many argue poses such complex problems that it cannot be likened to the subject matter of the natural sciences. Thus the positivist stands accused not only of

TABLE 2.3.1   *Summary statement of central assumptions and criticisms of positivism*

Positivist Assumptions	*Criticisms*
Social phenomena have an existence external to the individuals who make up a society or social group and can thus be viewed as objective facts in much the same way as natural facts . . .	Social phenomena are of an essentially different order to natural ones owing to their symbolic nature and the subjective interpretations of social meanings by individuals in a society . . .

hence	*hence*
An observer can identify social facts relatively easily and objectively . . .	Identifying social phenomena is a very problematic exercise which involves the assumption that an action has a single unchanging meaning for all people, times and situations . . .
hence	*hence*
Numerical and other 'scientific' techniques can be adapted to 'measure' social facts . . .	Attempts to 'measure' will gloss over the above problems and lead to the imposition of observers' definitions on to a situation where the extent to which these are shared by actors under study is unknown . . .
hence	*hence*
Hypotheses which relate observer-defined variables can be tested . . .	To construct hypotheses is to assume that the problems listed above are either trivial or have been overcome . . .
hence	*hence*
Social theories can be constructed on the basis of discovered 'relationships' or tested by deducing testable hypotheses from some general theoretical statement . . .	The bid to explain social phenomena which are seldom adequately described in terms of actors' orientations is at best premature and at worst a total misrepresentation of the problem of social reality . . .
hence	*hence*
Sociology can proceed with methodologies based on natural science models.	Sociology must develop alternative methodologies appropriate for studying subject matter which poses problems not faced by the subject matter of the natural sciences.

reifying social phenomena by regarding them as things but also of assuming that, once identified, it is appropriate to search for general laws which explain the particular 'fact' or 'object' under study. This latter, of course, involves the further assumption that such laws themselves also have an existence external to the individuals who make up a society and that these can be uncovered given enough time and effort from sociologists. Thus 'sociological theory' became an important and prestigious activity in a sociology directed to the discovery of social laws. Researchers are exhorted to 'unite theory and research', to 'test hypotheses' and to consider the 'theoretical implications' of their studies and, if they show too great an interest in producing detailed descriptions of their chosen subject matter, they run the risk of being branded 'crass empiricists'. And implicit in such criticism, of course, is the assumption that it is perfectly clear what it is that is to be explained and that the only problem is to arrive at satisfactory explanations, notwithstanding the fact that there is a high degree of disagreement among sociologists about precisely what constitutes an adequate explanation, and a low degree of consensus about where examples of studies which achieve such a goal are to be found. Indeed, as has already been noted, it was one of Durkheim's major achievements that he produced a theory of suicide which satisfied more sociologists than most other researchers put together can claim to have done.

In spite of the general absence from sociology of widely acclaimed examples of adequate general theories, it was nevertheless to become part of the conventional wisdom of the sociologist that his main task was to *explain* the events he saw in the social world around him. The fact that such events are subjectively experienced both by the actors involved and by the sociological observer, and that they may have different meanings attributed to them by all who experienced them was largely ignored, the problem of categorizing social actions being relegated to a rather mundane technical one (Operationalization, Questionnaire Design, Coding, etc.) compared with the real problem of locating the laws determining the actions. Two examples of the way such an orientation has survived among contemporary sociologists interested in suicide are the following:

the problem is approached from the sociological angle, which means that the investigator has concentrated on the underlying reasons for differences in suicide rates [Kruijt, 1965, p. 44].

the foremost task of sociological studies of suicide is to explain differences in rates [Gibbs, 1966, p. 228].

Gibbs, the author of the second of these has recently revised the general paper on suicide in which it appears (Merton and Nisbet, 1971, pp. 271–312), at least to the extent of mentioning the first extensive critique of the Durkheimian approach by Jack Douglas (1967). The location of this one-page discussion by Gibbs suggests that he thinks it only important in so far as it casts some light on the technical problems of using suicide statistics, about which he says, 'Douglas deserves credit for bringing the issue to the forefront, but his argument is not convincing' (Gibbs, 1971, p. 278; this theme is returned to in the next chapter). More interesting than the casual way in which the anti-positivist case is brushed aside, however, are the crudely positivist statements which Gibbs feels able to make at as late a stage in the history of sociology as 1971. A good example of this is the summary paragraph of his section on the theory of status integration expounded by himself and W. T. Martin (1964), in which the 'scientific' terminology implies a total acceptance of the view that sociologists can and should proceed in exactly the same way as natural scientists:

> Because status integration can be measured, the major theorem can be subjected to systematic tests. An initial series of tests has produced positive results, but an adequate evaluation of the theory must await further tests and judgement by impartial critics [ibid., p. 309].

Thus not only can status integration and suicide be 'measured', a 'series of tests' be carried out on a 'theorem', but there also exist social actors who can be regarded as 'impartial'. Furthermore, Gibbs seems to be in no doubt about the existence of a 'truly general theory' and a 'common denominator' of high rates which sociologists must discover, and his consideration of 'Future Sociological Investigations' (ibid., pp. 309–10) leaves out any reference to the problems summarized in Table 2.3.1:

> However real the case for multiple causation may appear, the very idea defeats the quest for a truly general theory through a search for a common denominator that underlies all instances of high rates. This quest carries on the tradition of Durkheim's approach. But future investigations must not slavishly follow Durkheim, if only because the search must go beyond the generation of indefinite concepts. Little is accomplished by suggesting that the common denominator is 'anomie,' or some equally vague term. Future investigations must not only locate a common denominator and describe it conceptually; they must also specify the operations necessary for assessment of its prevalance in populations [ibid., p. 309].

Taken for granted in all this, of course, is that suicides are the sorts of 'thing' which are sufficiently similar for us to be able to group them together and study them all as if they were identical. Taken for granted also is the existence of some law which accounts for this 'thing'. The full absurdity of such crude positivism, however, becomes manifest when one begins to contemplate the study of other actions to which the same name can be given. To express an interest in doing research into hole-digging, for example, in order to construct a general theory to explain why people dig holes would be to put one's judgement severely in question: clearly it would be ludicrous to try to explain the digging of a hole to plant a rose bush and the digging of a hole to bury a murder victim by reference to the same theory of hole-digging, for although 'hole-digging' may superficially appear to refer to an identical form of action, the symbolic meanings which can be associated with the various activities falling into that linguistic category are so many that to talk about 'hole-digging' without being more precise about these meanings makes little sense.[10] When it comes to talking about suicide, however, sociologists and experts from other disciplines have been notably uninhibited by the sorts of constraints this would seem to imply, and have never been slow to make general statements about actions which can be called 'suicides'.

Of the issues posed by Durkheim in *Suicide* which were to fascinate subsequent generations of sociologists, then, his apparent demonstration of the validity and potential of a positivist approach to the study of social phenomena was probably the most important for the development of the discipline. For the debate about positivism is one which cuts across the other issues he raised which are discussed below; thus psychology has not been notably less positivist in orientation than sociology, while attacks on functionalism typically posit an equally positivist alternative (Sharrock, 1970).

In conclusion we may note that suicide has maintained its position as a central reference point in the general debate about positivism with the emergence of ethnomethodology which casts even more of sociology as 'positivist' (or to be more precise 'constructive analysis') than does Douglas. Thus two of the most important figures in ethnomethodology, Garfinkel (1967a; 1967b) and Sacks (1966; 1972b), have both done work on suicide. In emphasizing the differences between positivism and ethnomethodology, then, it seems likely that the attention of sociologists may continue to be directed towards suicide.

2.4 SOCIOLOGISM

In addition to the debate about positivism, the suicide problem in sociology has also been central to the debate concerning what I referred to earlier as Durkheim's 'sociologism', by which I mean his stress on the supremacy of explanations in terms of social rather than psychological factors. In this context, Durkheim was involved in an ongoing, and still continuing, argument about the relationship between individuals and society and the relative merits of sociological and psychological modes of explanation, and his preference for the former stemmed logically from the view that social facts have an existence external to the individuals that make up a society. Thus, as has been widely recognized, his polemic against his contemporary psychologists was one of the main reasons why so much of the early part of *Suicide* is taken up with refutations of alternative theories. The extreme position to which this led him had been signalled in much of the discussion in *The Rules of Sociological Method*, and is typified by the following extract:

> We arrive, therefore, at the following principle: *The determining cause of a social fact should be sought among the social facts preceding it and not among the states of the individual consciousness* [Durkheim, 1938, p. 110; his italics].

In the subsequent debates which have preoccupied sociologists and philosophers of social science, it is arguable that this part of Durkheim's contribution has never been held in such awe as other aspects of his work. Rather it has been seen as an extremist position to be contrasted with alternative extremisms such as the following example from Popper (1945, p. 98):

> all social phenomena, and especially the functioning of all social institutions, should always be understood as resulting from the decisions, actions, attitudes, etc. of human individuals and we should never be satisfied by an explanation in terms of so-called 'collectives'.

But while it is easy to find quotations from Durkheim to show that he took an extremist position which apparently denied the validity of any sort of psychological explanation, it is just as easy to make a case supporting the view that, when he actually got down to the problem of explaining suicide, he did in fact invoke notions of individual psychology. For it would seem that he was aware that, although he had demonstrated statistical relationships between suicide rates and social integration, there remained the problem of explaining precisely how it was that a relative lack of integration led to a greater tendency towards suicide. In other words, he realized that there was a need to locate 'intervening variables' which would provide the link between the degree of structural integration and the variations in the suicide rates, and his answer to this was, according to Inkeles (1959, p. 252) to introduce an embryonic theory of personality:

> To the question of how the origin of suicide could lie in the degree of integration of a social structure, he [Durkheim] replied by referring to man's 'psychological constitution,' which, he said, 'needs an object transcending it'. This object is lacking in the weakly integrated society, and consequently 'the individual having too keen a feeling for himself and his own value . . . wishes to be his only goal, and as such an objective cannot satisfy him, drags out languidly and indifferently an existence which henceforth seems meaningless to him'.

While this may seem inadequate in accounting for why certain individuals engage in suicidal rather than some other sorts of actions, and primitive though a theory of personality which asserts the need for identification with a collective consciousness as a precondition for survival may seem, the important point to note is that Durkheim invoked any psychological notions at all. It is also of interest in the present context that Inkeles follows the above observations with a more extended discussion of Durkheim's and subsequent studies of suicide in introducing his paper on 'Personality and Social Structure' (ibid., pp. 252–6). That he did so gives support to our contention that suicide has continued to be used as a *resource* in sociological discussions of this issue.

As was noted earlier, Giddens (1965) showed how the debate in French sociology centered on the debate between psychologism and sociologism, and later attempted to integrate psychological and sociological approaches to suicide (Giddens, 1966). The problem has also been raised by most of the American sociologists who have done research into suicide,[11] a notable exception being the status-integration studies by Gibbs and Martin (1964), which follows Durkheim in its near-total commitment to sociologism. The most explicit attempt at achieving some kind of synthesis was provided by Henry and Short's (1954) adaptation of the frustration-aggression thesis to the problem of suicide which was outlined earlier. Elsewhere in sociology, the problem persisted in a number of guises. At a high level of abstraction, the debate about methodological individualism has held a predominant place in the philosophy of social science (see, e.g., Lukes, 1970), while other sociological 'theorists' have been consistently obliged to confront the issue. This has applied to consensus and conflict theorists alike, so that even writers as opposed as Parsons and Mills have agreed on the importance of exploring the relationship between personality and social structure (c.f. Parsons, 1964; Gerth and Mills, 1953).

The volume and content of subsequent discussions of the relationship between social and individual explanations of behaviour and related issues can leave the reader in no doubt that Durkheim's choice of suicide as a topic which would allow him to make his contribution to the debate was a brilliant success. For as he rightly observed and as is constantly reiterated in the literature, the suicide problem is one which poses the individual-social dilemma in a particularly obvious way. As such it can be taken as a topic for discussion by anyone claiming an interest in the nature and explanation of social action, and hence it becomes easier to understand why it is that it is so frequently referred to in sociological treatises even though so few sociologists have taken it as a major research interest. For the present, the debate about the relative merits of psychologism and sociologism simmers on though perhaps in a less extreme form than before. Thus the revival of interest in the social psychology of G. H. Mead (e.g. 1934; 1964) and symbolic interactionism can be seen as an indication of an increased willingness on the part of sociologists to look for a version of social action which does not assume that all can be explained exclusively in terms of social structures. Similarly, the following statement from Stinchcombe's recent book on theory construction, displays a degree of eclecticism towards the problem which, in earlier periods of sociological history, would surely have been hailed as 'heresy' by adherents to both sides of the debate:

> I have a firm conviction that some things are to be explained one way, some another. Trying to explain a phenomenon by a strategy inappropriate to the empirical terrain, because one thinks that a strategy is a 'theory' which must either be true or false, leads into ambushes. Some things are to be explained by personality dynamics, some things by their consequences, and some things by ecological causes. Some personality theories are true, and some ecological theories are true. Which kind is true of a particular phenomenon is a matter for investigation, not for debate among 'theorists' [Stinchcombe, 1968, p. 4].

2.5. FUNCTIONALISM

Another matter which has been taken as a topic worthy of debate by 'theorists' is the extent to which Durkheim can be regarded as a functionalist. Here, as with the debate referred to in the previous section, the literature is full of examples of the professional theorists' apparent delight with the kind of conceptual juggling which is so important to the sociologically initiated and so irritating to the novice. Thus Albert Pierce points out that the appropriateness of applying such a label to Durkheim's thought depends largely on what is meant by functionalism, and concludes his assessment by saying 'it would be erroneous to regard Durkheim as a functionalist in any of the commonly accepted contemporary meanings of the term' (Pierce, 1960, p. 165). Whatever the merits of such a statement, however, many features of the formulations proposed by Durkheim in *Suicide* can be related in important ways to the growth and content of functionalism in sociology.

The crudest form of functionalism is normally held to be that which likens societies to organisms and attempts to locate the functions which its various parts perform in contributing to the stability of the organism. Though this may not, according to Pierce, be one of the 'contemporary meanings of the term', substantial parts of Durkheim's writings reveal exactly such a view of societies. His extended discussion of 'normal' and 'pathological' social types in Chapter 3 of *The Rules of Sociological Methods* abounds with organic imagery and explicit statements which stress the similarities between organisms and societies. Initially he invokes the notion of old age in what seems to be a case against the crude version of functionalism presented above:

> People argue about this question as if, in a healthy organism, each
> element played a useful role, as if each internal state corresponded
> exactly to some external condition and, consequently, helped to
> maintain vital equilibrium and to diminish the chances of death. But
> it is, on the contrary, legitimate to suppose that some anatomical or
> functional arrangements are of no direct use, but are merely the
> products of the general conditions of life [ibid., p. 51].

But having proposed that certain types of apparent pathologies can be
regarded as 'normal', Durkheim goes on to suggest that once the
'average type' has been designated it is then possible to isolate those
features which can be regarded as pathological. And in this way he
arrives at a somewhat modified version of the extreme form of functionalism outlined above: 'It is the functions of the average organism
that the physiologist studies; and the sociologist does the same' (ibid.,
p. 56).

Thus Durkheim proceeds to a position where it is possible for him to
present his celebrated and much-cited case for viewing crime as 'normal' (ibid., pp. 64–75). The catch is, however, that if the crime rates increase too rapidly then it is to be considered as pathological. The same
theme is found in *Suicide* (p. 362):

> A necessary imperfection is not a disease; otherwise disease would
> have to be postulated everywhere, since imperfections exist
> everywhere. No organic function, no anatomical form exists, some
> further perfection of which may not be conceived.

As with crime, suicide is to be regarded as normal – so long as its frequency does not increase too rapidly:

> It is then very possible and even probable that the rising tide of
> suicide originates in a pathological state just now accompanying the
> march of civilization without being its necessary condition.
>   The rapidity of the growth of suicide really permits no other
> hypothesis . . . we know their connection with the most ineradicable
> element in the constitution of societies, since they express the mood
> of societies, and since the mood of peoples, like that of individuals,
> reflects the state of the most fundamental part of the organism. . . .
> So grave and rapid an alteration as this must be morbid [ibid., pp.
> 368–9].

Not only were rapid increases in the rates of crime and suicide to be
regarded as pathological, then, but they were also to be conceived of as
manifestations of a more general sickness of societies as a whole, as is
evidenced by his reference in the preface to *Suicide* to 'the general
maladjustment being undergone by European societies' (p. 37). Hence

he shared the view of his predecessors in the statistical analysis of suicide that the rates could be regarded as a barometer which measures the prevailing moral climate.

Though these ideas may differ in subtle ways from the contemporary meanings of functionalism, the connections between Durkheim's thought and modern versions of consensus theory are as important as they are numerous. The stress on balance, equilibrium and pathology are features of functionalism which have invoked the wrath of its critics. In tracing the evolution of societies, Durkheim focused on the changing bases of social solidarity rather than on the Marxian emphasis on the changing bases of conflict. His distinction between the 'normal' and the 'pathological' involves an equilibrium model of social structure in which 'social types' like crime and suicide are 'normal' features only so long as the rates remain at a level which is low enough not to upset or threaten that equilibrium. And in his later work on religion (Durkheim, 1954), it was its cohesive functions rather than its more divisive characteristics which interested him most. In the history of sociology and social anthropology, Durkheim's influence on the development of functionalism was profound and lasting. Writers like Radcliffe-Brown, Parsons and Merton, who have been among the more influential of the protagonists of functionalist analysis, reveal in their works heavy debts to Durkheim. His thought, it has been argued, struck a special note for American sociologists during the 1930s, before which it seems to have had relatively little impact in the United States. Durkheim had been writing at a time of great social upheaval in France, and it was during the similarly uncertain post-depression years in America when social order presented itself as being particularly problematic that the functionalism of Parsons and Merton began to take shape.

It was not just that Durkheim's work as a whole made an important contribution to the growth of functionalism in general, for his treatment of the suicide problem had a far-reaching effect on particular lines of sociological enquiry which emerged under the umbrella of consensus theory. His method of analysis provided a model for the investigation of variations in the rates of other social 'pathologies' and 'Social Pathology' emerged as one of the specialisms of sociology. Similar theoretical formulations to that provided by Durkheim in *Suicide*, however, proved less easy to come by than the statistics for computing the rates, but when the theoretical breakthrough did come, it was derived directly from what Durkheim had had to say about suicide. Thus in 'Social Structure and Anomie', Merton (1938) rediscovered for sociology one of the central concepts employed by Durkheim in his theory of suicide, and adapted it to produce what purported to be a theory which accounted for a range of different types of deviant behaviour. Both versions of anomie have been treated to extended discussions in the sociological literature, which is one measure of the immense impact it was to have on the discipline. For the sociology of deviance, the currently preferred name for what was previously known as 'social pathology', Merton's formulation seemed to provide a way of accounting for some of the more regularly found variations in the various forms of deviance studied, and was influential in the development of much subsequent theorizing on deviance (see, e.g., Clinard, 1964). For sociology at large, or more particularly the consensus or functionalist variety, anomie theory suggested a way out of the difficulties involved in trying to account for social conflict and change in terms of a supposedly stable integrated social system.

In his discussion of anomic suicide, Durkheim poses the following question, which it will be noted is phrased not in terms of conflicts between groups within a social structure but in terms of the 'adjustment' of the system:

> Whenever serious readjustments take place in the social order, whether or not due to a sudden growth or to an unexpected catastrophe, men are more inclined to self-destruction. How is this possible? . . . No living being can be happy or even exist unless his needs are sufficiently proportioned to his means [Durkheim, 1952, p. 246].

In the ensuing discussion, he considers how the necessary balance is achieved, adopting his favoured practice of ruling out all possible accounts but the social. The passions, he says, have to be limited and can only be limited by some force external to the individual which 'must play the same role for the moral needs which the organism plays for physical needs', a force which 'can only be moral' (ibid., p. 248). From this he leads into what is an embryonic functionalist theory of social class in which he states that there are:

> degrees of comfort appropriate on the average to workers in each occupation. . . . A genuine regimen exists, therefore, although not always legally formulated, which fixes with relative precision the maximum degree of ease of living to which each social class may legitimately aspire [ibid., p. 249].

In other words, people know what it is that they may strive for so that in 'normal times' everyone is 'in harmony with his condition, and desires only what he may legitimately hope for as the normal reward of his activity' (ibid., p. 250). This, then, is the 'goals' or 'ends' side of Merton's means-ends scheme.

It is not enough, however, for levels of aspirations to be regulated, and 'another, more precise rule, must fix the way in which these conditions are open to individuals' (idem.), which is the origin of the 'means' side of the Mertonian version. According to Durkheim, these sets of rules may become temporarily out of step with social conditions, so that, for example, in times of both economic boom and slump, needs and aspirations have to be modified. The trouble is that 'society cannot adjust them instantaneously' so that a period ensues, which he characterizes as anomie, and during which the system readjusts itself to a state of equilibrium. This process has specific and dramatic effects:

> when society is disturbed by some painful crisis or by beneficient but abrupt transitions, it is momentarily incapable of exercising this influence; thence come the sudden rises in the curves of suicides which we have pointed out above [ibid., p. 252].

Merton's main contribution was to attempt to specify the goals which were aspired to in American society and to separate more explicitly the two sets of rules elaborated by Durkheim. This leads him to consider some of the possible permutations which may occur when there is a disjunction between the goals and the means and to claim that the different possibilities lead to different sorts of deviant behaviour. Interestingly, suicide does not get a mention as a possible mode of adaptation to anomie, as Merton prefers to commit himself only to very general categorizations of actions (conformity, rebellion, retreatism, etc.). His rediscovery of anomie subsequently provided a way for sociologists to devise accounts of all manner of behaviours and social upheavals, without resorting to the more controversial language of class struggle, conflict and power employed by conflict theorists.

Although suicide may not have been used as a resource for discussing functionalism in a continuous way, as was argued to have been the case with respect to positivism and sociologism, Durkheim's original analysis was crucially important in providing a way for subsequent sociologists to account for deviant behaviour and social upheavals in terms of an essentially stable and integrated model of society. In the sociology of deviance, however, it did and still does hold its place as an example by reference to which anomie theory can be discussed, rather than as a topic for research (see, e.g., Cohen, 1966, pp. 74–5).

2.6 CONCLUSIONS

I began this chapter by observing that sociological interest in suicide can best be characterized as 'fascination from a distance' and it should now be clear what was meant by this. For it was the *issues* posed by Durkheim in a book which just happened to be on suicide, rather than the *phenomenon of suicide* itself which has stimulated most of the sociological interest. Paradoxically, the extensiveness of that interest is of little help to the would-be researcher into suicide. For from whatever stance one approaches the research, one is faced with fundamental and unsolved methodological problems which appear so obvious that it initially seems strange that they have been given so little attention in the past. That is, whether one's interest is in the relationship between sociological and psychological modes of explanation or in anomie theory, and whether or not one considers oneself a positivist, functionalist, conflict theorist or whatever, important decisions have to be made about the status and adequacy of the data chosen for analysis. In this sense the methodological concerns of the following chapters are to be regarded as *prior* to the kinds of theoretical interests summarized in Sections 2.4 and 2.5 above, and it is for this reason that what have traditionally been considered the most important aspects of the suicide problem in sociology receive little further attention from this point onwards.[12]

We may note in conclusion that not only is the widespread interest of sociologists in suicide of little help in solving the methodological problems faced by the empirically oriented researcher,[13] but that the character of that interest probably accounts for how it is that such fundamental and obvious problems were ignored for so long. For the difficulties to be discussed below are only likely to emerge as obvious *at the point of designing or attempting to do empirical research*, and hence to remain hidden from the view of the philosophers, theorists and teachers who use suicide as nothing more than a 'substantive' example in debates about ideas.

Chapter 3
Suicide Research and Data Derived from Official Sources

3.1 INTRODUCTION

The conclusion reached in the previous chapter was that the suicide problem, and particularly Durkheim's formulation of it, has been used by sociologists as a resource for making general points about sociological procedures rather than as a topic for research. That sociologists and others have seen fit to discuss the kinds of issues referred to implies further that they have also been ready to use data derived from official sources as an unexplicated resource for their work, as all the debates presuppose that it is fairly obvious what constitutes 'suicide', so that the interesting questions centre upon the manner in which suicidal actions may be *explained*. As I have noted elsewhere, however, anyone who takes suicide as the topic for research is necessarily faced with making a number of important decisions with respect to the data he uses (Atkinson, 1968), and it is to a consideration of these that the present chapter is devoted. In this first section I shall briefly indicate why the problem is more appropriately referred to as concerning 'data derived from official sources' rather than simply one of 'official statistics'. Section 3.2 then deals with the ways in which the problems relating to the use of such data can be formulated. The way one type of formulation has been treated by sociologists with reference to topics other than suicide is discussed in Section 3.3. It is then suggested that such problems have been of little concern to most suicidologists, whose almost exclusive interest in the problems of accuracy and reliability is examined in Section 3.4. A separate section (3.5) is devoted to Douglas's (1967) important discussion of official statistics and suicide, where it is argued that, although he has been alone among suicidologists in formulating the problem in terms of validity and meaning, his argument is somewhat equivocal with respect to the problem of accuracy.

In so far as official statistics have been regarded as problematic by suicide researchers, it has been because the rates which have been subjected to analysis have been calculated from published official statistics. That the rates themselves have to be *calculated* provides a clue to the way in which the formulation of the problem as one of 'official statistics' rather than one of 'data derived from official sources' gives an over-simplified view of the way in which much of the source material has been used in suicide research. The published statistics seldom give more than the annual number of suicides tabulated according to a very limited range of variables, which means not only that the researcher has to work out the rates for himself by reference to other demographic data, but also that if he wishes to follow Durkheim and the nineteenth-century moral statisticians by computing the rates of a wide variety of different groups, he has to resort to materials other than the published official statistics. This typically involves gaining access to the much more detailed records assembled during the process of in-vestigating the actual deaths counted in the final statistics. Maris, for example, went beyond the published statistics in his study of 2153 suicides in Chicago by obtaining the actual death certificates. Even then, however, he found the data to be lacking and had to resort to the coroners' records:

> The information on a death certificate is limited. Some of the sociological basics are there; age, sex, race, marital status, and oc-cupation. Nevertheless, we were forced to rely heavily on secondary sources to explain many of the patterns that developed from our analysis. For example, coroners' inquest records helped since they included addition information on the sample not recorded on the death certificate [Maris, 1969, p. 65].

Thus it is not so much the official statistics themselves which are or may be regarded as problematic, as the records of the officials whose decisions are counted for the purposes of compiling the official statistics. The researcher has to devise a way of coding information from these before he can compute the rates he wishes to analyse, and hence is dependent not so much on the published statistics as on the procedures of those who work to produce the evidence on which the official decisions are based. The data for research purposes, then, can be viewed as derived from official sources in two senses. First the pop-ulation to be studied or sampled is defined for the researcher by the decisions of the officials involved in categorizing deaths; and, second, the main body of data on which analyses are based may be obtained from records made available by such officials.[1]

To focus solely on 'official statistics', then, would be to ignore the diverse ways in which data on suicide have been derived from official sources, and hence to imply that the issues to be discussed below only have relevance for that relatively limited number of studies which are based exclusively on officially published mortality and other demographic statistics. It would imply also that one particular style of research which explicitly attempts to go beyond the data available in official records is exempt from the kinds of criticisms to be developed in later sections. These are the relatively few studies which are based on interviews with the relatives or friends of persons who have committed suicide, of which the American studies of Breed (1963), and the British studies of Barraclough and his associates (1967) are examples. On the strength of his having been the first sociologist to have set about collecting his own data on suicide rather than relying exclusively on the evidence contained in coroners' records, Breed is singled out by Douglas (1967, p. 120) as having a special place in the development of the sociology of suicide. Douglas does note, however, that Breed's sample of 103 suicides was provided by *official* categorizations of suicide, and suggests also that Breed overlooks the possibility of his own results being in error in the same way as those he finds in the coroners' records:

> The first finding of Breed's interview approach was that the official reports on occupations, marital status and unemployment-employment of these 103 suicides were very much in error. In terms of employment and types of employment, there seems to have been a very significant tendency for the official reports to overestimate the social prestige ranking held by the suicide. When one considers the strong possibility that the significant others interviewed by Breed may have also overestimated in this way, we have a strong bit of information against the use of national official data ... [Douglas, 1967, p. 120].

As will be shown in later chapters, statements made by significant others immediately after the death are a crucial part of the official records, and hence the scepticism expressed by Douglas about the alleged superiority of sociological over official interviews seems justified.

While Breed's aim in using interviews rather than coding data from records was to obtain 'better' sociological data, Barraclough's source of discontent is with the records as sources of psychiatric data.[2] The researchers attend inquests and, if a suicide verdict is returned, approach the relatives and/or friends of the deceased and request permission to conduct interviews. On the basis of these, special abbreviated psychiatric summaries are prepared and presented to a panel of three psychiatrists not involved in the research. Independently of each other, they each fill in a further questionnaire, in which they are asked to make diagnostic judgements about the deceased on the basis of the abbreviated list of symptoms. Where there is disagreement, a majority decision is taken as to the diagnosis, so that all the suicides can be categorized according to whether or not they were suffering from a mental illness prior to their deaths. If the answer is that they were mentally ill, then the panel also has to specify a more precise diagnosis of the illness. In this way, it is argued, it will be possible to arrive at a much more accurate estimate of the proportions of suicides suffering from different mental illnesses immediately prior to their deaths. While such a research strategy may, like Breed's, be regarded as a major departure from the traditional reliance on coroners' records, the researchers' data is nevertheless derived from official sources in that the populations studied are defined by the decisions of officials. In short, what they regard as problematic is the *contents* of the coroners' records rather than the *decisions* made by coroners as to which deaths are suicides, and on this later issue they appear to be in total agreement with earlier investigators.

For the most part, then, suicide researchers have found it necessary to do something more than merely analyse the published official statistics, whether this be by examining the records of coroners or by conducting interviews with the significant others of people whose deaths have been officially defined as suicides. To talk of problems relating to the use of official statistics, therefore, is to imply that the studies being referred to are only those relatively rare ones which rely exclusively on published official statistics, and hence that any comments do not apply to those which require more preliminary work to be done prior to the calculation of rates. To avoid such an implication, then, it would seem preferable to refer to the studies as ones based on data derived from official sources rather than on official statistics.[3]

3.2 FORMULATIONS OF THE PROBLEM

Discussion of the problems posed by the use of data derived from official sources has a long history in the sociology of deviance and criminology (Wiles, 1971), which, until very recently, depended almost exclusively on such materials as their main source of data. That the shift away from the near-total dependence on official sources for the data to be analysed has also involved a major reorientation of approach to the study of deviance is, it can be argued, no coincidence, and is itself dependent on a total reformulation of the problems traditionally discussed with reference to such data. Rather than detail the history of these various debates, then, the intention here is to summarize the major differences in approach to the problems and in particular to propose that there are two main ways in which officially generated data can be viewed as problematic. These, it will be argued, are mutually exclusive in that an acceptance of the second position, which has been summarized most succinctly by Kitsuse and Cicourel (1963), makes the issues which have been a traditional source of concern essentially uninteresting.

The first conceptualization of the problems relating to the use of official data for research purposes is one which leaves the basic assumptions about what is to be studied and how it is to be studied intact. That is, the central assumptions of positivism are not questioned. Actions are inherently deviant or non-deviant, can be readily identified as such and can be explained by the scientific observer. Furthermore, in order to accomplish such explanations, the appropriate place to look is at samples of actors who are known to have committed deviant acts, so that characteristics which they can be shown to possess can be compared with those of actors who are 'known' to be conformists. The discovered differences then provide the necessary materials for the formulation of explanatory propositions. In spite of the apparently 'scientific' character of such procedures, the results of such studies have been more notable for the rich variety of the types of causes claimed to be the 'real' causes than for any widely agreed generalizations, a point which Box has discussed in the following deliberately polemical tone:

> Depending on the fashion of the day or the fad of the researcher, his subjects had their heads measured for irregularities, their bodies somatyped, their unconscious probed and analysed, their intelligence rated, their personalities tested and assessed, and, in recent years, their gene structure investigated. . . . Millions, perhaps billions, of pounds and man-hours were, and still are being, expended in this manner. The result, however, hardly bears the fruit of these efforts; no consistent and valid differences between official deviants and a control group of conformists have been revealed. . . . Unfortunately, like their non-sociological counterparts, sociological accounts of deviance have been dazzling in their rich variety, but disappointing in their substantiveness [Box, 1971, pp. 4–5].

The major assumption in such approaches is that members of society can be and are divided into 'equivalence classes' which contain individuals who are 'alike' or 'identical' enough for them to be regarded as manifestations of the same 'type' of person (cf. Cicourel, 1964). Methodologically, then, there is the problem of how far the equivalence classes generated by those whose work results in official statistics or provides sampling frames for interview or other studies approximate to the 'real' equivalence classes in which the researcher is interested. For the conscientious researcher operating within such a perspective, this poses two sets of technical problems, the first relating to the definitions being used, and the second relating to the inclusiveness of the officially generated equivalence classes.[4] The process of determining whether or not to use data derived from official sources, then, involves an investigator in two separate decisions which may or may not be explicitly discussed in the ensuing research reports. First it must be decided whether or not the official categorizations can be accepted as appropriate indicators of the investigator's theoretical concepts (cf. Lazarsfeld, 1959). If it is decided to accept them as such, a second decision is required about the efficiency and accuracy of the officials in

classifying units in the appropriate classes. Thus the fact that data
derived from official sources have been so widely used in studies of
suicide implies that the researchers have decided that the death
registration category 'Suicide' is defined in a similar way to their own
theoretical conception of what constitutes a suicide, and hence that it is
an acceptable indicator. To say that these decisions are 'implied'
reflects the apparently normal practice of researchers who propose a
definition of suicide at the start of their work which is unaccompanied
by any reference to what the legal definition might be or how that
definition relates to the definition being proposed. Durkheim (1952, p.
44), for example, includes 'all causes of death resulting directly or indirectly from a positive or negative act of the victim himself, which he
knows will produce the result'. Cavan (1928, p. 3) has it that suicide is
'the intentional taking of one's life or failure when possible to save
oneself when death threatens', while Stengel (1964, p. 12) gives us 'the
fatal . . . act of self-injury undertaken with conscious self-destructive intent, however vague and ambiguous'. All these authors then proceed to
offer extensive generalizations about suicide based on data derived from
official sources without reference to the legal definitions in use in the
various countries concerned. Though this may be regarded as a fairly
serious violation of the rules for operationalizing concepts as advocated
by sociological methodologists like Lazarsfeld, it is worth noting at this
stage that such procedures may themselves be based on erroneous
notions of how members of society go about making definitions. For, as
will be shown in Chapter 5, it is possible for a coroner to be ignorant of
the legal definition of suicide and at the same time to perform as a
perfectly competent coroner.

This problem of the relationship between the definition considered
sociologically relevant by the observer and those employed by the
officials who generate the data on which research may be based is one
which has been treated extensively in other areas of the sociology of
deviance and, in particular, by criminologists (e.g. Tappan, 1947;
Cressey, 1951; Wiles, 1971). For these latter, the problems have been
especially obvious, for, as Cicourel (1968, p. 27) has noted:

> Law-enforcement officials, statisticians attached to rate-producing
> agencies, criminologists and sociologists have long known and com-
> mented on official statistics as misleading.

Thus it is not unusual for a sociologist who consults policemen about
the possibility of doing research of a statistical nature to be treated to
an extended lecture by the policeman himself on the methodological
problems posed by such an exercise. Similarly, a constant topic for concern among statisticians attached to one British rate-producing agency
(the Home Office Research Unit) used to be the difficulties involved in
using rates of reconviction as measures of success or failure of different

forms of punishment and treatment.[5] But just as sociologists have not let such 'difficulties' prevent them from undertaking studies and making generalizations as if the difficulties were either trivial or had been solved, so also are the same policemen and the same Home Office researchers able to make such statements in spite of the apparently 'known' problems. To the extent that sociologists who have used data derived from official sources in this way have attended to the difficulties raised by official definitions, they have addressed the question of the extent to which such definitions are 'sociologically relevant'. Thus Merton (cited in Kitsuse and Cicourel, 1963, p. 133) has said of such materials on juvenile delinquency:

> These are social bookkeeping data. And it would be a happy coincidence if some of them turned out to be in a form relevant for research. From the sociological standpoint, 'juvenile delinquency' and what it encompasses is a form of deviant behaviour for which the epidemiological data, as it were, may not be at hand. You may have to go out and collect your own appropriately organized data rather than to take those which are ready-made by governmental agencies.

As to why officially generated data may not be in a form 'relevant for research' and what those who share Merton's view have proposed as an alternative, Sudnow (1965, p. 255) is somewhat more explicit:

> One position, which might be termed that of the 'revisionist' school, has it that the categories of the criminal law, e.g., 'burglary', 'petty theft', 'homicide', etc., are not 'homogenous in respect to causation.' From an inspection of penal code descriptions of crimes, it is argued that the way persons seem to be assembled under the auspices of criminal law procedure is such as to produce classes of criminals who are, at least on theoretical grounds, as dissimilar in their social backgrounds and styles of activity as they are similar. The entries in the penal code, this school argues, require revision if sociological use is to be made of categories of crime and a classificatory scheme of etiological relevance is to be developed. Common attempts at such revision have included notions such as '*white collar* crime' and '*systematic* check forger', these conceptions constituting attempts to institute sociologically meaningful specifications which the operations of criminal law procedure and statutory legislation 'fail' to achieve.

Thus the researcher may extract sub-categories from the official categories, such as 'robbery' or 'football hooliganism' from 'crimes of violence', 'murders followed by suicide' from 'homicides' or '*serious* motoring offences' from 'motoring offences' (e.g. McClintock and Gibson, 1961; Taylor, 1971; West, 1965; Willett, 1964), and treat those as the sociologically relevant categories to be studied and explained.

Alternatively, actions not readily available from the official categorizations may be claimed to be nevertheless 'really deviant' or at least analysable 'as if they were deviant', examples being particularly plentiful among ethnographic studies of deviance such as Becker (1963) on dance musicians, Polsky (1967) on pool-room hustlers or Weinberg (1968a; 1968b) on nudists.

This approach to the problems posed by official definitions, then, may involve the selection of 'relevant' categories from *within* the official categories or the selection of other categories which are not provided at all by the official categorizations. Both strategies are to be found in the literature on suicide, examples of the first being those studies of groups of suicides deemed by the observer to have a special significance in their own right such as student suicides (e.g. Atkinson, 1969), elderly suicides (e.g. Gardner *et al.*, 1954; Walsh and McCarthy, 1967; Barraclough, 1970) or suicide pacts (e.g. Cohen, 1961). This style of study frequently derives from a larger-scale project being conducted by the investigator who draws smaller samples from his main sample and publishes separate analyses of these special sub-groups. The most notable examples of the second strategy of studying groups which are not obtainable from the official categorizations are the many studies of attempted suicides which have been carried out, mostly by members of disciplines other than sociology.[6] Both ways of approaching the definitional problem, however, implicitly involve the assumption that researchers can and should assert some specification of the limits of what is to be regarded as 'relevant' to be researched. Thus some studies based exclusively on the official categorizations involve an assertion that they provide the 'relevant' definitions of suicide, while others (e.g. McCarthy and Walsh, 1966), as will be seen in Section 3.4 below, revise some of the official categorizations for research purposes. Similarly, studies of attempted suicide may involve attempts to define the relationship between suicide, attempted suicide and other suicidal phenomena (e.g. Stengel *et al.*, 1958; Stengel, 1964) to argue the case for some revised definition such as Kessel's (1965) 'self-poisoning', or they may propose that other forms of behaviour such as drug-taking, risk-taking or alcoholism are properly to be regarded as relevant for consideration under the auspices of suicide research (e.g. Farberow, 1967, pp. 316–55). As such, the solutions to the problems associated with official definitions of suicide have followed a very similar pattern to the kinds of solutions described by Sudnow (1965) with reference to other areas in the sociology of deviance.

The second major issue which faces researchers who rely on data derived from official sources is, as was noted earlier, the extent to which the officials succeed in allocating all those actions eligible to be defined as suicides into the official category 'suicide'. This has been variously characterized as the problem of accuracy, reliability, or, in criminology as the 'dark number' problem (Wiles, 1971; Hood and

Sparks, 1971). In statistical terms, the problem can be summarized as this: given that the conditions of statistical tests and inferences require that the tester can make formal statements about the relationship between his sample and the population being sampled, how can a researcher proceed to such inferences if his sample is itself a sample of a universe which cannot be specified?[7] Large numbers of the studies of crime and delinquency, for example, are based on samples of institutionalized offenders who are known to represent only a minute proportion of all those dealt with by a particular judicial system. Furthermore, even if all those found guilty during a particular period are taken as the population to be sampled, there remain the problems of how to cope with the unknown number of innocents who were mistakenly found guilty and vice versa. And even if samples are extended to include the entire population of 'crimes cleared up' or 'crimes known to the police', the researcher must still remain in a state of ignorance about the size and nature of the 'dark number'. Yet in spite of, or perhaps because of, the apparent insuperability of such problems, researchers have not hesitated to make very general statements about 'criminals', 'delinquents' and the like on the basis of such sampling procedures. The suggestion is made that this may have been done because of the extreme difficulties involved, on the grounds that attempts to deal with the statistical problems involved require a degree of sophistication in mathematical techniques which is seldom in evidence in studies primarily concerned with asserting general statements about particular groups of deviants (cf. Hirshi and Selvin, 1967).

The decision to go ahead and make general inferences from data derived from official sources in spite of such obvious difficulties has been rationalized in a number of ways. Perhaps the simplest is to assert, as Gibbs (1971, p. 278) does with respect to suicide, that 'there is no feasible alternative'. This appears to be naïve in the extreme, as that is clearly not so. Thus it has already been noted that Breed (1963) attempted to avoid reliance on official statistics by interviewing relatives, while Jacobs (1967) has demonstrated that interesting sociological work can be done on the basis of suicide notes, Firth (1961) has shown how traditional anthropological techniques can be used and, though they have barely been touched by sociologists, there are other sources such as psychiatric case materials which have also been extensively used in suicide research. In the light of these, then, the statement by Gibbs, which is explicitly intended as meaning that there is no feasible alternative to *official statistics*, seems somewhat curious. Alternatives have also been tried in other areas in the sociology of deviance, notably the attempts to gauge the extent of unreported crime or to study samples of self-confessed law-breakers (for example, see Box, 1971, Chapter 3). The aim in such studies is to improve on the accuracy and the reliability of the data available from official sources. Thus accuracy is increased by locating the criminals or delinquents not known to the police and hence not identifiable by reference to official categorizations, while reliability is improved by avoiding the usual dependence on officials to collect other data about the individuals concerned. By collecting their own data, therefore, sociologists can claim first that what is collected is 'sociologically' rather than 'bureaucratically' relevant, and second that the same data is collected in every case.

A second proposed justification for the use of official statistics is that at least they are accurate as far as they go (Wolfgang, 1969). This involves the claim that, although we may not know about the degree of representativeness of our sample, at least we do know that what we have got is a sample of murderers, robbers, thieves or whatever. The problem with such claims, however, is that studies of the way the law is administered suggest that in varying degrees this is precisely what is not available from official categorizations, for the widespread practice of plea-bargaining means that the eventual list of convictions produced by a particular judicial system may bear little resemblance to the original list of charges (cf. Newman, 1956; Sudnow, 1965). Thus the claim that a sample of larcenists, for example, are at least all guilty of larceny is to miss the fact that many of those included in that official categorization may not have committed larceny at all but have agreed to plead guilty to such a charge in the hopes that the guilty plea to a lesser charge would result in a lighter sentence. Even without such evidence, however, the argument that at least one had a sample of a particular group of deviants would not suffice to solve the statistician's problem of specifying the relationship between the sample and the universe sampled. Thus, although it may seem that the studies of plea-bargaining are irrelevant to suicide research given that suicides are in no position to strike such bargains, the problem of statistical inference still remains.

It has been argued to this point that, to the extent that traditional research into the sociology of deviance has posed questions about the near total reliance on data derived from official sources, the questions have been of a kind which leave the assumptions of the positivist paradigm intact. In particular, it has been assumed that the appropriate way to study deviance is to locate samples of persons who are known to have acted in a way which can be categorized as one or other type of deviance, so that the main problems for the researcher are to check on the way his sample was defined in the first place and on the extent to which it is or is not 'all-inclusive'. This involves a further assumption which has seldom been questioned, namely that the most rational way to group individuals into equivalence classes for social-scientific purposes is by reference to some act or acts which they are known to have committed at some time in the past so that other features of their lives can be compared with those of groups not known to have committed those acts, in order to uncover some kind of explanation of the action in question. As Cicourel has observed, this involves a view of social action which begs some fundamental questions about the status of the phenomena being studied:

> for years sociologists have complained about 'bad statistics and distorted bureaucratic record-keeping', but have not made the procedures producing the 'bad' materials we label 'data' an object of study. The basic assumption of conventional research on crime, delinquency, and law is to view compliance and deviance as having their own ontological significance, and the measuring rod is some set of presumably 'clear' rules whose meaning is also 'ontologically and epistemologically clear' [Cicourel, 1968, p. 331].

The focus on 'bad' statistics in the traditional concerns of sociologists, then, presupposes that 'good' or 'better' statistics are in principle obtainable and hence that the testing of explanatory hypotheses is still a viable goal for research. As will be seen below, however, the alternative formulation of the problems associated with the use of data derived from official sources is not concerned with the problem of 'good' or 'bad' statistics, but rather with the *validity* of the approach to the study of social phenomena implied by taking those problems seriously. That this is so means that the many studies of suicide which have totally depended on such data can be assessed from two different perspectives: it can be asked first how far such work measures up to the rules of operationalization and sampling which provide the rationale for being able to make generalizations on the basis of quantitative data, and second whether or not those rules are worth following at all. The ways in which this latter problem has been treated by sociologists of deviance are considered in the following section, and the ways suicide researchers have responded to the former problem is dealt with in section 3.4.

3.3 VALIDITY AND MEANING

In their important critique of the way in which sociologists had used official statistics for research purposes, Kitsuse and Cicourel (1963, pp. 134–5) are explicit about the need for a reorientation of approach away from deterministic studies towards the analysis of the social organization of the rate-producing processes:

> We suggest that the question of the theoretical significance of the official statistics can be re-phrased by shifting the focus of investigation from the processes by which certain forms of behavior are culturally and socially generated to the processes by which rates of deviant behavior are produced. . . . Thus the explanation of rates of

deviant behaviour would be concerned specifically with the
processes of rate construction. . . . The theoretical conception which
guides us is that the rates of deviant behavior are produced by the
actions taken by persons in the social system which define, classify
and record certain behaviors as deviant. . . . From this point of view,
deviant behavior is behavior which is organizationally defined,
processed and treated as 'strange', 'abnormal', 'theft', 'delinquent',
etc. by the personnel in the social system which has produced the
rate.

They go on to point out a number of consequences of this. In the first
place, the specification of definitions becomes an empirical problem.
Second, it becomes problematic as to whether or not the actions included in a particular category are homogenous. Third, a different perspective on the problem of the reliability and accuracy of official statistics is
provided, as they can now be taken to be accurate records of the
numbers of officially defined and processed deviants. Finally, the fact
that the rates are constructed by identifiable organizations means that
the relevant structure which produces them can be clearly specified and
examined. They are, therefore, clearly proposing a move away from the
traditional concern of sociologists with attempting to explain how certain individuals come to engage in various forms of deviant behaviour
towards a consideration of how it is that they come to be categorized as
such.

These ideas were very consistent with those of other sociologists
whose dissatisfaction with traditional positivist approaches to the
sociology of deviance had found expression in the advocacy of an interactionist perspective on deviance (e.g. Lemert, 1967; Becker, 1963,
1964; Matza, 1964, etc.). The ways in which the Kitsuse-Cicourel formulation of the problem of using data derived from official sources were
adapted in subsequent studies, however, were not always in keeping
with the particulars of that formulation. Thus Sudnow (1965, p. 256)
was able to observe some time later that their perspective 'has been on
the whole more promissory than productive, more programmatic than
empirical'. His paper on 'Normal Crimes' is presented as an attempt to
go some way towards remedying that situation, and it is still one of the
relatively few detailed studies of the way in which members of a rate-
producing agency go about doing categorizations which eventually
become 'official statistics'. Other major works in this area were done by
Kitsuse and Cicourel themselves with respect to educational
categorizations (1963) and by Cicourel alone (1968). At its most
general, the importance of these studies was their demonstration that
the processes by which official categorizations are generated are far
more complex than had previously been imagined. The problem of
operationalizing definitions, for example, emerged as a primary practical problem for the officials as well as being simply a technical matter

for researchers, so that Cicourel (1968, p. 104) notes with respect to the police:

> Virtually every instance of categorization requires decisions that transform a truncated behavioural description of 'what happened' into some precoded, but almost never unidimensional, category that enables the police to invoke legal language.

In order to make those decisions, the officials are shown to rely on background expectancies, commonsense theorizing and typifications which enable them to make sense of and objectify the phenomena with which they are faced. By making problematic the procedures employed in assembling accounts of what happened, such works have sought to establish a case for the study of hitherto unexplicated phenomena by sociologists.[8] They have also posed important questions about the meaningfulness of traditional studies of deviance, central among which is the apparently circular reasoning that is involved by asserting that correlations based on officially generated data can be used to validate particular hypotheses about deviance. If, for example, probation officers' decisions to recommend a court appearance rather than some form of discharge for a delinquent are based on his 'knowledge' that delinquents typically come from broken homes and that the particular delinquent being processed is from such a home, then clearly studies based on court statistics will reflect that knowledge. Furthermore, the officials themselves take note of the statistics that their work produces and hence find confirmation of their reasoning in the very results of their own reasoning. The possible implications of such activities for traditional studies based on official statistics seem far-reaching indeed, and it is noticeable that there has to date been no attempt by writers who continue to undertake such studies to reply to such observations.[9]

Doing detailed studies of features of the social organization of particular rate-producing agencies, however, has been only one way of responding to the problems elaborated by Kitsuse and Cicourel. Another is to accept the case against using data derived from official sources and to propose instead that other types of study are indicated which may have little or nothing to do with studying how official categorizations are done. Thus the pleas by Becker (1963, p. 170) for studies of deviants 'in their natural habitats' and by Matza (1969, pp. 3–14) for a 'naturalistic' approach to deviance involve a rejection of the positivist reliance on official data and offer a programme of ethnography in its place (see also Douglas, 1970b).

Such a solution, however, has found its critics even among those who are ready to accept much of the interactionist critique of positivist studies of deviance, and particularly from those who fear that interactionism may misdirect sociology away from its traditional concerns with macro-structural issues towards ever more detailed 'micro' analyses (see, e.g., Gouldner, 1968; Taylor, Walton and Young, 1973).

For some of these, official statistics are still a matter of some concern, but what is at stake is what they mean and what they tell us about social structures. The logic of this style of response to the problem can be characterized as follows. Traditional studies have made the mistake of accepting official categorizations as designating social problems to be studied. The ready availability of such data, coupled with the sociologists' acceptance of the layman's question 'Why do they do it?' (Becker, 1963, pp. 3–4) has led them to look to samples derived from official sources for the theoretical solution. The 'correctional perspective' (cf. Matza, 1969, pp. 15–40) constituted by this approach leads researchers to ignore some of the important features of deviance stressed by the interactionists. In particular, the actor's orientation to his actions are ignored in the quest for the 'real' causes, which are held to lie almost anywhere other than in his expressed utterances. Similarly, the role of the other side of the interaction, namely the 'labellers' or 'agents of social control', are ignored. When all these are taken into account, the meanings of the official statistics can be reassessed. The 'agents of social control' become the 'agents of the powerful', their task being to maintain the *status quo* on behalf of their sponsors. The deviants become the 'oppressed', their 'real' reasons for acting in the way they do being denied by the expert researchers, who claim to have found other accounts which do not raise the possibility that the deviants may somehow be in the van of an awakening revolutionary consciousness. The official categorizations can then be held to reflect those types of actions which the powerful are determined to stamp out, or conversely as those most likely to disrupt or threaten the *status quo*. An astute observer can then point out how the actions which get categorized in the criminal statistics are for the most part offences which are only likely to be committed by members of the working class, while other forms of 'white collar' crime tend to be ignored or simply categorized as non-crimes.[10]

A further mode of response to the problem of officially generated data is less explicitly radical than the foregoing, but similarly invokes connections between different parts of the social structure. The 'deviance amplification model' as formulated by Wilkins (1964) has roots going back at least as far as Tannenbaum (1938), and has been modified subsequently with reference to a variety of deviant activities (e.g. Young, 1971a, 1971b; Cohen, 1967, 1972). According to this, irrespective of the accuracy or otherwise of official statistics, they may be read as meaning that a particular form of deviance is on the increase or is emerging as a special problem. This may be given publicity in the media or elsewhere, which in turn may have the effect of encouraging the relevant officials to take special action with respect to that form of deviance. It may also result in a 'real' increase in the particular activity concerned as a result of the publicity so that this, coupled with the more vigourous action of the officials, results in more cases being recorded in the official statistics. These 'more' cases may then receive further publicity, which may again set the spiral in motion. There are, then, strong deterministic overtones in this approach, the implication being that the model can account simultaneously for the actions of the officials and the actions of at least some of the deviants. And, as with most deterministic models, there is a very obvious problem of over-determination, as it is seldom specified how the spiralling amplification process is ever supposed to come to a halt, let alone how it might be set in reverse.

To this point, then, I have tried to show how there have been a variety of ways in which the problems of using data derived from official sources have been tackled by sociologists who can all be regarded as influenced by or sympathetic to what has come to be known as 'labelling theory'. The common feature of their responses to such data is that they share a rejection of the orientation to the problem outlined in Section 3.2. Officially generated data is no longer to be taken at its face value and treated as 'hard, objective data' on the incidence of deviance or on the location of deviants, for this is to ignore the complexities of the interactions which lead to the official categorizations as well as the possible meanings which the actors involved may attribute to their own actions and the actions of others. Thus the degrees of relatedness between theoretical and operational definitions cease to be matters for concern, the question of whether particular types of action are to be regarded as deviant being not the theorist's construct, but an empirical one to be decided by reference to the way different actions are responded to in everyday life. In keeping with that view, the concern with problems of accuracy and reliability becomes irrelevant for the sociologist, as it derives from the assumption that there are clearly defined equivalence classes of deviant actions which have an existence independent of the activities of members of society who categorize certain activities as deviant. An acceptance of that assumption, therefore, is a necessary condition for believing that some assessment can be made of the extent to which officials succeed in including all, most or some specifiable sample of these actions eligible for categorization in the official equivalence classes.

But while there may be agreement that the issues discussed in the previous section are technical problems, of interest only to those who have settled for a mistaken conceptualization of the nature of social action, there has not been total uniformity among labelling theorists as to the most appropriate response to the problems posed by data derived from official sources. As this book increasingly becomes focused on the problem with reference to suicide, and as its title implies a preference for the study of the social organization of the rate-producing processes as exemplified in the studies by Cicourel and Sudnow, some comments on the relative merits of the responses described in this section are in order.

The 'ethnographic' option has, as was noted, concentrated on areas of deviance which are not necessarily of interest to any clearly defined official agency. Thus the studies by authors like those in the collection *Observations of Deviance* (Douglas, 1970b) have shown how it is possible to conduct studies of groups of deviants who are not readily available in samples derived from official sources. As such, they can in one sense be seen as providing an alternative to traditional studies which have concentrated on officially defined deviants, and hence they do not provide any obvious solution to the problem of how sociologists should regard the official categorizations.[11] The solution they propose is also of very limited potential as far as the study of suicide is concerned, for the chance of doing participant observation with people who are about to commit suicide seldom presents itself, and, by the time that an action has been identified as a suicide, it is by definition too late to engage in the necessary ethnographic work. In general, then, this response provides a way of escaping or avoiding the problems of using officially generated data rather than any constructive advice on how the issues should be faced, while with reference to suicide it is hard to see how an investigator is to conduct such studies. This is not to say, however, that ethnographic methods may not be used to study the rate-producing processes, as clearly they can be and have been used for such purposes (as in Sudnow, 1965; Cicourel, 1968).

The style of response characterized above as involving a revised interpretation of the meaning of officially generated data (hereafter referred to as the 'revisionists')[12] not only differs markedly from the detailed empirical focus on the rate-producing processes or on particular groups of deviants, but also has more in common with the positivist view of such data than is generally admitted. In the first place, the revisionists, like the positivists, seem ready to make far-reaching generalizations about official definitions, statistics, rates and the like, in spite of a widespread lack of detailed empirical studies of the processes by which such data are generated. It is especially noticeable, for example, that the number of British studies, which include critiques of the approach to official data by positivist sociologists of deviance and criminologists, has been increasing (see Atkinson, 1974) even though no studies comparable with the American studies by Cicourel (1968), Sudnow (1965), Newman (1956) or Skolnick (1966) have been published in Britain. One revisionist who shows an awareness of this lacuna is Box, who is also disarmingly honest as to why this should not worry us:

> In chapter 6 I . . . refer to much supportive data, drawn mainly from research conducted on American police, although I have included references to English police wherever possible. I am not convinced that I should now await similar research in this and other industrialized countries before suggesting that 'this is how it is'. To do

so would be to deceive you into thinking that sociologists proceed from facts to theories. This is not so. They either collect 'facts' and never get around to relating these to theories, or, like me, they start with theoretical perspectives and then attempt to illustrate them [Box, 1971, p. vii].

While it may seem reasonable to claim that the findings of American research have an identical or near-identical relevance for British society, Box does not draw attention to the *similarity* between the assumptions on which the assertion is based and those which permit positivists to make, for example, international comparisons between rates of deviance. Furthermore, his concern for suggesting 'this is how it is', together with his remarks here and later about 'facts', might be taken as prima-facie evidence for believing that here is a fairly traditional positivist at work. That is, it appears that the *form* of his argument is similar to that of the positivists, the only differences being those of content and interpretation.

This line of criticism can be developed further to apply to the methods used by revisionists to arrive at their revised interpretations of officially generated data. In particular, it appears that both the positivists and the revisionists are alike in their unreflecting use of the documentary method, of which Garfinkel (1967a, p. 78) writes:

According to Mannheim, the documentary method involves the search for '. . . an identical homologous pattern underlying a vast variety of totally different realizations of meaning'. The method consists of treating an actual appearance as 'the document of', as 'pointing to', as 'standing on behalf of' a presupposed underlying pattern.

Thus Box is unusually honest about the 'presupposed' character of the underlying pattern for which he seeks documentary, or in his terms 'illustrative', evidence. The problem is that the revisionists and the positivists differ as to the underlying pattern of which the officially generated data are a document, the difference being centered on the sociologists' preferences with regard to the appropriateness of a consensus or conflict model of society. Thus positivist criminologists take the legal categories as a 'document of' shared values, while the revisionists take them as a 'document of' the values of the dominant group in society. Similarly the rates generated from official sources can be seen either as 'documents of' the real amount of changes in amount of rule-breaking (deviance) or as documents of the extent to which certain forms of action are deemed undesirable by the ruling class. There are of course many alternative possible interpretations available, all of which face the common problem of how a particular one is to be considered 'better than' the others or as *the* interpretation. Currently there seems to be agreement among sociologists of deviance that there is an underlying pattern behind data derived from official sources and that this can be located. There appears also to be a tacit agreement between proponents of different perspectives that the way to warrant one interpretation as correct or better than its competitors is to rely on or to work to convince an audience that one set of epistemological assumptions is preferable to another and that, given that this is recognized, the particular interpretation being proposed fits better than the alternatives.

3.4 ACCURACY AND RELIABILITY

So far the discussion has centered on general problems which confront *any* social researcher concerned to make sense of or use data derived from official statistics. In this and the subsequent section I want to turn to the ways in which such problems have been matters of concern to suicide researchers. The present section is concerned with the majority group of experts engaged in active research into some aspect of suicide, most of whom are not sociologists.[13] I want to propose *first* that there has been a great increase in the amount of attention given to problems relating to the use of officially derived data; *second* that, in so far as there is an interest, it is concerned with the problem of accuracy; and *third* that the problem has not been solved with sufficient rigour to guarantee the validity of findings based on such research even if one were to accept the scientific norms on which such studies are based.

As has been noted earlier, formulating the problem of officially derived data as one of accuracy involves the assumption that there is some clearly defined thing called 'suicide' which can in principle be identified and counted. A bunch of statistics can then be said to be more or less accurate according to the observer's assessment of the efficiency of the officials responsible for the decisions which later come to constitute the statistics in locating all or nearly all of the deaths which should be categorized as suicides. Sometimes one finds instances where investigators are unhappy with the assessments of the particular official or officials who have provided the data, an example being McCarthy and Walsh's (1966, p. 1393) ecological study of suicide in Dublin:

> Permission was obtained from the Dublin City Coroner and the County Dublin Coroner to examine their records for the years 1954 to 1963 inclusive to find every case coming to the courts during that period *irrespective of the verdicts they returned*. To this end we examined, in the first place, the registers of both coroners for 1954–1963. Entries in these registers in each case described briefly the mode and circumstances of death, and if any of the entries were such as to in-

dicate the possibility of self-inflicted death then the records for that case were scrutinized in detail and *suicide was either confirmed* or excluded [my emphases].

It is to be noted that no clue is given as to the procedures used in 'confirming' or 'excluding' suicides nor is anything said about what it was that led them to scrutinize certain cases in the first place. Whatever the procedures were, however, they certainly made a marked difference to the rates which are cited, for after presenting their tables they offer the following conclusion:

Our investigation has shown that the rate of suicide based on all cases of sudden death coming to the coroners in the Dublin area for the same time [as that covered by the official rate] was 4:5 per 100,000, and thus *twice the official rate* [ibid., p. 1394; my emphasis].

The possible implications of this remarkable finding for other studies based only on suicide verdicts, however, are nowhere considered and McCarthy and Walsh concentrate on comparing their statistical findings with those of other studies (in spite of the fact that their method of arriving at their sample is a notable exception to the normal total reliance on coroners' decisions). They engage also in the kind of dubious statistical reasoning so typical of suicide researchers, where consistency of rates from year to year is taken as being a definite indicator of reliability and where generalizations are made beyond the limitations imposed by the particular sample in question:

We have no reason to suspect that there is any difference in the recording practices in the rest of Ireland . . . the consistency of the official Irish suicide rates from year to year . . . suggests that such is not the case. In consequence we felt justified in assuming that the true suicide rate for the whole of Ireland for the period under study was in keeping with our Dublin experience, twice the official rate [ibid.].

In this example, then, we have a clear statement that the problem to be faced is one of accuracy and reliability. There is a 'true rate' to which the official rate approximates. In order to improve on the approximation provided by the official verdicts, the authors embarked on their own repair work, and the fact that they did not spell out how their decisions were arrived at suggests that they regard the identification of 'real' suicides as a problem sufficiently straightforward to merit no special comment. One important implication of their study is that it puts in doubt, at least as far as Dublin is concerned, any claims to the effect that the errors in the official suicide statistics are small or trivial, for they are claiming to have evidence that the official rate for that city is no more than half what it should be. In other words, investigators, who accept the possibility of making a distinction between 'real' and official rates and hence that accuracy may be a problem, are likely to be faced with serious discrepancies if they endeavour to measure what that difference might be. Given the widespread assumption that it is appropriate to generalize about 'suicide in general' from officially derived samples, findings such as these cast serious doubt on the extent to which it is legitimate statistical procedure to do so, when the samples may be no more than very poor approximations to what the researcher may regard as the 'true' population.

Although there has been more concern with such problems in the recent past the question of the accuracy and reliability of official statistics on suicide is not a new one. Thus one of the most outspoken attacks on research which regards them as unproblematic was published even before the post-war boom in suicidology. Gregory Zilboorg (1936) had sought to disprove what he refers to as the 'pseudo-scientific' view that suicide increases with the development of modern civilization, and the way he developed his argument depended on his showing first that the statistical sources on which that thesis was based were not to be taken seriously. Early in his argument (p. 1350) he states boldly that 'statistical data on suicide as they are compiled today deserve little if any credence'. Foremost among his reasons was that too many suicides go unrecorded. Families, he claims, conceal suicides, while automobile accidents and delayed deaths following suicide attempts are never recorded as suicides, and he goes on to conclude:

> it is obvious that under these circumstances the statistical data available cover the smallest and probably the least representative number of suicides; one is justified, therefore, in disregarding them as nearly useless in a scientific evaluation of the problem [ibid., p. 1351].

Thus Zilboorg's critique took the statistical studies on their own ground, charging them with bad statistical practice in using small and unrepresentative samples for their generalizations. His comments were later taken up by George Simpson in the introduction to his English translation of Durkheim's *Suicide*, where again the problem is formulated as one of reliability and accuracy:

> It appears inescapable to state that until we have better records and more literate statistical classification in terms of psychiatric nomenclature, we can draw few binding conclusions concerning regularity in terms of age, ethnic groups, social status, etc. [Simpson, 1952, p. 19].

In spite of such warnings, however, sociologists and researchers from other disciplines paid little heed, and the analysis of suicide rates has continued in the same uninhibited way as the analyses of the pre-Durkheimian moral statisticians did in the nineteenth century. Even those who, like Zilboorg and, as we shall see later, Douglas, have levelled strong attacks against such work have relied more on argument than on empirical research. Zilboorg, for example, bases his case on *suggested* sources of error which can readily be imagined by his readers. That is, he appeals to plausible reasons for error in a manner *no different in form* from the statisticians' appeals to plausible reasons for believing that the data can be relied on. Thus neither side of the debate proposed much in the way of empirical evidence on the way statistics were compiled or estimates made of the degrees of error until a little over a decade ago.

That some of the earliest systematic attempts to examine possible sources of error and their effects on the official rates were conducted in Scandinavia may have had something to do with the focus of world attention on the alleged high suicide rates there following President Eisenhower's famous observation that Sweden's suicide problem was a consequence of too many years of socialist government. Such claims certainly led American suicidologists to take a special interest in Scandinavia (e.g. Hendin, 1956, 1962, 1964), and may also have led the Scandinavians themselves to seek an alternative explanation of the high rates by reference to the possible greater degree of efficiency and accuracy of their procedures for registering sudden deaths. Thus in 1962, the Danish journal *Sociologiske Meddelelser* contained two papers which addressed the suicide statistics problem with much greater attention to detail than had been usual in earlier discussions. Dalgaard (1962) tackled the problem of international comparisons between rates and argued that figures from the Anglo-Saxon coroner system are not directly comparable with those from countries using a different system. He also suggests, as does Douglas (1967), that the kinds of sociological factors usually invoked to explain differences in the rates of suicide may also explain differences in registration practices. He proposes further that Denmark has a particularly 'objective' system for recording suicides in that death certificates in all cases of unnatural death have to be signed by independent health officers. This is apparently not the case in Norway, where the suicide rate for 1959 was less than half the Danish rate (Weiss, 1964), a difference which Dalgaard suggests may be partly explained by the differences in registration practices. A similarly large difference between the rates of two other countries which, like Norway and Denmark, appear to have a great deal in common culturally is found when the rate for Scotland is compared with that for England and Wales. As with the two Scandinavian countries, the procedures for registering sudden deaths differ considerably, and the rates derived from the Scottish Procurator Fiscal system are much lower than those derived from the English coroner system. With respect to this difference, Stengel (1964, p. 19) makes the following observation:

> The latter [the Scottish suicide rate] has been consistently lower than the former [the suicide rate for England and Wales] by one half to one third. Dr. Neil Kessel, working in Edinburgh, has checked on the recording of an unselected sample of known cases of suicide in Scotland and found only one half of them so recorded.

As with the Dublin study referred to earlier, no reference is made to how the decision was made as to what constitutes the 'real' suicides which were not officially recorded, and Kessel himself has not been more explicit about his findings in any of his published work.[14] It is noticeable again, however, that the observation about the possibility of 'error' in the recording procedures is based on the assumption that deciding between what are 'really suicides' and 'non-suicides' is a simple enough matter to be unworthy of extensive comment or elaboration, and that the problem is one of accuracy and reliability of the official procedures.

Another Danish sociologist, Kirsten Rudfeld (1962) conducted an empirical study into the reliability of the Danish suicide statistics by looking specifically at the 'borderline between suicides and accidents'. She began her study by taking a sample of 'doubtful' suicides on the one hand and accidents which could have been suicides on the other, and proceeds to analyse these according to age, sex and other face sheet variables. This led her to the conclusion that, where a case is doubtful, there is a slight tendency to record women as 'suicides' and men as 'accidents'. With respect to age, she detected a tendency to classify the dubious cases of the very young (less than twenty years old) and the very old (over seventy years old) as accidents rather than suicides. In the very old age-group, she claims that the trend towards misregistering suicides as accidents is large enough to challenge the widely observed tendency for suicide rates to reach a peak at age sixty and then to decrease again in extreme old age. In spite of these findings, however, she is able to present a conclusion which provides some rationale for the continuation of statistically based research by arguing that the dubious cases in each category just about cancel each other out. And two years later, another Danish sociologist (Weiss, 1964) began a Durkheimian study of suicide with the observation that Denmark was a particularly appropriate place to test Durkheim's theories on the grounds that the statistics were particularly reliable in that country.

By 1967, the problem of accurate certification had achieved sufficient importance in suicidology for a plenary session of the Fourth International Conference for Suicide Prevention to be devoted to 'Certification of Suicide Around the World' (Farberow, 1967). Speakers from the U.S.A., Britain, Mexico, Sweden and Czechoslovakia presented papers concerned with the general difficulties and with the specific merits and defects of the official procedures in different countries. The seriousness of the doubts which were in evidence at that Conference as well as the pervading concern with the assumption that there is some 'true' rate to which the recorded rates approximate, is exemplified by the first and most ambitious paper of the session:

> In recent years the reliability of mortality statistics in general and of suicide rates in particular has been questioned. According to Louis Dublin, still the leading expert in suicide statistics, the United States suicide rates understate the *true incidence of suicide* by about one third. This is a very conservative estimate compared with one made by the Mental Health Division of the City of Chicago. Two investigators, Kostrubala and McIerney, surveyed the deaths of all persons in Chicago investigated by the coroner. They formed the opinion that the official suicide rate is only one third or one fifth of the *true figure*. They believe that the attitudes to suicide on the part of the public, and of the Coroners and their juries, are responsible for the enormous degree of concealment, and that only a drastic change of the public attitude to suicide could remedy this situation. Dr. Ettlinger of Stockholm and some others have expressed grave doubts about the value of suicide statistics today. Surely, time has come for a serious study into this problem [Stengel and Farberow, 1967, p. 8; my emphases].

Statements like this, together with the observations on particular problems relating to differences in laws and attitudes, between systems involving medical and legal officials and the more specific problems raised in this and subsequent papers, suggest that at least the lack of concern about such problems is a thing of the past. It is interesting to note, however, that at the same time as they were reported on some documented research on the 'inaccuracy' of the Chicago registration procedures, a large-scale sociological analysis of over 2,000 recorded suicides was being conducted in that same city. When the report was published two years later, however, Maris (1969) made no more than the minimal observations referred to earlier and certainly does not refer to the study cited at the Conference.

Given the sentiments expressed in the above quotation from Stengel and Farberow's paper, and given the apparently high degrees of error they quote, it might have seemed that the last vestiges of faith in the appropriateness of using officially derived data for scientific research would have been shattered. The commitment to the idea that the statistics were an essential tool for doing a science of suicide, however, seems to have been greater than any commitment such experts might have had to the kind of methodological rigour which appears to underlie the concern for the problems posed by the certification processes. That is, in spite of evidence to suggest that the degrees of error were large enough to make very dubious any sampling procedures based on populations of officially recorded suicides, such obstacles were *argued away* or at least not deemed sufficient to call a halt to further research based on the suicide rates:

> What are the implications of our findings for suicide research and prevention? Should we ignore suicide rates and discard statistical methods altogether? Certainly not. But we ought to strive to make them more meaningful and more truthful [Stengel and Farberow, 1967, p. 13].

The implications of the last sentence here is that they are currently 'meaningful' and 'truthful' in some degree but that there is some room for improvement. The extent of the 'meaningfulness' and 'truthfulness' of the present rates is neither defined nor specified, which seems somewhat surprising given the kind of evidence about high degrees of error they present. Also unspecified is just how 'meaningful' or 'truthful' they *ought* to become in the future or how one is supposed to know when some adequate level has been arrived at. All that is given are pieces of advice for the continued use of such data and policy proposals for improving the standards and comparability of death-registration procedures:

> We ought to adopt the principle that only comparable data should be compared and that the onus of proof of comparability falls on those who use the data. Obviously, the study of changes in the suicide rates in the same population over periods of years and the comparison of suicide rates of different populations are valuable even if they understate the truth, provided the methods of case finding are the same. . . . We should press for the certification of suicide being entirely freed from its associations with the criminal law and to be made a medical responsibility with proper safeguards. . . . And we should aim at uniformity of certification procedures and the adoption of common operational criteria for case finding [ibid.].

Thus Stengel and Farberow's message seems to be that research can continue even though the data may leave much to be desired. Whereas in the past suicidologists could do analyses of suicide rates without reference to any of the problems relating to how they had been compiled, they must now 'pay attention to them', 'take care' and provide a rationalization or using them *in spite of* known difficulties. The way of doing science, therefore, was to remain intact. Issues relating to the problems of measuring social phenomena according to natural science procedures which were increasingly becoming matters of concern to sociologists were never raised at the Conference, and the discussions took place within a consensus that suicide was amenable to being identified, measured and analysed statistically, the only difficulty being that unknown numbers of 'real' suicides were escaping the official net.

With one or two notable exceptions, such as the already referred-to study by Rudfeld (1962) cited earlier, discussions of the certification problem up to and including most of those at the Los Angeles Conference had been based more on impressions about possible sources of error and anecdotal evidence than on extensive empirical research. This situation, however, has been gradually changing and more studies explictly directed at throwing new light on the problems have been undertaken and attempted in recent years.[15] An early example of this was Wayne's (1969) study of the certification procedures in different areas of the U.S.A. Initially, he reports, he was faced with the problem of doing research in a situation where there was 'enormous variability in local practice', as different systems of death registration are used in different areas of the U.S.A. (ibid., p. 11). His study, therefore, aimed at comparing suicide rates between areas with a medical examiner and areas with a coroner, as well as a questionnaire survey of the two groups of officials. The coroners complained in the survey of the widespread failure of other relevant personnel to report deaths to them. some estimating that as many as 25 per cent of sudden deaths were not being reported. Wayne calculates on the basis of this that there may be as many as 16,000 deaths annually which should be considered by coroners or medical examiners but which never reach them. Of the deaths the officials did handle, the mean estimated proportion of 'equivocal cases' was 2 per cent, while the mean of their estimates of the proportion of unrecorded suicides was 13:5 per cent. The result of three separate tests of the hypothesis 'that medical examiners should produce a higher proportion of suicide verdicts than coroners' (because of their greater medical sophistication) failed to show any significant differences in rates between the jurisdictions of the two types of official. The only notable difference was that the medical examiners recorded 8 per cent more suicides from poisoning than did the coroners.

Considering the novelty of doing this kind of research, and the apparent importance of so doing which was emphasized at the Los Angeles Conference, it is somewhat surprising that Wayne's report ends with almost no reference to the wider implications of his work for suicide research, and the reader is left to speculate on whether this is a manifestation of the author's discontent with the relative inconclusiveness of his study or of his desire to be the 'ideal scientist' who merely presents his results for interested parties to use as they wish. More surprising, perhaps, is the research design adopted, which aimed at looking at so many different jurisdictions, for, given that no detailed study had to that time been done of any one jurisdiction, it might have been a more appropriate starting point to concentrate on an examination in one area rather than attempting to collect the impressions of a large number of officials and to do statistical comparisons of their areas. In this sense Wayne's study, like the others done to explore the accuracy problem, seems to share with the studies for which accuracy is a problem a primary concern with quantitative data and only a minimal interest in qualitative materials.

The same emphasis on providing statistical evidence is to be found in the most important British study so far published, in which Sainsbury and Barraclough (1970) seek to provide a statistical proof of the appropriateness of continuing to use official statistics for research purposes.[16] As it has been claimed recently in a major British sociological journal that, as a result of the Sainsbury and Barraclough study 'the reliability of these official statistics, both in Britain and internationally, has been vindicated' (Bagley, 1972, p. 397), their work must be considered in some detail. Two questions were subjected to statistical scrutiny:

> (a) whether differences between national suicide rates are independent of the method by which suicide is reported, and (b) whether differences between coroners' districts in England and Wales are independent of the coroner who determines the verdict [Sainsbury and Barraclough, 1968, p. 176].

Though their approach to the first is highly ingenious, it is to be noted that its logic rests on an unquestioning acceptance of the Durkheimian conclusion that 'a nation's rate of suicide is determined by its social characteristics (idem.). That this conclusion itself was allegedly based on an analysis of the official rates in different countries is an observation which Sainsbury and Barraclough leave on one side when it comes to elaborating on the reasoning behind their test:

> The method used . . . was to correlate the suicide rates of immigrants from different countries to the U.S.A. with the rates of their countries of birth. Each immigrant group will, of course, have its suicides ascertained by the procedures used in the U.S., but if their rates correlate with those of their countries of origin, each of which will use its own particular national procedure, then the differences between countries are occurring in spite of their different methods of reporting suicide [ibid., p. 177].

The rates of eleven groups of immigrants to the U.S.A. in rank order of suicide rate from the highest to the lowest are than presented in a table together with the national rates of their countries of origin. A mathematical calculation is then all that is needed to 'solve' the complex problem of international comparability:

> The product moment of correlation of 0:87 is highly significant (P 0:001). The differences between the suicide rates of these countries cannot therefore be accounted for by their differing procedures for reporting death [ibid.].

Similar statistical tests are then done on data from areas of England and Wales where there had been a change in coroner and on the basis of these they reach with similar ease the conclusion that the coroner has almost no impact on the suicide rate, except that they detected a small degree of 'under-reporting' in the case of open verdicts.

Yet though Sainsbury and Barraclough seem to provide an impressive 'scientific' proof that a 'science of suicide' can be legitimately based on certain uses of the official statistics, their study leaves much to be desired even in terms of the scientific standards with which they claim to be operating. To begin with, it is claimed that the statistics they use, which were gleaned from a distance with minimal direct reference either to the systems of death registration operating in the different countries referred to or to the persons involved in working those procedures, provide a legitimate rationale for making far-reaching generalizations about the impact of those persons' attitudes and actions on the procedures and on the ensuing calculation of suicide rates. Furthermore, the immediate leap from the correlation coefficient to the conclusion as quoted above suggests that no alternative interpretations of the finding need to be entertained by the reader, it being assumed that the figures presented bear directly and unequivocally on the questions posed by the authors. In particular, there is a failure to consider the possible effect that other statistical relationships available from the kinds of study which they are attempting to validate on their tests. Given the importance ecologists normally give to 'known correlations' between particular variables and suicide rates, the most surprising feature of their work, not to mention Bagley's blind acceptance of it as a 'vindication', is the total absence of any attempt to control for the possible effects of these other correlations in their comparison between national rates and those of groups of U.S. immigrants from the countries considered. It seems reasonable to assume that the national groups will differ both among and between themselves according to dates of migration, patterns of settlement in the U.S., religion, education and occupational status, and, as Sainsbury and Barraclough ought to know, important statistical relationships are frequently found between these 'variables' and suicide rates. But they not only fail to give any attention to the possible influences of these other 'ecological factors' on the rates of migrants, but also their failure to control for dates of migration coupled with the choice of a particular annual rate for the countries of origin seems to imply that there is a mysterious form of telepathic communication at work, whereby the migrants keep 'tuned in' to the latest available national trends in their homelands. In short, this first part of their 'vindication' falls a good way short of the standards of adequacy normally associated with the kinds of analyses which their study is claiming to vindicate.

Similar objections can be made to the conclusions drawn from the second part of the 'vindication'. This is based first on the somewhat dubious assumption that if the overall number of deaths categorized as suicides remains constant or nearly constant when there is a change in coroner the accuracy and validity of the certifications is guaranteed. Without a more detailed study of cases than they provide, however, it is difficult to see what the basis for such an assumption could be, for it is presumably quite possible that the *types* of death being so categorized may be quite different, even though the quantities may remain approximately the same. An even more dubious assumption on which their analysis is based is that the coroner's role is the only important one. That is, their analysis rests for much of its apparent force on providing a 'before-after' situation such that readers will recognize that different systems of registration are operative during the two periods. As will become clear in later parts of this book, however, many others are involved in the process. The coroner makes his decision on the basis of evidence which has been collected, edited and written up by coroners' officers, other policemen, chemists, pathologists, ballistics experts and the like, and, unless all of these change at the same time as the coroner (which they do not), Sainsbury and Barraclough can again be charged with ignoring the possible effects of too many important 'variables'. Further problems also seem to be posed by their use of the suspect measuring rod (suicide rates) to check on the degree of suspicion with which it (i.e. suicide rates) should be treated. Given difficulties such as these, and given the extreme brevity with which their vindication has been proposed, it is not easy to see how the claim that their work constitutes a green light for continued research based on the manipulation of rates can be maintained. That is, the standards of 'scientific' procedure to which they are clearly committed would require a much more detailed and careful examination of the rate-producing processes before the kinds of unequivocal judgements they make could be deemed valid.

I began this section by proposing that there has been an increasing degree of concern for the problems of using officially generated data for research among suicidologists, and went on to look at some of the studies which I take to form part of this trend. The content of these provides support for the view that, in so far as the statistics have been regarded as problematic, the problem has been conceived as one of accuracy and reliability. Running through all the studies is the assumption that suicides are relatively clearly defined events and that the only problem is the technical one of how far the official procedures are efficient in recording all such events that take place. In keeping with this Durkheimian view of suicide as a 'fact', is a view of doing a science of suicide along fairly traditional Durkheimian lines by using procedures of sampling, statistical testing and the like drawn from the natural sciences. Asking questions about the appropriateness of that way of doing science is *in no way a part* of the scientific enterprise which has come to be known as 'suicidology'. With respect to the studies relating to the problems of using official data, several conclusions can be drawn. In the first place, results which reveal serious degrees of error do not lead to the conclusion that other research based on official data is scientifically inadequate and that further similar research should be discontinued. At the very least, one might expect that a temporary halt to such work might be recommended while the possible sources and extent of 'error' were examined in more detail. Where such examinations are done, a curious willingness to stay several steps removed from the probable sources of error is in evidence, so that statistical manipulations, like that by Sainsbury and Barraclough (1970), or addressing a few questions to coroners about their opinions on the degrees of error as was done by Stengel and Farberow (1967) and Wayne (1969), is deemed an adequate way of approaching the problem.

In short, then, there emerges a profound inconsistency between the ideals of 'good scientific procedure' which lead such researchers to an awareness that there might be serious sampling problems involved in using official statistics, and the responses of such workers to the results of studies which do indeed reveal serious problems. The implications of these latter studies would seem to be *not* that research can be continued 'with care' but rather that detailed analyses of the registration procedures must be the necessary preliminary to any further work of that kind.

3.5 DOUGLAS ON SUICIDE STATISTICS

The only extensive discussion of the problems associated with using data derived from official sources for the purposes of suicide research which stands apart from those discussed in the previous section is that by Jack D. Douglas (1966; 1967). One central difference is that Douglas does find the problems so severe as to reject further research

based on the analysis of rates and to propose an alternative approach to
the study of suicide. That alternative will be considered further in the
next chapter, and in the present context I shall confine myself to some
observations about the differences and similarities between his discussion of official statistics and those considered in Sections 3.3 and 3.4.

Douglas begins by examining the arguments traditionally offered by
sociologists in support of using such data in their studies. He notes that
there had not only been no serious attempt to examine or overcome the
kinds of problems already discussed in this chapter, but that there had
also been a remarkable lack of concern for establishing any relationship
between the formalized meanings of suicide adopted for analytic purposes and the meanings used by officials and others involved in registering the deaths as suicides. In a highly original section, he shows how
such problems were at least in evidence in the writings of Durkheim
and the other early writers, but that they and their successors continued to proceed with their work in spite of such unsolved problems. In
response to possible claims that such issues are unimportant or only of
small significance, Douglas elaborates on the problems posed by the existence of different official definitions of suicide and different search
procedures designed to assess whether or not the official requirements
are met. He also closely scrutinizes the statistical arguments
traditionally invoked in defence of regarding the official data as reliable
enough for scientific purposes, concluding that all such cases rest on
very dubious logic and generally lack support from systematic empirical
research of the sort which would be required to establish such
propositions. In relation to this theme, Douglas also raises a number of
possible difficulties which could have important implications for the
official rates such as the role of concealment and attempted concealment by families and significant others. He also raises the problems
posed by the necessity for coroners and other officials to impute motives
to deceased persons in order to categorize deaths as suicides and shows
how such a process may have very serious implications for research
based on data derived from their decisions.

Douglas's treatment of the problems involved in using official
statistics can be distinguished from those discussed in the previous section in a number of ways. His examination of the logic underlying the
traditional defences of doing analyses of suicide rates is so extensive and
so critical in its conclusions that the possibility of continuing to conduct
such research 'in spite of' known difficulties is ruled out. While his case
is heavily dependent on exposing fallacies in the traditional justifications of statistics, it is given added strength by his suggestion of
further difficulties which were almost completely new to suicide researchers. Thus his discussion of the possible connection between social
integration and rates of concealment and attempted concealment and
of the influence that this may have on the resulting suicide rates

suggests that a radical reinterpretation of Durkheimian and much subsequent theorizing on suicide may be needed. If the official suicide rate
is dependent on rates of concealment and if rates of concealment are
highest among those who are more socially integrated, then we are
faced with the possibility that Durkheim's theory, not to mention others
based on the official rates, account only for the official rate and not
necessarily for the 'real rate'.[17] And if that is so, the need for research
which would expose the 'real rate' would be clearly indicated if the aim
were still to be to explain suicide rates in such a manner. A further
novel problem which is not normally discussed in consideations of the
suicide statistics is the way in which coroners have to impute motives to
the deceased as part of their analyses of the situations with which they
are presented. Thus he proposes that coroners examine the cases they
are presented with for their 'suicidal meanings', and that their verdict
will depend on how far these can be located in a particular case. How
they do this involves them in highly complex interpretive procedures
which include the need to refer to their knowledge of what constitutes a
suicide,the circumstances under which people are most likely to commit
suicide and so on. His argument here is closely related to that Cicourel (1968) and, not surprisingly, the implications for attempts to
'verify' theories by reference to official statistics are very similar.

In making points such as these, Douglas is raising issues in the context of suicide research very similar to those which have been subjected
to more extensive debate within the sociology of deviance and which
were discussed in Sections 3.2 and 3.3. Not surprisingly, then, he is involved in raising more general questions about the validity of research
procedures based on officially derived data in addition to
demonstrating the technical problems which stand in the way of such
research. To the extent that his critique leads him to reject such
research 'in principle' as well as on technical methodological grounds
which, if solved, might provide for doing analyses of rates, his work is
an important and radical departure from conventional discussions of
the problems.

In so far as sociologists and other suicide researchers with a commitment to the view that officially derived data can fruitfully be used to do
a science of suicide have replied to Douglas, their comments when
taken together point to some of the weaknesses of his critique of suicide
statistics. This is not to suggest that any such researcher has engaged in
a detailed examination of his arguments or in a carefully argued reply,[18]
but rather that the different interpretations of his thesis which are to be
found suggest that there may be ambiguities in his treatment of the
problems. In a brief reply to the problems posed by Douglas, Bagley, as
has already been mentioned, invokes Sainsbury and Barraclough's
study as a vindication of the official statistics:

Since Douglas is preoccupied with the social meaning of suicide, he fails to come to terms with the statistical work of Gibbs and Martin, and is in fact generally sceptical of work based on official statistics of suicide. It is an important point that the reliability of these official statistics, both in Britain and internationally, has been vindicated [Bagley, 1972, p. 397].

That he does this suggests a belief that a reply referring to reliability is an adequate reply to what Douglas has to say. Another attempt to cope with the critique is to read his formulation of the problems as being different from and not necessarily incompatible with those relating to the problems associated with analysing rates: 'In part Douglas's criticism is just a plea for different sources of data (Maris, 1969, p. 169). Gibbs begins his one-paragraph reply to Douglas by suggesting that Douglas's contribution was concerned with reliability:

> Jack Douglas has articulated the most sweeping condemnation of official suicide statistics, and the evidence he presents indicates that some rates are grossly unreliable. Douglas deserves credit for bringing the issue to the forefront, but his argument is not convincing [Gibbs, 1971, p. 278].

The claim that Douglas fails in making his case is backed by the lack of systematic empirical evidence in his study. Gibbs goes on to observe that:

> Above all, Douglas's epistemology negates the very notion of a 'reliable rate' . . . from Douglas's perspective there are as many suicides in a population as there are divergent categorizations of deaths, and hence no rate is any more or less reliable than another. Indeed, the very notion of a reliable rate is alien to his perspective. Now the true incidence of suicide is unknown and unknowable, but it can be considered inferentially. For example, suppose that, working independently, several investigators gather data and compute a suicide rate for the same population. If those rates correspond closely, there is reason to regard each as fairly reliable. Douglas has no conception of a 'true' rate, and he asserts that 'great disagreement' exists among officials, investigators and laymen . . . in categorizing deaths as suicide. But he presents no systematic evidence on the question, and that is precisely the kind of research we need [ibid., 278–9].

There are curious inconsistencies evident in these two extracts from Gibbs, for, having claimed that Douglas deserves credit for having brought before the issue of reliability to the fore, he then proposes that reliability is not an issue for Douglas anyway. Gibbs then uses the same grounds for dismissing the second formulation of the problem as he used for ignoring the first, namely the lack of 'systematic evidence'. His other device for dismissing the epistemological issue is to propose in very vague terms a hypothetical investigation which, if certain results were found, would give 'reason' for believing the rates were 'fairly reliable'. Quite apart from the fact that no clear guide is given as to how such research could be done, why no one has done such 'needed' work, in what sense the possible results would give us 'reason' to assume reliability or how reliable 'fairly accurate' is or has to be, Gibbs effects a sleight-of-hand which resembles that by Bagley. That is, having recognized that Douglas is concerned with something *other than* the problem of reliability, Gibbs resorts to arguments about reliability to make a case against the more general epistemological stance of Douglas. He is therefore able to avoid having to consider the implications of Douglas's arguments for the kind of statistical work to which he is so committed.

That his critics have been able to respond by confusing the problems of accuracy and reliability with the broader problems of epistemology can be seen as a consequence of the way Douglas presents his case on official statistics. That is to say, there is an important sense in which Douglas himself fails to make a clear distinction between the two sets of issues he deals with. Thus his extended examination of the arguments typically used to defend the *reliability* of the rates gives the impression that he too regards this as a relevant issue and that if his objections were met something approaching a reliable rate could be obtained. At one stage in his argument, for example, he writes:

We shall never be very sure about the reliability of the official statistics, and certainly not about their validity, until a great many good studies have been made of the methods used by officials to categorize deaths, their assumptions, their methods of collecting data and tabulating it, and of the 'real' community rates of suicide [Douglas, 1967, p. 297].

Here the tension between his concern for the two sets of problems is quite explicit. He distinguishes between the reliability and validity of the official statistics and clearly implies that some 'real' rate is potentially knowable. Elsewhere in his discussion, he sometimes concentrates on the wide variability in definitions and meanings of suicide and sometimes on variations in patterns of concealment. The former kind of argument takes the whole problem of imputing meanings to actions as problematic and hence suggests that the ways actions get categorized as suicides must be the central focus for research, while the notion of concealment implies that it is in some way obvious what are 'really' suicides, or at least obvious enough for families to attempt to cover it up when it happens. Thus the 'concealment' problem seems to be one which is closely parallel with the 'dark number' problem referred to in the earlier discussions of criminal statistics, and which is a problem only if the investigator starts from the assumption that some 'real' or 'true' rate is approximated by the official rate. The fact that he refers to the need for research into patterns of concealment is a further instance where it seems that he is advocating possible solutions to the problems of accuracy and reliability. Furthermore, pleas for further research such as this lay him open to the charge made by Gibbs that his case is lacking in empirical support, though what Gibbs does not note is that this omission is something which Douglas clearly admits when he says that his rejection of the statistics is primarily based on 'an abundance of negative plausible arguments'.

Douglas, then, can be criticized both for failing to clarify the distinctions between the nature of the problems he deals with and for relying more on logic and argument than on the findings of empirical research. It does not follow from this, however, that his critique need not be taken seriously or that an adequate reply to his discussion of the problems associated with social meanings can be made by reference to arguments about reliability, as is done by Bagley and Gibbs. Such responses not only fail to address the wider epistemological issues, but also fail either to note how little empirical research has been directed to the problem of accuracy, or to subject what work has been done to any serious critical assessment.

3.6 CONCLUSIONS

In this chapter, I have attempted to show how the problems of using data derived from official sources can be formulated in a number of different ways, and how the kinds of solutions sought will be, or at least should be, dependent on which formulation is adopted. It was then suggested that, with the exception of Douglas, suicide researchers appeared unaware of or unconcerned with any formulation other than that which conceives of accuracy and reliability as the only issues which need to be addressed. I went on to subject studies of that problem to a critical assessment in which I suggested that there is still no evidence which warrants the conclusion that analyses based on officially derived data can be continued as if there were no significant problem.

By clarifying that there are different ways in which the problems associated with using data derived from official sources can be approached, I hope to have resolved some of the ambiguity found in Douglas and to have shown the inadequacy of the few brief dismissals of his work which perpetuate that ambiguity by referring to arguments about reliability in replying to the epistemological issues posed by Douglas. There is, however, some justification for the charge that Douglas relies more heavily on logic and argument than on the results of empirical research, but this is a charge which can equally be levelled against those who claim that official statistics really are accurate and reliable enough to warrant continued research in the Durkheimian tradition. In other words, the general lack of research into the way in which official data is collected is an important omission which is common to the different formulations of the problem. In the next chapter, therefore, the form such research might take will be considered.

Chapter 4

Alternative Sociological Approaches to Suicide Research

4.1 INTRODUCTION

It may seem from the discussion so far that there has been no sociological work on suicide other than that which is based directly or indirectly on data derived from official sources. But while it is true that the majority of studies have relied almost exclusively on such sources, there have been a small number which have used or proposed the use of rather different methods. These, together with their implications for empirical research, are the concern of this final chapter in Part I.

4.2 SEQUENTIAL MODELS OF THE SUICIDE PROCESS

In a celebrated passage of his book *Outsiders*, Becker (1963, pp. 19–39) distinguishes between what he calls 'simultaneous' and 'sequential' models of deviance. The former is used to characterize the traditional positivist studies of deviance which, by claiming to locate large numbers of 'variables' which correlate with deviance detected at some later date, involve the assumption, first, that all the 'causes' are operating simultaneously and, second, that explanations are to be found by taking two points in time (e.g. early childhood and the time at which the detected deviant act occurs) and inferring that the things that happen at the later date are in some way determined by characteristics found at the earlier time. Becker, like others associated with the interactionist approach to deviance, is highly critical of such a model and proposes as an alternative what he calls the 'sequential' model. Here deviance is formulated as emerging from a continuing process in which interactions between the individual, agents of social control and others may lead, via the attribution of labels and the like, to the individual adopting a deviant identity and becoming 'committed' to a deviant career. Very similar themes also run through the work of Lemert (1967, pp. 40–64) on primary and secondary deviation and of Matza (1969) on 'signification'. This kind of distinction between approaches that focus on variables which may be located at separate and unrelated points in time and those which focus on an ongoing process provides a useful way of clarifying a general difference between the kinds of studies of suicide criticized in the previous chapter and those to be considered here. This is not to say that the distinction is always a very clear one or that the authors referred to below are necessarily explicit in setting their work within one or other perspective, but rather that the studies to be considered can be read for their relevance to the sequential model of deviance so that, when taken together, such a model of the suicide process can be generated.[1]

An early reading of these works, coupled with those by sociologists who were proposing the alternative 'sequential' model of deviance suggested the model of the suicide process presented in Table 4.2.1 below.[2] The general contention was that at the different stages different things could happen which would lead a particular individual towards or away from proceeding to the next stage and ultimately to finishing as an officially recorded suicide statistic.

TABLE 4.2.1   *Three stages in the processes leading to suicides being recorded as such**

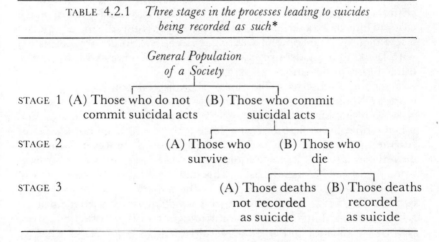

* Source: J. M. Atkinson, 'On the Sociology of Suicide', *Sociological Review 16*, (1968, p. 89)

Thus prior to the suicidal act, warnings and the responses to them were seen as crucial, after a suicidal act the probability of intervention to save life seemed most important and, after death, the possibility of differential concealment patterns was cited as a determining feature of official registration. What I want to do now, then, is to look at the kinds of works which led to the construction of this model before going on to consider how far it provides any clear directions for conducting empirical research.

Stage 1 in the model refers to the period up to and including the suicidal act. From the point of view of doing research, this is, as was mentioned earlier, probably the most difficult point where it would be possible for anything approximating participant observation to be carried out, for it is seldom possible for persons to be located during a pre-suicidal phase. From the point of view of the sequential model of deviance proposed by Becker, however, it is clearly crucial, as it would be during this period that the interactions between the individual concerned and others would be so crucial. Not surprisingly, then, the only study which even remotely approximates an analysis of the sort that might be advocated by those who stress the need to focus on the processes of becoming deviant was conducted by psychiatrists, who had close contact with a small number of mental hospital patients who subsequently attempted or committed suicide. One of Kobler and Stotland's main interests in their book _The End of Hope_ (1964) is with making a connection between a change in administrative policy in a small private American mental hospital and a 'suicide epidemic' which followed the arrival of the new superintendent of the hospital who instituted the changes. They do report, however, in extensive detail on the cases of four patients who engaged in suicidal actions during a period of a few months, and some of what they say seems to be very consistent with the kind of model proposed by Becker and others with respect to other forms of deviance.

Prior to the change at the top of the hospital administration dealt with by Kobler and Stotland, patients who were regarded as suicide risks were not singled out for special attention from the nursing and other staff, and, while that policy lasted, there had been no suicides or suicide attempts. A new policy was introduced, however, which required special 'suicide precautions' to be taken in cases where patients were deemed to be suicidal risks. This included things like a notice with a large 'S' being placed on the door to the patient's room as well as the confiscation of razors and other objects which might be used in an act of self-assault. Within a year of the introduction of these practices, there were three suicides and one near-fatal suicide attempt. Thus what we seem to have is the introduction of activities which amount to fairly explicit labelling of particular individuals as 'potential suicides' followed by those individuals engaging in suicidal acts and, although the references cited by Kobler and Stotland reveal no familiarity with the sociological literature on interactionism and labelling theory, the interpretation they offer is that this practice was in major part responsible for what they describe as the 'suicide epidemic'. Using detailed case notes and transcribed interview materials with one of the patients who survived, they argue that the suicide precautions viewed from the point of view of the patients represented the 'end of hope'. The patient who survived, for example, describes how he had come to the hospital as a last desperate attempt to have his problems solved and how, on finding that he was treated as though he was about to commit suicide, he took this to mean that the doctors and staff also regarded his case as hopeless. On having his spectacles confiscated, he had tried to imagine how it was that he was supposed to harm himself with them. The only thing he could think of was that he could perhaps use the stems to poke out his own eyes, whereupon he started to poke at his eyes with his fingers, which promptly led to his arms being tied to the bed by the hospital staff.

Kobler and Stotland, then, present evidence which seems to support strongly the contention that the reactions of other people to suicidal warnings are crucial determinants of whether or not a suicidal attempt will follow. During the period when there was no explicit or public labelling of patients as suicidal, there had been no suicide problem in the hospital, but, following the introduction of special suicide precautions there was what they describe as an 'epidemic'. Furthermore, in the case of the survivor referred to above, we seem to have clear support for there being a point at which a potential suicide becomes 'committed', in Becker's terms, 'to a suicidal career'.

There are, however, a number of problems with the kind of analysis provided by Kobler and Stotland. The first of these relates to one of their interests referred to earlier, namely that their object was to expose what they deemed to be bad psychiatric practice and indeed they wrote a separate book documenting the successes and failures of the same hospital (Stotland and Kobler, 1965). The reader, therefore, cannot be sure how far the selection, presentation and interpretation of their materials are influenced by that interest and hence how far their attribution of responsibility for the suicides to the policies of labelling patients as potential suicides is exaggerated. It is furthermore difficult to see how a sociologist might check on their findings or engage in another study designed to explore the process in a similar way, for not only would there be severe practical constraints on getting the kind of access to a mental hospital that would be needed,[3] but the focus on particular individuals who were viewed by hospital staff as being suicidal might, particularly if Kobler and Stotland's thesis is correct, lead to a self-fulfilling prophecy for which the researcher might be held responsible. In addition to these practical and ethical problems, there are at least two further important methodological difficulties. The first is that if one were to enter a hospital situation where some patients were regarded as suicidal, with a view to analysing the effect of such labelling on those individuals' subsequent conduct, the question of how such ascriptions were made in the first place would be wholly begged. There would be a tendency to assume that such ascriptions were clearly and systematically made so that the staff and the observer would, at any point in time, have a fairly good notion of which patient fell into which category. This in turn might imply that the recognition of suicide warnings or tendencies was also a fairly unproblematic process which was carried out prior to any suicidal actions which might be committed. As I hope will become clear in later parts of this book, however, it is extremely difficult to prove that such ascriptions are made in any unequivocal way prior to the occurrence of suicidal actions. After such actions have occurred and have been categorized as 'suicidal', utterances and actions of the individual prior to the act may be recalled and reassessed as 'signs', 'warnings' and the like. In other words, what I am saying is that attempts by sociologists to conduct such enquiries are likely to lead very early in the research to a realization that there are other possibly more fundamental questions being begged, or left unanswered, by proceeding straight to an analysis of the reactions to the labelling.[4] A further constraint on such research would be that, even if it were possible to conduct such a study of persons deemed to be suicidal within a hospital setting, it is difficult to imagine how it would be possible to study the reactions to suicidal warnings and the subsequent actions of those giving the warnings in any other setting. In crude sampling terms, therefore, one would be able only to cover a very small group of 'pre-suicidal' persons, who may well already have experienced interactions in which suicidal intimations had been given and responded to prior to entry into hospital.[5]

Some of these problems, however, only emerged as a result of having attempted to embark on similar research and as a result of observations made in mental hospitals in connection with another research project.[6] Initially, the work of Kobler and Stotland seemed to provide the promising beginnings of an interactionist interpretation of suicide. This promise was enhanced by the results of the research by psychiatrists into the high frequency with which suicidal warnings are given by persons who subsequently commit suicide (e.g. Robbins, *et al.*, 1959; DeLong and Robbins, 1961). Thus there seemed to be evidence to support the view that large numbers of persons who commit suicide give some kind of warning at some stage in their pre-suicidal career. Coupled with this, the apparent prevalence of the saying 'people who say they are going to kill themselves never do' and its variants seemed to provide at least some prima-facie evidence for believing that the reactions of others to such warnings might prove an interesting and, from the interactionist perspective, potentially fruitful subject of study.[7] Hence, in formulating a sequential model of the suicide process, it seemed that the identification of reactions to suicidal warnings must play an important part in determining who proceeded to the second stage in the process.

That there might be a second stage in the suicidal process during which intervention of some kind might make the difference between life and death was, when first made, a novel proposal within sociology. As

James Wilkins noted in his detailed and extensive review of the psychiatric literature on attempted suicide, sociologists had almost completely ignored the phenomenon of uncompleted suicide attempts in their analyses of suicide. Given that most authorities estimate that there are many times more attempts than suicides,[8] it is particularly surprising that statistically oriented researchers, and particularly those aware of the special problems posed by the use of small samples, did not turn their attention towards this subject. That they did not implies either ignorance of its relative prevalence compared with completed suicide or that they considered attempted suicide to be an essentially different 'thing' from achieved suicides. This latter argument has certainly had its attractions for psychiatric researchers, who have argued that suicides and attempted suicides are most appropriately to be studied as separate phenomena. Stengel is perhaps the best-known protagonist of such a view, though he does tend to qualify it when asked to provide rigid distinctions between the two. There are also even finer distinctions to be found in other psychiatric writings with Kessel (1965), for example, arguing that 'self-poisoning' is properly to be regarded as a special pattern of behaviour which can be objectively distinguished from other kinds of suicide attempts. Sociologists, however, have for the most part been totally silent on the matter, which means that the reasons for ignoring the possible relevance of apparently more widespread suicidal phenomena than the achieved suicides recorded in the official statistics are largely obscure. Thus Wilkins (1967, p. 296) is highly critical of any sociological works on suicide which fail to consider warnings and attempts:

> . . . little more can be learned about suicide by adhering to the traditional methods and assumptions for its study – especially those which prohibit or discourage analysis of attempted suicide and suicide communications.

The alternative approach advocated explicitly involves conceptualizing suicide in terms of a process:

> Between (1) exposure to conditions which appear to generate suicidal impulses and (2) registration of a suicidal death, there are many pathways; and, for by far the greater number of persons who enter, these pathways do not lead to suicidal death. Systematic differentials in the pathway selection would obviously bear upon continuing work to explain the suicide rate. With this point in mind, we have turned to work on the entire suicide process [Wilkins and Goffman, 1966, p. 4].

In addition to drawing attention to the general neglect of attempted suicide by sociologists, Wilkins also criticizes the traditional sociological approach to suicide for failing to take any notice of other widely reported suicidal phenomena such as warnings and gestures. A third important part of the process, which is provided for in the model presented in Figure 4.2.1, is the possibility of intervention to save life after a suicidal action has taken place:

> According to the evidence, it is a very small proportion of those who do complete suicide who have not been exposed to some opportunities for intervention. . . . It is clear that completed suicide is affected by opportunities for effective medical intervention . . . [ibid., pp. 8–9].

Just as there is evidence in the non-sociological literature on suicide which points to the importance of suicidal communications and attempts, so are there some pointers to the crucial role which may be played by intervention during this second stage in the suicide process. In his study of suicide and risk-taking in Tikopia, Raymond Firth (1961) showed how the society's 'rescue services' played a crucial part in determining whether or not death resulted from the suicidal-risk-taking activities of its members.[9] He describes how the young men of the tribe may put out to sea in unworthy boats for a destination which can only be safely reached when the sea and weather conditions are exceptionally kind. On learning that such a trip has started, the other tribesmen set out in an attempt to bring them back. If these rescue services are instituted very soon after the risk-taking voyages begin, there is a good chance that the men will be brought back safely. On the basis of this, Firth argues that the suicide rate is dependent on the efficiency of the society's rescue services and goes on to speculate on this as a possible determinant of suicide rates in other societies. Evidence to support such a thesis, though not originally presented with that in mind, can be found in some of the psychiatric literature on attempted suicide. One of the biggest differences between the samples of suicides and attempted suicides studied by Stengel, Cook and Kreeger (1958), for example, was that intervention by others after the suicidal act was many times more frequent in the case of the attempts than in the case of the completed suicides. It was also the case in this and other studies that the samples of attempters appear to be markedly less isolated than the suicides, a finding which is clearly consistent with the higher rates of intervention and which also poses the possibility of a reinterpretation of the Durkheimian theory of suicide.

The final stage in the process, then, is that between suicidal death and official registration as such which provided the basis for much of the discussion in the previous chapter. Initially it seemed that this sequential model of the suicide process could be used to orient empirical research into suicide which attempted to overcome some of the more important mistakes and omissions of the traditional sociological studies. I have already referred to some of the problems, such as access to settings in which the first stage could be examined, which emerged early in the research. A further practical problem stemmed from the fact that the model derived from an attempt to synthesize a considerable amount of different materials which had been gathered in different ways. The result of this was that all attempts to design a research project involved the proposing of several separate projects which were certainly beyond the capacity of a single researcher to conduct on his own. That is, the model seemed to point to a programme of research which could last many years rather than to any clearly defined and manageable work which could be carried out fruitfully by one researcher over a limited number of years.

In addition to this, there were a series of worrying theoretical problems which will be examined further in Section 4.3 below. The ones most relevant in the context of this section are these. First, all the attempts to derive directives for empirical research from the sequential model required that at some stage definitions which the work of Douglas (1967) suggested were crucially problematic had to be taken as given. Finding samples of people who had given warnings, for example, would require a reliance on assessments which had already been made by others involved in particular settings. Assessing the role of intervention would necessitate some prior operationalization of what was to count as intervention. Similarly one would be very heavily reliant on retrospectively formulated accounts of what happened by others who had been involved in the suicidal sequences. This poses serious methodological problems, for, as Henslin (1970) has pointed out, accounts of such sequences by survivors seemed to be characterized by the speakers providing explanations of what happened which absolve them from any responsibility for the suicide. In other words, it can be argued that significant others of the suicidal typically formulate stories of the events which are at least partly designed to show the hearer that the speaker 'did all that might have been reasonably expected of him', and is not to be seen as having played a significant part in the causal sequence. If this is the case, and indeed some of my own data would tend to support it, then it would be clearly very difficult for the sociologist to decide on the validity of such retrospective accounts as means of providing data for assessing responses to warnings, interventions and so on.

Finally, the argument referred to earlier that social integration may play a significant part at each stage in the process is not so much providing an alternative interpretation of the suicide rates to that of the traditional Durkheimian studies as it is merely filling in some of the intervening variables not alluded to in such studies. In other words, it suggests that suicide rates are indeed correlated with social integration, or the lack of it, but that this results from much more than features of an individual's situation prior to any suicidal act being committed. The observation that traditional sociological studies of suicide have drawn a sample from 3B in the model in order to make generalizations about the difference between populations 1A and 1B may be correct, but if social integration is as crucial at each stage in the process as was suggested in that early paper (Atkinson, 1968), then all that is being done is to propose a rather more complex causal chain than is implicit in the traditional studies. How far this can be said to constitute an alternative approach to suicide research, therefore, is questionable, as it shares with Durkheim a deterministic focus on the official suicide rates. [10]

4.3 SUICIDE AND SOCIAL MEANING

The most detailed and explicit attempt to provide an alternative approach to the sociology of suicide is that presented by Douglas (1967) in his *The Social Meanings of Suicide*. In the early sections of the book, where he offers extended critiques of earlier sociological studies of suicide, he had relied heavily on observations to the effect that researchers had either ignored or relied unknowingly on their own commonsense understanding of the social meanings of suicide and on their readers' ability to recognize and accept these in a similar way. With respect to the final section of the book, he says that it is 'the culmination of the whole argument and, if my argument is convincing, the beginning of a new sociological approach to suicide' (ibid., p. xiv). What I want to do here, then, is to consider the basis for such an ambitious claim with particular reference to the empirical solution he proposes and to the directions for further empirical research provided in his work.

That Douglas begins his final section by invoking Weber's definition of social action in terms of the subjective meanings of activities to social actors may not seem very original in the context of contemporary debates in sociological theory. It comes as no surprise, however, for very early in his thesis (ibid., p. xiv), Douglas had noted that the approach he would be advocating would not be altogether new as far as sociology as a whole was concerned, but that it was certainly an innovation for the sociology of suicide. At its simplest, then, Douglas seems to be advocating the adoption of a Weberian rather than a Durkheimian approach to the study of suicide. In places, however, he seems to want to go beyond this by 'putting right' the mistakes of Weber and his latter-day interpreters. Thus he begins by distinguishing between what he says Weber was advocating and what later interpreters have said he was advocating:

There is, however, a difference between what Weber was calling for and what these later sociologists interpreted his work as calling for. Weber was concerned with obtaining the 'inside story' or 'meaning' of events as the actor himself saw or interpreted it. These later, semi-Weberian sociologists have, on the other hand, been quite unconcerned, in the particular when not in the abstract, with determining the meaning of things from the standpoint of the actor [ibid., p. 236].

The most important exceptions to this criticism cited by Douglas were the ethnographic studies of the Chicago school of the 1920s, and he goes on to argue that the sub-cultural theories of deviance which followed much later provide a beginning to the return to a 'purer Weberian goal' (ibid.). Douglas suggests that the main reason for the failure of later sociologists to read Weber's methodological recommendations correctly was that the interpretive procedures which seemed to be indicated were 'very much in opposition to the strong tide toward highly "objective", formalized methods in American sociology' (ibid., p. 237). The result, according to Douglas, was two sorts of allegedly Weberian sociology, the first being an increasing tendency to formulate abstract typologies of social phenomena, which derived from Weber's writings on ideal types and which were characterized by no more than remote references to how things may look to the actors involved in the situations being referred to. The second is what he calls the 'average building-block approach' to the analysis of meanings, which involves locating general patterns of meanings which, taken together can then be said to constitute a society's culture. These two responses to Weber, he suggests, are not at all surprising given certain fundamental ambiguities in Weber's own writings:

First, Weber himself seems not to have resolved the conflict between his demand for studying meanings concretely, which, presumably would call for the study of individual meanings, and his concern with very generally shared patterns of meanings. Second, for all his concern for the subjective meaning of events to the individuals involved, Weber did not conceive of these meanings as being constructions of the individuals; quite to the contrary, he looked at the statements, actions, etc. of individuals only to discover the underlying, causal, general (or 'average') patterns of meaning which he considered to be the basic components of culture [ibid., p. 238].

There is, then, a problem with respect to the relationship between meanings at the level of the individual and general shared patterns of meanings. The typologizing solution takes little or no account of individual meanings, while the 'building-block' option fails to specify how individual and shared patterns of meaning are related or how to move from one to the other.

Douglas, then, expresses a deep concern for the empirical problems involved in moving from observable phenomena to general statements about shared patterns of meaning. Sub-cultural writers such as Albert Cohen and Gresham Sykes are given some credit for their attempt to make inferences about the orientations of delinquents and prisoners respectively, but Douglas raises further objections to their style of analysis which can be levelled against a very large proportion of the work carried out within sociology. His remarks are very similar to sections of Cicourel's (1964) critique of conventional research methods in sociology, though that work is not cited during this part of Douglas's analysis. Thus he writes (ibid., p. 241):

> my particular criticism of this type of representational analysis of meaning is that it *infers* that the 'things' or 'meanings' lying behind (or under) the linguistic categories (or whatever they take as their data) are the grand abstractions of some sociological theories. . . . These sociologists do not infer from linguistic categories any images, thoughts, feelings, beliefs, etc., which one might actually observe or experience indirectly by communications with the actors or directly as a social actor himself. Rather, they simply assume that the observable phenomena are representations of their theoretical categories. Such analyses of social phenomena really tell us nothing of a scientific nature: they consist primarily of merely imposing upon the immediately observable phenomena an abstract set of assumptions about the nature of society, assumptions which can be applied anywhere to any social phenomena.

This view that much of sociological methodology involves a sustained attempt to show how observations are in some way consistent with the particular theoretical assumptions of the researcher is one which has caused sociologists a good deal of trouble in recent years. The solution suggested by Cicourel and other ethnomethodologists has been to propose a kind of analysis not traditionally known or used by sociologists which, not surprisingly, has invoked a good deal of opposition from other sociologists (see Chapter 8). Similarly, other attempts to find a solution, such as Matza's (1969) appeal for a 'naturalistic' sociology, have caused a good deal of debate and, unlike ethnomethodology, have been more programmatic than productive of analyses which demonstrate the 'how' of the solution being proposed. It is, then, with a good deal of interest that the reader awaits an answer from Douglas to the kinds of problems he has isolated to this point in his argument.

Unfortunately, from this stage onwards, Douglas's thesis seems to diminish in clarity at the very point when his 'new approach' to the sociology of suicide was to have been articulated and demonstrated in action. Somewhat surprisingly, in view of his comments about the dangers of abstract generalizing about ideal types, he introduces his solution by stating:

> It is not my intention to argue that general or abstract theoretical propositions are irrelevant or necessarily bad in such work. On the contrary, I shall be quite concerned with *certain* general propositions and arguments concerning the nature of suicidal meanings and the way one should study them [ibid., p. 242].

These general statements, however, will not, he promises be of the sort whereby an analyst argues from general propositions about the nature of social systems, actions or meanings 'down to' the specific details of suicidal meanings. Rather the concern is with:

> *certain* ideas concerning the general dimensions of suicidal meanings and of the general properties of suicidal processes. In fact, my whole method of analysing social meanings leads us to try to see the general in the particular and the particular in the general; and certainly one of the fundamental ideas of this method is that the particulars are frequently comprehensible only in terms of the general context in which they occur, so that one must have some idea of the general context in order to understand the particular. (We might call this *the principle of contextual determination of meanings*.) And this general context is not something that is necessarily part of the *meanings* available to the social actors themselves: they may be, and almost certainly are most of the time, quite unaware of such general dimensions as we shall be considering. But it is of the greatest importance that these fundamental dimensions of suicidal meanings are intended to be directly relatable to concrete, observable suicidal phenomena in this culture [ibid.; his italics].

This passage has been quoted at length here because it is the place at which Douglas is as explicit as anywhere else in his work about the nature of the approach that he is advocating. Coupled with his subsequent refusal to define or even attempt to define what it is that we are to regard as 'meanings', these statements seem remarkably unhelpful to anyone seeking directions as to how to undertake research consistent with the new approach he is advocating. What he seems to be saying is that there are important *general* patterns of meaning associated with suicidal phenomena, and there are *particular* meanings which are available to and invoked by persons involved in suicidal episodes. Such persons may not be aware of the general dimensions, but the general dimensions may nevertheless be located and subjected to analysis by sociologists.

Having noted that there is a general vagueness about the formulation of this 'new approach' to the sociology of suicide, I now want to be a little more Precise about the nature of that vagueness. To begin with, it is remarkably unclear just what it is that the sociologist following Douglas would look for which has not been looked for by earlier suicide researchers. Nor does he say in any detail whether some features rather than others are more appropriate data for the analysis of social meanings. What he does say in this context is: 'The statements, cries, actions and whatever other real-world phenomena one can come up with are the data one must use to study and analyse meanings . . .' (ibid., p. 43). In other words, we seem to be provided with an infinite range of choice of what can be gathered and analysed. This in turn poses further problems for the would-be social meanings analyst. First, it is not made clear what features of such data constitute the social meanings in which we are supposed to be interested. Is it the 'statements, cries', etc., themselves, is it interpretations of those phenomena by actors involved in suicidal episodes, or is it something which is available only after the researcher himself has engaged in interpretations of such data? In other words, there are no directions as to how the investigator is to recognize social meanings or to be sure that what he has located is a social meaning. Nor are there any directions as to what he should do if his claims with respect to what he has found are questioned or denied by others encountering those claims. That is, though Douglas appeals to appropriate modes of doing science in his critique of traditional studies of suicide, he fails to provide for his own approach a crucial component of any methodology with scientific pretensions – namely, he provides no warranting procedures for researchers to apply to their data and analyses. A second related problem is that he is not clear about what one is supposed to do with the social meanings once they have been located (assuming, of course, that the researcher has overcome the above problems to an extent which allows him to assert that he has indeed located certain meanings, whether they be 'individual' or 'general patterns of meaning'). Thus an analyst may be supposed to produce some kind of catalogue of meanings which he might claim constitute part of, or the beginning of, some kind of total description of a particular culture. Alternatively, he might be supposed to elevate what he has found to the status of 'causes' of suicide, arguing aginst Durkheim that it is not some 'reified structural situation', but, rather, 'social meanings' which cause suicide. A third possibility constitutes something of a combination of these two, namely that having generated some kind of catalogue of different types of suicides according to the different meanings they have or manifest, one proceeds to look for different theories to account for the different types of suicide.[11] And running through all these difficulties is one which was referred to earlier in this chapter, which is that before getting to a stage at which such data can be collected and analysed, the actions, etc., which constitute the data have already been defined as suicidal by persons other than the researcher. It is all the more surprising that Douglas seems content to ignore this feature of the kind of data he seems to be recommending, since he, more than any of the other sociologists referred to whose work deviates from the traditional Durkheimian approach to suicide, raises the problematic nature of such definitions as a crucially important issue, particularly in the context of his discussion of official statistics.

Now it may seem a little unfair to raise these kinds of criticisms of the Douglas approach at the point where he is offering a programme rather than a demonstration of how to conduct research into the social meanings of suicide, for it could be argued that the proof of the pudding must be in the eating. As his programmatics proceed towards the analysis of some data, however, the kinds of confusions referred to above seem to become more rather than less marked. In his chapter on 'The Construction of Social Meanings', for example, he turns his attention to the importance of language in the analysis of social meanings, arguing first that there is a very close correspondence between linguistic categories and social meanings, and second that language provides for immense ambiguities in interpreting the meanings. At one stage he observes that:

> there seems to be no very clear set of rules either for *ordering* the linguistic terms or applying them to specific phenomena: i.e. *there is variability, ambiguity, and conflict in the imputations of the linguistic categories, including the fundamental category of 'suicide,'* (or 'suicidal') *itself* [ibid., pp. 247–8; his italics].

This statement is a particularly interesting one from the point of view of the ethnomethodologist, for it points to an empirical problem which has provided an increasingly important focus in recent years (e.g. Sacks, 1963, 1966, 1972a, 1972b; Schegloff, 1972). That is to say, although it does indeed appear at first sight that there are no such rules for ordering linguistic categories and that they are irredeemably ambiguous, most members of society do appear to conduct their everyday lives with such a degree of definiteness and *unambiguousness* that they not only achieve things as a result of linguistic communications with one another, but also seem to display a degree of definiteness in their actions which has allowed generations of sociologists to do analyses of those actions *as if* they were reified things. In short, if it were the case that the use of linguistic categories is as ambiguous and uncertain as Douglas suggests, then it becomes impossible to imagine how sociologists could ever have engaged in the kinds of positivist analyses of social actions of which he is so critical.

These remarks have important consequences both for the type of research proposed by Douglas and for that reported in the remainder of the present book. For his observations about the absence of any clear rules for the ordering of linguistic categories (and hence, in his terms, also of social meanings) and on the immense ambiguity of suicidal meanings, in particular, points to at least two kinds of research. One can either take it as a prima-facie fact of life that there are no organized procedures for assembling categories such as suicide, or one can regard that as problematic and orient research towards discovering whether or not there are such procedures and, if so, what they might consist of. Douglas seems to take the former view, which is somewhat surprising given his discussion of official statistics in which he does indeed imply that definitions of suicide are arrived at in an ordered and patterned way. The research that he goes on to report then consists of his presenting interpretations of various situations which had already been defined as suicidal, in which he proposes that the suicide had this or that meaning. The relationship between what he says the meanings were and what they appeared to mean to the participants is left unclear, as is the status of his own interpretations. In presenting what he regards as 'common patterns of meaning' in Western cultures, for example, he states that he will analyse these by:

> concentrating our attention on the analysis of those patterns of ac-
> tions and meanings which seem, from a general survey of the
> literature of the Western world on suicide, to be most frequent [ibid.,
> p. 284].

There follows a list of sub-headings, which seem to constitute the kind of typologizing activity of which he was critical earlier, and under which he collects various examples derived almost exclusively from secondary sources of one sort or another which he claims can be suitably characterized by the particular sub-heading under which they appear.[12] In so far as this is as close as he gets to demonstrating his new approach to suicide in action, the method seems to consist of the researcher sifting through the ambiguities of the social meaning in order to 'iron out' some of them to a point where a particular construction can be put on them such that they can be gathered together under a heading which it is the claimed constitutes a 'common pattern of meanings'. What the analyst seems to be required to do, then, is to examine the ways in which particular suicidal events (already defined as suicidal by others) can be or were interpreted by the actors involved in them and then to arrive at a conclusion as to 'what they *really* meant'. As already noted, how to move from the data to the conclusion is by no means explicit, but perhaps more important even than this is that the method appears to be an invitation to do something else of which Douglas was, at an earlier stage, highly critical. That is, the observer is still being expected to put a construction on his data in a manner not very different from that to which he refers in the quotation cited earlier on p. 78. At the end of that, he noted:

> Such analyses of social phenomena really tell us nothing of a scientific nature: they consist primarily of merely imposing on the immediately observable phenomena . . . an abstract set of assumptions about the nature of society, assumptions which can be applied anywhere to any social phenomena [ibid., p. 241].

If we substitute 'phenomena reported by other observers' for 'immediately observable phenomena', and the 'nature of culture' for the 'nature of society', we are left with what is arguably a very apt characterization of the approach to suicide advocated and demonstrated by Douglas himself. In short, I am suggesting that in showing how to do research under the auspices of his 'new approach', Douglas can be faulted first on the grounds that what he does is not so very different from what previous researchers have done, and second that his demonstration is inconsistent with his own programmatics. His biggest failing seems to have been that, having articulated the problematic nature of the way in which linguistic categories are organized, he does not proceed to take this as his research topic with reference to suicidal categorizations, but attempts to provide a series of interpretations designed to render more clear the ambiguities to which he refers.

I have suggested that Douglas's 'new approach' to suicide tends to involve a number of important mistakes, including some for which he had criticized earlier sociologists. From the point of view of continuing research into suicide, the main criticism is that his work provides no clear directives as to how new empirical work should be done or what form it should take. The research reported in Part II of this book, then, was done in an attempt to find ways of studying what seemed to be among the more important of the problems Douglas poses.

PART II

Suicide
and the
Social Organization
of Sudden Death

Chapter 5

Registering Sudden Deaths: Official Definitions and Procedures

5.1 INTRODUCTION

One of the main criticisms of the work on suicide by Jack Douglas which was raised in the previous chapter was that, although he deals at some length with the problematic nature of definitions of suicide in his section on official statistics, he focuses on situations already defined as suicidal when it comes to demonstrating his research method. In other words, like previous suicide researchers, he leaves the question of *how* suicides become identified and categorized as such empirically open, in spite of pleas such as the following that research into the work of the officials responsible for registering sudden deaths should be carried out:

> The final and most certain answer to the question of the reliability and validity of the official statistics on suicide can be given only by intensive and extensive empirical investigation of the methods, implicit and explicit assumption, etc., of the officials who are responsible for the statistics on suicide ... [Douglas, 1967, p. 229].

The idea that there are or may be many different definitions and different types of definitions of suicide leads immediately to a bewilderingly complex situation from the point of view of doing empirical research into the subject. We have already referred, for example, to possible differences between the formal or theoretical definitions used by researchers and the official legal definitions used by those responsible for registering deaths. For both groups, there was also the question of how those formal definitions are operationalized with respect to individual cases. There was, further, the probability that different researchers and different officials would be operating with different definitions. If one adds to these two groups with an interest in suicide those actually involved in suicidal situations such as significant others and medical personnel, the range of choice as to where to begin research becomes even wider. This is illustrated schematically in Figure 5.1.1. The situation portrayed there is such that for most sorts of definitions, there are an unknown and possibly quite large number of

FIGURE 5.1.1   *Schematic representation of different types of definitions of suicide*

Definition used by	Type of definition	
	Formal	Operational
Researchers	A1	A2
Registration officials	B1	B2
Persons involved in suicidal situations	C1	C2
Other members of society	D1	D2

available definitions. The empirical interest with which this research began was in the way in which suicides are officially registered, and the schematic representation in the table suggests that there is a prima-facie case for believing that Type B would be the most straightforward area with which to begin, for it initially seemed obvious that at least there would be only one relatively clearly stated official definition of suicide in England and Wales.[1] Having established that, it would then be possible to look at the ways in which this was operationalized by coroners and others in the practical work of registering sudden deaths. Such a research procedure had the added attraction that in all the discussions of the problems associated with official statistics, no previous researcher had attempted to locate any official definition of suicide or to study empirically how it was applied in practice. By focusing the research on this aspect, then, it seemed not only that the potentially vast range of research programmes envisaged earlier could be kept on a scale managable by a single researcher, but also that some new and original ground might be covered.

The work done in the early stages, however, suggested that some of the central assumptions about how definitions of suicide were arrived at were in need of major revision, and indeed that the representation presented in Table 5.1.1 not only oversimplifies but also misconstrues the way in which definitions are made. These early conclusions are discussed in Section 5.2, at the end of which a formulation of our central research problem is presented. Section 5.3 gives an account of some of the formal and informal procedures involved in death registration in England and Wales, based partly on documentary materials and partly on field research. The final section then describes a preliminary research design and some problems that emerged in attempting to carry out the research.

5.2 AN OFFICIAL DEFINITION OF SUICIDE?

The long history of the English legal system and its heavy reliance on precedent means that locating precise legal definitions of particular actions is seldom the straightforward task it may initially seem to be. In the case of suicide, it is further complicated, as we shall see below, by the existence until 1961 of the felony *'felo de se'*. Before such complications were discovered, it seemed reasonable to expect that one place where a concise definition of suicide would be found would be in the main legal handbook for coroners (Jervis, 1957). Such an assumption, however, was quickly proved false and although that book stresses the need for coroners to take 'special care' in cases of possible suicide and only to bring in a suicide verdict when there is really firm evidence, it nowhere specifies what features should normally be present for such a verdict to be returned. The word 'normally' is used here because it is not true to say that no definitions of suicide are to be found in the book. The ones that are there, however, are of considerable interest from the point of view of the expectation that there would be only one fairly clear official definition of suicide, for situations are referred to which have probably never been thought of by most members of the society. One of these refers to the length of time which can elapse after a suicidal act for the death to be categorized as a suicide. Thus if death can be shown to follow directly from such an act having been committed, then the death is a suicide. If death occurs after a year and a day, it is not a suicide. It may be noted, then, that although a specific situation is elaborated, the crucial feature from our point of view of how the act would be categorized as suicidal in the first place is not elaborated. A second and probably even more obscure situation is also technically to be regarded as a suicide. If a person A points a gun at person B with intent to kill B, and the gun explodes killing A instead of B, then A is deemed to have committed suicide.[2]

From this initial search, then, we were left with two somewhat surprising results. First it appeared that in official terms there was more than one way in which suicide was defined. The second was that the coroners' main legal handbook provided us only with what seemed to be rather obscure definitions, presumably taking it for granted that 'normal' suicides were obvious enough to be easily identifiable. A further search was therefore started in Halsbury's *Statutes*. On finding 'suicide' listed in the index, it seemed that the quest was on the point of being ended. It emerged, however, that suicide was there defined as being the same as 'homicide' except that the victim was the 'self'. This was to complicate the situation even further, as the homicide law is itself complex, distinguishing for example between 'murder' and 'manslaughter'. In so far as it was possible to derive a succinct definition, it seemed that it involved the killing of another person with malice, malice apparently meaning something like 'intent'. Inferring from this to suicide, then, we seemed to have it that suicide constituted killing the self while intent to do so was present.

Although it seemed that at least a close approximation to an official definition of suicide had been discovered, a number of further factors emerged which introduced new doubts. The first was that following the Suicide Act of 1961 suicide had ceased to be a felony, the main practical result of which is that it is no longer a criminal offence to attempt suicide.[3] The definition derived from Halsbury's *Statutes*, however, referred to the pre-1961 situation, which raised the possibility that the act in question had resulted in the removal of the official definition of suicide, so that there is currently no such thing as an official legal definition. A further related complication also emerged from an examination of annual comparisons of the coroners' returns to the Home Office, which show that until 1938 two types of suicide were listed: 'Suicide while insane' and '*Felo de se*'.[4] What had initially appeared to be a relatively straightforward task, then, was becoming increasingly complex, in that the evidence seemed to point simultaneously to there being on the one hand *no* official definition of suicide and on the other *several* such definitions. While this seemed to suggest the need for a more detailed and diligent search through the legal literature, it also suggested that our initial assumptions (as well as those of Douglas and others who had discussed the problem of official definitions) about the problematic relationship between formal and operational definitions had been at fault. This latter conclusion seemed more appropriate in the light of other preliminary investigations which were going on at the same time as the search through the legal literature and it was after the following encounter with a coroner that it was decided to abandon the search for an official definition or a list of definitions.

While discussing the possibility of gaining access to his records and to other parts of the death registration process not normally available to the public, I 'casually' asked a question about my then current obsession: 'By the way, what is the legal definition of suicide?'[5] He replied hesitantly with frequent 'well's, 'er's and 'um's. Reaching for his copy of Jervis (the handbook referred to above), he said, 'well, it will be in here.' I told him that I had already examined it fairly carefully and that I had been unable to find it. He replied by saying 'But it's bound to be in here . . .' and a lengthy pause followed while he skimmed passages of the book in search of an answer to my question. Finally he closed the book and said, 'I don't seem to be able to put my finger on it at the moment,' implying that it was indeed to be found in Jervis, and that it was only shortage of time which prevented him from locating it. 'But anyway, it's straightforward enough, it's – er – it's – um – er – "death while the balance of the mind was disturbed".' Both the answer itself and the manner of its giving are of great interest in the context of the problem with which we are concerned. First, the fact that he regarded it as 'straightforward' seemed wholly consistent with the absence of the definition from Jervis, which itself could be taken as an indication that the problem of definition was more generally regarded as 'straightforward', so much so that there was no need to spell out with any precision what actions should be so categorized. Second, his hesitation immediately following the observation that it was straightforward, is of interest in that it suggests he was unable to formulate a definition immediately *in spite of the fact that he was regularly and routinely involved in categorizing deaths as 'suicidal', 'accidental', and so on.* The significance of this is further added to by the nature of the definition he then proposed, namely one which left out *both* of the central features of the closest approximation to a legal definition that I had been able to come up with, namely the *killing of the self* and *intent.* That he did include the familiar 'rider' often added to suicide verdicts by coroners was also of interest, given that it adds nothing, as far as the law is concerned, to the verdict.[6]

The significance of the response described above is open to a variety of interpretations. One could for example argue that it provides evidence of a very wide discrepancy between the official-legal definitions of suicide and that used by the particular coroner in question, and perhaps go on to conclude that analyses of official data derived from *his* records would be especially dubious.[7] In a more general way, one might be tempted to take his reply as evidence of his incompetence to do his work, for here it seems is a person officially responsible for registering suicides who is not only unaware of the official definition of suicide, but is only able to formulate one which leaves out any reference to 'intent' or 'killing of the self'. Indeed, some of his other practices might be taken as further evidence in support of such a conclusion. On several occasions, while attending inquests, I observed that he sent the jury out to decide between verdicts of 'misadventure' and 'accidental death', having first provided them with instructions as to how to distinguish between the two. In the official mortality statistics and in the coroners' returns to the Home Office, however, no such distinction is to be found, both verdicts being grouped together as accidents. In other words, the wording with which 'accidental deaths' are recorded seems to have no significance as far as the official statistics are concerned, and yet here was a coroner going to considerable lengths to make a distinction between deaths by 'accident' and by 'misadventure'.

Now were we to opt for some conclusion which was critical of the coroner like those suggested above, the position would be complicated by certain other evidence, which suggests not only that this particular coroner's competence compared favourably with that of others, but that he was also held in a degree of special esteem by his colleagues. Thus, with respect to the first point, as far as I was able to ascertain, there had never been any semblance of a complaint made against his work either by the public or by the official agencies to whom he was responsible. And one can take as evidence which is at least suggestive of his enjoying special esteem among his colleagues the fact that he had served for several years on the committee of the coroners' professional association, the Coroners' Society. On a more day-to-day level, he was variously described by persons involved in processing the deaths he dealt with as 'a damn good coroner', 'very conscientious', and 'far better than the one I worked for in Xtown'.[8] To propose a conclusion that the coroner was in some sense incompetent, then, would involve us in extending our accusations far beyond him to his staff, his colleagues and his masters at the Home Office and Somerset House, for we would be saying that it was time they took note of his incompetence.

An alternative, and in my view, preferable conclusion to be drawn from these data is that they point more to a common inadequacy of sociological research practice than to any inadequacy on the part of the coroner in question. For it may be noted that the 'critical' conclusions depend for their sense on an acceptance of the observer's formulation of how official definitions get done. Thus if we say that there are available the different definitions of the type listed in Table 5.1.1, and that the research problem is to identify, for example, the 'formal definition' and the 'operational definition' and then to see how these compare, then the question as to *how* deaths get categorized as suicides *in practice* is being completely begged. It is being assumed that more or less 'clear' definitions are available and that they are somehow 'used' by officials in their work. In this way, the processes of death registration are being formulated in an idealized way and in advance of doing any research. Once this has been done, any research is likely to be directed towards making assessments with respect to how far observed practice matches up to the ideal type, judging from the degree of consistency between 'formal definitions' and the 'coroners' definitions', and between the 'coroners' formal definitions' and 'operational definitions'. Formulating the research problem like this will then almost inevitably lead to making moral assessments about skill, competence, consistency, etc., assessments which rest wholly on the observer's *a priori* assumptions about how the categorization process works. The data reported on above, however, seems to place such assumptions in serious doubt, for we are faced with a situation where categorizations are being routinely done in a way which arouses no criticism (other than that which might be raised by a sociologist who chooses to stay with his original formulation of the problem of official definitions) by a coroner who is unable to provide the official definition when asked, who claims that it is 'straightforward', and who formulates up a definition which leaves out what appear from our other investigations to be the key features of an official suicide definition (killing the self and intent). That official categorizations are being made in an organized and unproblematic way in spite of the presence of factors which, in the light of the 'research formulation' of the problem, seem very strange, suggests that they are being made in a way which is *different* from that conceived by those of us who have been concerned with the problem. It suggests that the empirical issue is *how* the categorizations are done and not how well do they get done, or how closely does their getting done match up to our ideal view of how they get done. In more general terms, it points to the error of discussions of the way in which official statistics are compiled which rely almost wholly on speculative versions of possible errors, practices and processes of the kind considered in Chapter 3, since to rely on such speculative versions is to run the risk of engaging in extensive analysis of phenomena which have no empirical reference beyond the construction of the analyst. For as far as categorizations of suicide are concerned, it is currently the case that there is very little of the kind of evidence on how the categorization process works to provide any basis for making generalizations either about the accuracy of official categorizations or about other interests specified as important by Douglas. The remainder of this book, then, is concerned with studies of *how* some deaths get categorized as suicides.

5.3 PROCEDURES FOR DEATH REGISTRATION IN ENGLAND AND WALES

Though it would be a mistake to think that a detailed description of the procedures of death registration in England and Wales would somehow make available an answer to our problem, I want to provide a brief outline of the system in order that the relevance of the later more detailed focus on coroners and coroners' officers may be clarified.

Prior to 1836, there was no provision for the registration of deaths in England and Wales. What records had been kept were the result of registering burials, which had been the duty of two persons, usually old women, known as 'searchers', who were appointed in each parish. According to the Registrar-General's *First Annual Report* (1839), that system had left almost one-third of all the deaths in England and Wales unaccounted for, and the periodic inflated returns which resulted from epidemic diseases such as cholera tended to result in states of panic in local populations.[9] It was partly in an attempt to overcome such problems that the Births and Deaths Registration Act of 1836 was passed. Precisely how and why the law was changed at that time could be subjected to the kind of analysis proposed by Becker (1963) in his study of 'moral entrepreneurs', though this is outside the scope of the present study. It is, however, worth noting that the whole system for registering deaths is complicated by and reflects the interests of the two professional groups who come together in the Medico-Legal Society. Thus much of the debate about possible changes in the procedures for registering deaths centers on the sometimes conflicting requirements for greater medical precision on the one hand and greater judicial rigour on the other (e.g. the Broderick Report, 1971). Encounters with officials involved in the process during the present research revealed alternative interpretations of the need for accurate and efficient death registration which reflected such interests. The medical version was expressed by a coroner who was qualified in both law and medicine:

> The main importance of our job is to monitor possible epidemics and other health hazards – industrial diseases, dangerous machinery and the like. It's also crucially important to know about causes of deaths in the interests of medical research.

The interest in research is reflected by experts in the field of social medicine and demography, for whom the problems associated with mortality statistics are a constant topic of concern. Another coroner with exclusively legal qualifications expressed a rather different view:

> The important thing is that people should not be left with any grounds for doubt about how someone died. If they were, you'd get all kinds of malicious gossip and speculation.

A somewhat different legal concern tends to be expressed by coroners' officers, as was evident in the following exchange between a coroner's officer and myself:

M.A.: . . . does it really matter to us whether somebody committed suicide or died from an accidental death?
C.O.: I would say that it was important in so far as was death by accident or by design, and, if it was by design, as a policeman I want to know what design it was. Was it intended murder or homicide or was it accidental or was it suicide?[10]

Another expressed a similar view: 'All deaths according to our books are treated, shall we say, as murder to start with.' Just as the first cited coroner's concern for research has its academic counterpart, so also has this concern for the possibility of murders going unnoticed, as is evidenced by academic studies such as Havard's *The Detection of Secret Homicide* (1960).

I have introduced these distinctions between medical and legal concerns at this early stage in order to emphasize that the process of registering deaths involves a constant interaction between the two professional groups, their activities and their orientations to the problems with which they are faced. The participants in the system include doctors, lawyers and policemen, while the procedures may include elaborate medical examinations such as post-mortems, and elaborate legal examinations in the form of inquests. In very general terms, then, it can be said that the final categorizations of deaths result from an interplay of two main professional traditions and are part of the routine practices of members of those professions. The relevance of this observation for the study of how deaths get categorized as suicides will hopefully become clearer as the analysis proceeds.

Following the Act of 1836 which required the official registration of all deaths, periodic changes took place before the system operating at the time the research discussed here was carried out.[11] The basis of the present system is the Births and Deaths Registration Act of 1926, which made it an offence to dispose of any body without a registrar's certificate for disposal or a coroner's order. Most deaths are dealt with in the former manner and only a minority come to the notice of coroners.[12] As it is a condition of the issuing of a registrar's certificate of disposal that the death does not fall into a category which requires the intervention of a coroner, I shall briefly outline what these latter deaths are before looking at the most common way in which deaths are processed.

The Coroners Act of 1887 provides that a death comes under the jurisdiction of a coroner if he receives information which suggests that a death is 'violent' or 'unnatural', or a 'sudden death, the cause of which is unknown', or that it comes under certain statutory requirements such as deaths on the roads, railways, or in prisons. Medical experts have pointed out that the precise scope of such terms is uncertain, and that they can give rise to problems in deciding which cases ought to be referred to coroners. 'Sudden' deaths, it has been claimed, have been interpreted as 'unexpected' deaths, so that some sudden deaths may not attract medico-legal investigation:

A person under treatment for coronary insufficiency may die 'suddenly' from coronary thrombosis, but his death may not have been 'unexpected'. In the medieval period, when the coroner's jurisdiction was established, the state of medical knowledge and the available medical services were such that any sudden death was regarded as unexpected. Under modern conditions a distinction must be made and the word 'sudden' should be replaced by 'unexpected' [B.M.A., 1964, p. 5].

With respect to 'violent' deaths, these same experts also suggest that things are less simple than in medieval times, and cite deaths from operations and certain types of birth injury as being technically violent deaths (ibid.). Most confusing of all, however, is the category 'unnatural death'. Originally, 'natural' deaths were all those not caused by violence, so that 'unnatural' was synonymous with 'violent'. Thus in medieval times, prisoners who died as a result of starvation were deemed to have died 'natural deaths', while by the seventeenth century such deaths had been recategorized as 'unnatural' (ibid., p. 6). Changes such as this led the B.M.A. special committee to conclude that: 'It follows that in the historical sense "Unnatural" death is a dynamic term which is determined by current trends and the attitude of the community' (ibid.).

The distinction between 'natural' and 'unnatural' deaths poses other severe technical problems which are less obsure than the example cited above. Thus there is a sense in which all deaths can be deemed 'unnatural' given that they can at least in theory all be traced to some malfunction or cessation of functioning of some part of the body. Conversely, even 'unnatural' deaths can be described in identical ways to 'natural' deaths. Pneumonia, for example, can be brought on by 'natural' or 'unnatural' events, so that two apparently very different deaths may be attributed to 'pneumonia'. Such medical difficulties have been much debated within the profession, and pose practical problems for the personnel involved in the procedures for registering sudden deaths. An attempt to resolve the ambiguities involved in attributing cause of death is found in the layout of death certificates issued by doctors and in post-mortem examination reports. Figure 5.3.1 reproduces part of a form which pathologists who conduct post-mortems have to hand to one of the coroners who features in this study. It will be noted from Figure 5.3.1 that there are not only two major sets of causes of death, but also three sub-types within the first set. The complicated business of attributing cause of death· is further reflected in the instructions contained in the footnotes to the form, which, in their attempt to achieve greater precision, can be viewed as underlining the approximate or equivocal nature of the problem. Thus there is a sense in which doubt is institutionalized or provided for in the legal requirements which have to be fulfilled in registering deaths, so that the form given as Figure 5.3.1, for example, qualified the apparent precision of the entries specified with the opening clause: 'In my opinion the cause of death was: . . .' Similarly deaths which are registered as a result of certificates issued by family doctors have the 'cause' qualified by the clause 'to the best of my knowledge and belief', and it is when a doctor is unwilling to make even such a qualified statement that most deaths are referred to coroners.

But just as it was argued earlier that a close examination of formal

---

FIGURE 5.3.1   *Extract from Pathologist's report form*

In my opinion the cause of death was:

<table>
<tr><td>I</td><td></td><td>I</td></tr>
<tr><td>Disease or condition directly leading to death*</td><td>a</td><td>. . . . .
due to (or as a consequence of)</td></tr>
<tr><td>Antecedent causes</td><td>b</td><td>. . . . .
due to (or as a consequence of)</td></tr>
<tr><td>Morbid conditions, if any, giving rise to the above cause, stating the underlying condition last</td><td>c</td><td>. . . . .</td></tr>
</table>

<table>
<tr><td>II</td><td>II</td></tr>
<tr><td>Other conditions, contributing to the death, but not related to the disease of condition causing it **</td><td>. . . . .
. . . .</td></tr>
</table>

---

* This does not mean the mode of dying, such as, e.g. heart failure, asphyxia, asthenia, etc.; it means the disease, injury, or complication which caused death.
** Conditions which do not in the pathologist's opinion contribute materially to the death should not be included under this heading.

definitions of suicide would provide no more than an idealized understanding of how some deaths get categorized as suicides, so also is this focus on the official requirements of the various forms which have to be filled in likely to lead to the obscuring of other important features of the way the process works. This may be illustrated by reference to a post-mortem examination I attended. The deceased had died before regaining consciousness after an operation, and I had been told by the coroner's officer with whom I went to the post-mortem that the case was 'very straightforward'. In spite of this claim, however, the deceased's biography, his illness, the necessity for the operation and the chances of survival provided the almost exclusive topics for conversation between the pathologist and the coroner's officer during the actual examination. In other words, it seemed that the 'straightforwardness' of the case was a matter which still needed to be confirmed or agreed on at the examination. Towards the end, the coroner's officer asked the pathologist, 'Well, have you found anything for me?' This question somewhat surprised me, given that I had been assured that it was all so 'clear'. The pathologist had paused after the question and had picked up the heart of the deceased which he seemed to be examining closely. The pause gave me the opportunity to ask, 'I didn't realize you were looking for anything in particular, what are you expecting to find?' The coroner's officer replied, 'The cause of death, I've got to have a cause of death.' At this point the pathologist looked up from his examination of the heart and said, 'Well, I'd like to give you "shock" – "shock" in the medical sense, that is, because the shock of the operation is what really stopped his heart beating, but this coroner doesn't like "shock" does he?' The coroner's officer confirmed that that was indeed the case, to which the pathologist replied: 'I could give you "heart failure" then – how would that be?' 'That'll do me fine, ' replied the coroner's officer. What we seemed to have here, then, was a cause of death which, though officially given on the basis of a professional scientific examination, had been negotiated and agreed upon by the two officials present at the examination. It had furthermore been arrived at by reference to some particular shared knowledge of the coroner for whom they were working, which was not immediately obvious to me as an observer. Afterwards I asked the coroner's officer what the pathologist had meant and he explained that the coroner was worried by the medical status of the word 'shock'. It suggested to him that the cause of death was 'unnatural', which would mean that he might insist on having an inquest. Evidently this happened three weeks previously when the same pathologist had enterd 'shock' as the main cause of death, and the coroner's officer observed, 'I'd had to go to all the trouble of arranging an inquest and Dr. X had to give up the best part of his morning giving evidence.' He also assured me that the distinction was a very fine one and the alternatives really meant the same thing.

Two sorts of interpretation could be put on this incident. On the one hand, it could be claimed that the pathologist and the coroner's officer were conspiring with one another to 'fiddle the books' or to deceive the coroner. On the other, it could be argued that what they did was made possible by, and was a reflection of, the complexities and ambiguities of specifying a cause of death with precision. That is, there were available to them alternative categorizations which were medically and legally defensible so that they could select that one which was most convenient to them. That they engaged in the exchange so casually in front of someone known to be doing research and that the coroner's officer was so willing to clarify the situation for me without any embarrassment or requests for me to 'keep it dark' would suggest that the 'deception' interpretation is hardly plausible. What mattered for the pathologist and the coroner's officer was that 'shock' might lead to an inquest, which would not only be inconvenient to them in a practical way, but would also come to a conclusion which could be arrived at without the necessity of holding an inquest at all, namely death by 'natural causes'. If the death could be shown to be due to 'natural causes' on the basis of the post-mortem, then the coroner would be able to dispose of the case without an inquest. The wording chosen by the pathologist, therefore, was selected in order to raise no hesitation on the part of the particular coroner concerned, so that no inquest was necessary.

The referral of deaths to coroners, then, hinges on a distinction between 'suddenness' and 'unexpectedness' of a death, and the consideration of a death at an inquest depends on a distinction being made between 'natural' and 'unnatural' deaths. For a death to be categorized as a suicide, then, it has first to be deemed 'sudden' and second 'unnatural', and the different channels through which deaths are processed may be clarified by reference to Figure 5.3.2.

FIGURE 5.3.2   *Schematic representation of the death registration process in England and Wales**

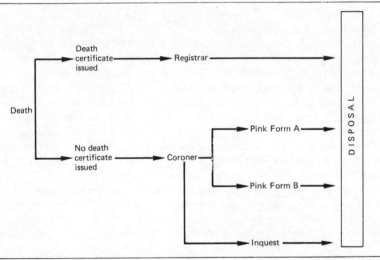

* Derived from descriptions in *Deaths in the Community,* London: British Medical Association, 1964 and *What to do when Someone Dies*, London: Consumers' Association, 1967.)

In order to issue a death certificate, a doctor must have either seen the deceased within fourteen days of the death or have seen the body after death. In normal circumstances, this will then be taken by a member of the family to the local Registrar of Births, Marriages and Deaths who then issues a Certificate of Disposal which gives the go-ahead for funeral or cremation arrangements to be made. There

may, however, be special problems which lead the registrar to withhold
the Certificate of Disposal and refer the death to the coroner as indicated by the arrow in Figure 5.3.2. As the B.M.A. special committee
observed on p. 7 of their Report:

> A 'last illness' can last a very long time, and it seems that death cer-
> tificates can be accepted without reference to the coroner in circum-
> stances where the doctor has not seen the deceased person for several
> weeks. Many things may happen in the meantime without the
> knowledge of the certifying doctor, and the absence of any statutory
> definition of attendance during the last illness constitutes a serious
> loophole in our system of medico-legal investigation. The only
> safeguard is the duty of the local registrar to notify the coroner where
> it appears from the death certificate that the certifying doctor has
> neither attended the deceased with 14 days before death, nor has
> seen the body after death. But if the doctor *has* seen the body after
> death, the 14 day rule does not apply and the coroner need not be in-
> formed.

The rules for the issue of a death certificate, then, do not require the
certifying doctor to see the body after death and he may issue one, for
example, on being informed of death by a relative of the deceased. According to the report cited above, 25 per cent of all death certificates are
issued without the doctor seeing the body (B.M.A., 1964, p. 8). Where
a doctor is unwilling to issue a certificate, either because the death was
'sudden' or appeared to be 'unnatural', and in those cases referred to
above which are noticed by the registrar, the coroner is informed. In
1969, 20 per cent of all deaths in England and Wales were referred to
coroners (Broderick Report, 1971, p. 5), and this proportion has
remained fairly constant at least since 1950 (B.M.A., 1964, p. 8).

Once the coroner has been informed, death certification may proceed
in four ways, according to whether or not a post-mortem is ordered and
whether or not an inquest is held, and the different possibilities are
shown in Table 5.3.1, which also shows the numbers of cases processed
in each way in 1969.

As indicated by the figures, there is wide variation between the frequency with which the different types of processing are used and, not
surprisingly, there is very wide variation in the practices of individual
coroners (see Broderick Report, 1971, pp. 388–94). Indeed that variation has been a source of much debate among medical and other
specialists with an interest in death registration.[13] Whichever course is
followed, a certificate for disposal will be issued to the deceased's
relatives and although there are special regulations for proposed crema-
tions as compared with cases where burial is intended these are not
directly relevant to our present interests.[14]

TABLE 5.3.1   *Official certification procedures used by coroners in England and Wales and the numbers processed in 1969*

	Without post-mortem	With post-mortem	Totals
Without inquest	14,506* ('Pink Form A' cases)	92,003* ('Pink Form B' cases)	106,509*
With inquest	1029**	24,101**	25,130**
Totals	15,535	116,104	131,639

* Exclusively deaths by 'natural causes'
** Mainly 'unnatural deaths', but with some verdicts of death by 'natural causes'
(The statistics used here are derived from those presented in Appendix 5 of the Broderick Report, 1971, p. 394. The particular way they have been tabulated here is my invention and is designed to clarify the options open to coroners.)

There are a considerable number of inquest verdicts available to coroners, as is shown in Table 5.3.2, which also shows the numbers returned in 1969. In some cases where a death results in criminal proceedings, a coroner may adjourn the inquest indefinitely, the verdict being returned as part of the conclusion of the criminal proceedings (e.g. murder, manslaughter, infanticide and death by dangerous driving). Although there are perhaps a larger number of possible verdicts than might be initially expected, the figures in Table 5.3.2 show that by far the most frequently used ones are *Accident, Suicide, Open verdicts, Natural causes* and *Industrial diseases* in that order, and these verdicts comprised 98.7 per cent of all verdicts returned by coroners in 1969. The high proportion which result in verdicts of *Accident, Suicide* or *Open verdicts* (83 per cent) means that much of their attention at inquests is directed to accidents and suicides and, by inference, to the distinction between them.[15]

The coroner's court is one of the oldest courts in England and Wales, and as such it operates according to a number of rules and traditions which are peculiar to it (see Jervis, 1957). In addition to investigating sudden deaths, coroners are also responsible for examining claims regarding treasure trove though such inquests are extremely rare occurrences. They also have much more discretion as to how the inquest should be conducted than is the case in other courts of law, and the absence of an accused and prosecuting and defence counsels means that the proceedings are typically structured very differently.[16] Usually the coroner has before him the completed statements given by witnesses to

TABLE 5.3.2   *Verdicts available to coroners, together with the*
numbers returned in 1969*

Verdicts	Totals for 1969
Death by wilful or criminal acts	
Murder	*42*
Manslaughter	*26*
Infanticide	*2*
Justifiable homicide	–
Suicide	*4369*
Attempted or self-induced abortion	*3*
Death by neglect, exposure or excess	
Neglect	55
Excessive drinking	123
Addiction to drugs	13
Want of attention at birth	15
Death from industrial diseases	783
Death by accident or misadventure	15,520
Death from natural causes	1563
Still born	32
Open verdicts	1602
Total	24,172

(* Derived from Appendix 4 of the Broderick Report, 1971, pp. 383–7)

the coroner's officer, and uses these as the basis for his cross-ex-
amination. As will be seen in the next chapter, this very often involves
him in reading out the statements and checking with the witness, who
in court is on oath, that the statement is correct. In general, the atmosphere is more informal than in other courts of law, with the coroner
and other officials apparently attempting to minimize the distress likely
to be involved for the bereaved.[17]

But as is evident from the statistics in Table 5.3.1, inquests are only a
small part of coroners' investigations, the main work of which is done
prior to and more usually without an inquest. The examination of the
scene of death, identification of the deceased, interviews with relatives
and other witnesses, arranging and attending the post-mortem,
collecting all this evidence together for presentation to the coroner and

organizing the inquest are tasks which are almost always delegated to the coroners' officers. These are usually policemen who specialize in the work either exclusively or as one aspect of their duties. In some big jurisdictions, a number of officers may work together for a coroner, while others may work in relative isolation. Though it may appear to be a very unpleasant sort of job, the police do not seem to have much difficulty in finding recruits. As the coroner's officer with whom I did observations commented: 'It's as near a nine-to-five job as you can get in the force.'

The coroners themselves mainly belong to local firms of solicitors who have traditionally provided a coroner for their area. There are 255 jurisdictions in England and Wales and all but fourteen of these are the responsibility of part-time coroners. There is very great variation in the number of cases dealt with annually by the different coroners, ranging in 1969, for example, from the 3 which were referred to the coroner in the Maelor Hundred area of Shropshire to the 4,597 referred to the coroner for Inner South London.[18] Not surprisingly, this latter jurisdiction has a full-time coroner, as is the case with most of the large centres of population. Thus the fourteen full-timers deal with about one-third of all the deaths referred to coroners annually. In order to become a coroner, a person must be qualified in law or medicine, and have been in practice for at least five years, and usually a new coroner will have acted as a deputy for the coroner he replaces, which means that he will have conducted the duties of coroner while his superior was ill or away from the area. Most of the full-timers are qualified in both law and medicine and, as was observed at the beginning of this section, the relative advantages of the alternative disciplines is a cause of discussion and debate between them. Put simply, the lawyers feel that doctors are not well enough acquainted with legal matters to be fully competent in holding inquests and conducting cross-examinations of witnesses, while the doctors feel that lawyers are unable to understand the implications of pathologists' reports on post-mortem examinations.

In this section, I have attempted to provide a general description of the official procedures for registering sudden deaths in England and Wales. 'Suicide' was seen to be one of the many available verdicts which could be brought in at an inquest on a sudden death, and inquests were shown to be only one of the procedures used by coroners. And the coroner system itself was seen to be only a part, albeit an integral part, of the more general system of death certification.

5.4 A PRELIMINARY RESEARCH DESIGN AND SOME PROBLEMS

It should be clear from the preceding section that the role of coroners in deciding on which deaths are to be categorized as suicides is of crucial importance, and hence that any research into how deaths get so categorized must at some stage be directed towards them. A further practical advantage from the point of view of the lone researcher also seemed to be evident from the organizational structure of the coroner system. That there are only fourteen full-time coroners means that the task of interviewing all of them in some depth about the way in which they decide how to categorize particular deaths should be an easily manageable one. By talking to them all, one would then have data from those responsible for registering a third of all the deaths referred to coroners in England and Wales each year. A more limited mailed questionnaire could then be sent to all the other coroners in the country, so that at the end of the research it could have been claimed that the whole, or at least very nearly the whole, population in which we were interested had been contacted. After preliminary talks with three coroners, and after asking one of them whether he thought there would be any objection to my embarking on such a study, I was advised to contact the Coroners' Society. After a meeting with two of their officials, certain problems emerged which had not seemed obvious at the outset and which made the possibility of pursuing research along the lines outlined above somewhat remote.

Practical guides to the gaining of access to research settings provided in methodology texts tend to be few and far between and, when present, are seldom appropriate for the particular situation with which one is faced. There is also the general problem which, as I suggested earlier, sociologists face in Britain, where there is no widespread awareness of the kinds of interests they have, and even where there is some awareness, there may be fear of some kind of 'exposure' job being done by the researcher. To an extent, I think this kind of consideration played an important part in my failure to gain permission to go ahead with the proposed study, for to express an interest in how official statistics are assembled will almost inevitably arouse some degree of suspicion on the part of those who assemble them. Given the kind of remarks so frequently made about official statistics, some suspicion seems to be wholly justified, for what many such studies seem to be engaged in is in commenting on, and usually criticizing, the efficiency of the officials in doing their daily work.[19] If, for example, a sociologist observes that 'police discretion' leads to far more offences of Type A being cleared up than is the case with offences Type B, then even if he does not say so in so many words, it is at least implicit that a possible remedy for the situation is to divert resources to offences of Type B. It might be argued that attention should be somehow evened out between the two types of offence, or that additional resources be brought in to bring the clearing up rate of offence Type B up to that of offence Type A. Whatever the particular conclusion or recommendation, however, an observation of this sort does seem to be directed towards criticizing and remedying procedures which can always be made to appear inadequate by a careful scrutiny of official figures.[20] In the same way, to express an interest in how the official categorizations of suicide get done may put one's informant on the defensive with respect to his own competence, that of his colleagues, and the efficiency of the system as a whole. If one offers assurances that one is not interested in criticizing coroners or the coroner system, then, as I shall suggest below, even greater problems may be posed for the researcher.

My meeting with the officials of the Coroners' Society began by my being informed that requests for assistance from coroners were on the increase and that it had been agreed that such requests should now be vetted and that the responsibility for this had been delegated to them. Their concern was to check that any research done had serious aims and was generally well-conceived. It was stressed that they had no objection in principle to helping researchers, but that they had had one or two complaints from individual coroners about the apparent pointlessness of some projects which had been proposed. As I wished to interview full-time coroners and send mailed questionnaires to all the others, I was told that my proposal would have to be particularly coherent so that they could justify it to their professional colleagues, should any of them raise questions about it. I was therefore invited to elaborate on what I wanted to do and why I wanted to do it. Now as I suggested above, it is very difficult to formulate a research interest in how official categorizations get done, particularly to a non-sociological audience, without making it sound as though one wishes to check on the efficiency or otherwise of the officials concerned. This issue was raised by the officials 'on behalf of' their colleagues who were 'less well-informed' about research than they themselves were, and it was noted that they would probably not be too keen on the idea of someone like me checking on the way they worked. By replying that my interest was not in making assessments about the efficiency or competence of coroners, I did not solve the problem but provoked a further and more difficult one. For if my interest was entirely academic and not concerned with making some kind of assessment of the practical work of coroners, then *what possible point could it have?* Thus I was faced with providing an intellectual justification for my proposed research which would be both understandable and recognizable to coroners as an adequate justification for doing it. It is arguable that the great difficulty I found in coping with this situation was in some measure a reflection of a general weakness in my rationale for wanting to do the research, for, if it seemed worth doing, then presumably I should have a clearly worked-out case which could instantly demonstrate that it was indeed a worthwhile project. But the trouble was that I had been led to this as a research topic by the kinds of issues discussed at considerable length in the first part of this book. The failure to view as problematic the way in which suicides get categorized as such was, as I hope now to have demonstrated, a common feature of almost *all* previous research on suicide. Clearly there was no time available to describe in any detail during a brief meeting precisely what had led me to a position where this seemed to be an important area for research, and any reply would almost certainly be bound to sound either intellectually inadequate or arrogant, or both. Thus to say something like, 'Well, I have carried out an extensive study of the literature on suicide and have come to the conclusion that this is the most common and the most important omission, which I now intend to rectify . . .' is unlikely to be convincing when said by a young graduate student to two middle-aged people with years of first-hand experience of registering sudden deaths.

In an attempt to resolve the dilemna outlined above, I suggested to the officials that it was surprising that, in all the research that had been done on suicide, no one had ever bothered to consult coroners about their thoughts on the subject, and that my initial talks with some coroners had suggested that their theories of suicide might be very similar to those of the expert researchers. This line of argument was met with comments to the effect that coroners did not have the time to do research into suicide and hence could not be regarded as experts, quite apart from the fact that suicides represented only a small proportion of the cases they had to deal with. It was also pointed out to me that, though my interest might be sincere and have some serious scholarly backing, it would be almost impossible to provide other coroners with a convincing case as to its worth. I was therefore invited to go away and prepare a more clear and concise proposal for them to consider. That I never did so was not simply a result of pessimism about the prospects of successfully gaining access, but also had to do with the fact that alternative research strategies were emerging at about that time.[21] As time went on, I also became increasingly sceptical about the usefulness of survey methods for the research topic. Before going on to present some of the findings of the research that was done, however, some brief remarks on the significance of these difficulties seem appropriate.

A central problem in my encounter with these coroners (and which also emerged later in research with a coroner's officer) was that of persuading those whose work one wanted to study that there was anything interesting or problematic enough about their routine activities for these to be worthy of the close attention of a sociologist. Thus, just as the coroners were at pains to tell me that their task was 'very straightforward', so also did coroners' officers later present me with a similar case. Even when something seemed unusual, it was likely to be portrayed by them as 'ordinary'. On one occasion, for example, I noticed an evening newspaper board with 'Man found shot dead in a wood' written on it. It was during a period when I had been spending a good deal of time with one coroner's officer with whom I had an arrangement to be informed if anything of special interest happened. Wondering why I had not been told of this, I telephoned him and asked, without reference to the shooting, if anything of interest was under way at that time. He replied 'No, everything's pretty quiet at the moment,' to which I replied, 'How about this shooting I read about in the papers?' His reply was, 'Everything's under control on that one; the body's been identified, we've had the P-M, and I've sent the gun off to the ballistics boys at Xton. Now it's just a matter of waiting for their report.' Another officer revealed a similar tendency to describe his work as 'straightforward' and 'uncomplicated' when I asked him what training was required to become a coroner's officer: 'It's not difficult – you are shown exactly what to do. There are official forms to fill in and quite honestly it's a commonsense thing to do.' That these coroners' officers and the coroners referred to above appeared to view their work in this unproblematic way is in marked contrast to the shifting ambiguous world of official and other definitions of suicide depicted by Douglas (1967, especially Chapter 12 and Appendix II). Thus for the officials it seems that the process of registering sudden deaths is a socially organized matter, characterized by *order* rather than by ambiguity and uncertainty.

It is possibly as a consequence of this that coroners and their officers will seldom talk at length about what they consider to be the mundane, ordinary, or in Sudnow's (1965) terms 'normal' cases. These tend to be referred to only in a general way, the detail being reserved for what they regard as 'specially interesting' cases. Thus the only actual example that the officials of the Coroners' Society talked about was the death of Judy Garland, which had received a great deal of publicity. Another instance of this tendency to go into great detail about the unusual is the following example, where a coroner's officer interviewed begins with a generalized observation about suicides by gassing and then proceeds to 'illustrate' it by reference to an 'interesting' case:

Someone who is committing suicide by gas generally tries to make themselves comfortable – they want to die in comfort. They put a cushion on the floor in front of the gas oven or in the gas oven for them to rest their head. One interesting case I can bring to mind – one man was suffering from tremendous depression owing to financial debt and he wrote a letter to his wife saying how much he loved her and how sorry he was, and that the insurances would cover him, and she'd be better off without him. He wrote one to the police explaining that he was committing suicide and apologizing for any inconvenience. He wrote one to the coroner saying it was suicide and therefore he could dispense with an inquest, and he wrote another letter to the pathologist and in this letter he tried to outline what it was like to die. It was very disturbing reading this letter because he set off quite plainly stating his case – why he was doing it, how he was going to do it – it was by gassing as it happens – and he tried to go through the physical feeling of dying, and as one read the letter, one could see the handwriting tapering away and staggering about the page. And he gave the times precisely every ten minutes and kept putting 'it's now 3.30 p.m.' or whatever it was until eventually you could almost see the point of unconsciousness where he was just writing and feeling very drowsy, and the pen just went off the paper. Umm – as I said, it was very upsetting reading this, to read about a man dying, but this is the sort of thing one comes across in suicide.

Thus a 'normal' pattern (the 'sort of thing one comes across') found in cases of suicide by gassing is illustrated by reference to a case which the coroner's officer admitted in subsequent exchanges to be an 'exceptional' one. An implication of this tendency (to detail the exceptional) for the research design proposed above is that the answer to the research problem of how deaths get categorized as suicides is unlikely to be obtainable simply by asking officials. This is not to claim that data like that presented above are without any relevance to the problem, but rather that they only provide generalized accounts of the 'ordinary', and some basis for making inferences about the 'ordinary' by noting what the officials consider to be 'extraordinary'. In the light of this, the difficulties involved in trying to make arrangements to survey coroners seemed less important, as it was unclear whether such interviews would provide much insight into the ordinary routine practices of the officials. The research reported in subsequent chapters, then, makes limited but not exclusive use of interview materials and includes analyses of other sorts of data, such as the contents of coroners' records, newspaper reports of suicides and observational reports on the work of a coroner's officer.

5.5 CONCLUSION

This chapter began with a consideration of the ways in which problems relating to the definition of suicide can be formulated. After finding it difficult to locate what seemed to be the least problematic of the different types of definition, namely the official legal one, it was suggested that such an interest was based on a mistaken formulation of the definitional problem. Thus it appeared from our evidence that it was possible for a coroner to be unable to provide even an approximation to the official definition of suicide (and also to operate with an unofficial distinction between deaths by accident and misadventure) and yet to be able routinely to generate official categorizations without arousing any criticism or doubts about his competence. The implication of this is that the procedures for categorizing sudden deaths are organized in some *unknown* way which cannot be anticipated in advance of research. To claim that research should be directed towards the supposed relationship between *formal* and *operational* definitions, for example, is to assume both that such a distinction adequately characterizes a distinction recognized by the officials, and that the problem has been researched to a sufficient extent to allow comparative statements to be made about the different types of definition.

By describing the official procedures for registering deaths in England and Wales, I hope to have clarified the place and importance of coroners and their officers in determining which deaths are suicides. And in considering the difficulties involved in trying to effect a research design which seemed particularly attractive in the light of the structure of the coroner system, I attempted to show how an answer to the research problem of how deaths get categorized as suicides would be unlikely to be forthcoming simply and exclusively from asking officials about their work. In the next chapter, therefore, data from several sources is examined in an attempt to outline some of the procedures used in deciding whether or not deaths are suicides.

Chapter 6

Some Relevant Factors in Imputing Suicide

6.1 INTRODUCTION

In this chapter I want to examine a series of factors which seemed in the light of our early enquiries to be important in leading coroners to a suicide verdict. Data is used from a variety of different sources, which include my initial contacts with coroners prior to the failure reported in the previous chapter, attendance at inquests in three different towns, and participant observation with a coroner's officer.[1] To have reported in detail on any one or all of these research endeavours would have been to write several books and for present purposes it will be enough to attempt some preliminary interpretations of the data, and to consider their implications for suicide research and for the subsequent research reported in Chapter 7. The following is based closely on the analysis presented in an already published paper, though some additional empirical materials are included which hopefully will provide added support for some of the contentions made in that earlier version.[2]

In that previous discussion of the issues to be examined in this chapter, I introduced the problem in the following way:

> Although in theory coroners have several possible verdicts open to them, in practice most inquests result in ones of accidental death or misadventure (which in law mean the same thing). The next most common verdict is suicide, which accounts for about a quarter of all verdicts. At the majority of inquests, therefore, it is almost a two-horse race, and the coroner can normally expect to return a verdict either of accidental death or suicide, and, for it to be a suicide, he must be convinced both that the deceased died as a result of his own actions and that it was intended.
>
> Compared with the judge who hears a murder trial, the coroner is in a specially difficult position at an inquest. The obvious impossibility of cross-examining the dead and the absence of prosecuting and defending counsels means that, in order to bring in a suicide verdict, intent has to be *inferred* 'post mortem'. His position is comparable with that of a judge hearing the trial of a dead man for murder

without any assistance from barristers. Thus coroners are forced to rely on cues which, for reasons which will be discussed below, lead them towards or away from a suicide verdict. That the problem of inferring intent is not always a simple one has been publicly recognized by the Los Angeles County Coroner, Theodore J. Curphey, who has enlisted the help of experts from the famous Los Angeles Suicide Prevention Center in the investigation of equivocal deaths. What they do has come to be known as the 'Psychological Autopsy', and involves gathering information on (1) the life history of the deceased, (2) his psychiatric history, (3) whether or not intent was communicated to other persons and (4) straight detective type data which may be relevant in pointing to a motive. Curphey has stated that one of the main advantages of employing trained social and psychiatric workers to carry out these 'Psychological Autopsies' is that the personnel normally assigned to coroners are insufficiently skilled to be of much use in helping to determine the presence or absence of intent. This interesting phenomenon has yet to arrive in Britain, but I would nevertheless argue that our coroners do *in fact* carry out 'psychological autopsies' anyway, and that the Los Angeles Experiment is merely an attempt to do what coroners have always done in a supposedly more efficient way. Indeed . . . the kinds of evidence they seem to use in inferring intent are very similar to those sought out by the psychological detectives of Los Angeles [Atkinson, 1971, pp. 173–4].

Now, although the formulation of the coroner's problem as that of the post-mortem inferring of intent may seem something of an over-simplification in the light of the discussion of definitions in the previous chapter, that they are engaged in searching for specific pieces of evidence to confirm or reject a particular verdict and that this closely resembles the work of the psychological autopsies has been argued by Garfinkel on the basis of his study of the Los Angeles Suicide Prevention Center's work with the coroner. On this he makes the following observations:

SPC inquiries begin with a death that the coroner finds equivocal as to *mode* of death. That death they use as a precedent with which various ways of living in society that could have terminated with that death are searched out and read 'in the remains'; in the scraps of this and that like the body and its trappings, medicine bottles, notes, bits and pieces of clothing, and other memorabilia – stuff that can be photographed, collected and packaged. Other 'remains' are collected too: rumors, passing remarks, and stories – materials in the 'repertoires' of whosoever might be consulted via the common work of conversations. These *whatsoever* bits and pieces that a story or a rule or a proverb might make intelligible are used to formulate a *recognizably* coherent, standard, typical, cogent, uniform, planful, i.e., a professionally defensible, and thereby, for members, a *recognizably* rational account of how the society worked to produce those remains. This point would be easier to make if the reader will consult any standard textbook in forensic pathology. In it he will find the inevitable photograph of a victim with a slashed throat. Were the coroner to recommend the equivocality of the mode of death he might say something like this: 'In the case where a body looks like the one in this picture, you are looking at a suicidal death because the wound shows the 'hesitation cuts' that accompany the great wound. One can imagine that these cuts are the remains of a procedure whereby the victim first made several preliminary trials of a hesitating sort and then performed the lethal slash. Other courses of action are imaginable, too, and so cuts that look like hesitation cuts can be produced by other mechanisms. One needs to start with the actual display and imagine how different courses of action could have been organized such that *that* picture would be compatible with it. One might think of the photographed display as a phase-of-the-action. In any actual display is there a course of action with which that phase is uniquely compatible? *That* is the coroner's question' [Garfinkel, 1967b, pp. 17–18; his italics].

In this depiction of how the coroner proceeds, then, is a process whereby 'bits and pieces', 'relics' and so on lead him towards a suicide or some other verdict. These I referred to in my original formulation as 'cues', and my concern here is with the kind of cues which specifically point towards a verdict of suicide.

6.2 SUICIDE NOTES AND THREATS

Communications from the deceased are particularly important cues for the coroner in deciding on whether or not a particular death is a suicide. Suicide notes can be seen as the only form of direct communication, while threats which are reported by third parties can be viewed as forms of indirect communication. That notes constitute such crucial relics may have led to the following exaggerated generalization taken from the transcript of an interview with a coroner's officer:

generally you find suicidals do leave notes . . . suicides are always in fact or quite often in fact indicated by notes. It's amazing that most people seem to leave notes that they are going to commit suicide.

Another policeman I interviewed expressed a similar view, but provided also a reason why studies based on coroners' records show that only a minority of officially recorded suicides leave notes. He observed that the first thing members of a family are likely to do on finding a suicide is to burn or otherwise destroy the note, an action which in his words was 'particularly likely in the case of Catholics'. The dual importance of notes and threats is further exemplified by the following exchange between myself and a coroner's officer. While doing participant observation with the officer, I arrived in his office and asked what cases he was working on. He replied that the body of a woman had been pulled out of the canal the previous day. 'Suicide?' I enquired, to which he replied: 'Yes it is – no, I shouldn't really say that – everything points to it, but I'm not sure we'll get that as a verdict.' On asking him why not, he elaborated further: 'Well she was a patient at [the local mental hospital], she was suffering from depression, and we know that she's tried it once or twice before. The trouble is I can't find a note, and she doesn't seem to have made any threats.' In this case, then, it seemed that the presence of a note or evidence of threats would have 'clinched' the matter beyond doubt, but that without them, a verdict of suicide might not even be returned.

In the light of evidence such as this, it is tempting to conclude that suicide notes and threats are almost enough in themselves to guarantee a suicide verdict, and indeed I tended towards that interpretation in my earlier paper on the subject (Atkinson, 1971). There are, however, at least two important qualifications which need to be added to so neat and simple a conclusion. The first of these is exemplified in the question and answer sequence which followed the earlier quotation from the coroner's officer who suggested that most suicides do leave notes. This led to the following exchange:

M.A.: And presumably if they do [leave a note] your investigations don't really have to look very much further.

C.O.: Well, they do – an investigation is continued in the normal manner. Just because a suicide note's been left it could disguise murder. If you remember as I said earlier it would be very difficult for someone to make a murder look like a suicide – it's not impossible – it's difficult but not impossible and this is where the coroner's officer's experience comes into play. If he thinks there's anything suspicious about that death he immediately informs the C.I.D. senior officers and a murder investigation is undertaken. If it turns out that it is in fact a suicide there's nothing lost, but those examinations or investigations must be made to make sure that the death is in fact accidental or suicidal and not due to the malicious intent of an individual, or third party.

This theme was raised by other coroners and coroners' officers met during the research, and it can be argued that it is offered more as a kind of defensive rationalization for their activities than any approximate description of their routine practices or concerns. Thus during my participant observation with the coroner's officer, it was in no way apparent to me that a dominant or ever-present concern on his part was whether or not a particular death was a murder. And yet when asked specific questions about his work, he would state quite clearly that the *first* task of the coroner's officer was to assess whether or not foul play was involved. Routine provision for such an assessment only seemed to be made in one kind of case, which was one where suicide was not even a possibility. This was in cases of 'cot deaths', where there 'was always the possibility that it resulted from "baby battering".' Here the officer would make arrangements for a C.I.D. officer to accompany him or meet him at the home while he was examining the body. 'If it's obviously a case of baby battering, I withdraw discreetly and leave it to them – otherwise they leave it to me.' The suggestion that replies from the coroners' officers which stress the need to assess the homicidal possibilities of each death may constitute a 'defensive rationalization' rather than an attempt to accurately describe their activities is based on the fact that such statements were invariably made in response to questions of mine which could have been construed as being in some way critical of the work they were doing. Thus the example given above follows what could be heard as a suggestion of mine that diligence may be lessened once a note has been found and can be seen as providing an account for why that does not happen. Towards the end of the same interview, I asked a more general question about the processes of sudden-death registration which provoked a similar response:

> M.A.: Why is it such an important decision? Does it really matter to us whether someone committed suicide or died from an accidental death?
>
> C.O.: I would say it was important in so far as was death by accident or by design and if it was by design, as a policeman I want to know what that design was. Was it intended murder or homicide or was it accidental or was it suicide?

Whether or not such statements do reflect an abiding practical concern on the part of officials involved in the death registration processes is not directly relevant to the present discussion. What is important, however is to note that references to the need to rule out the chance of murder being concealed means that any claim to the effect that notes are somehow sufficient in themselves to provide for a suicide verdict is not tenable.

A further qualification also needs to be made, which is that it would be a mistake to see the finding of specific 'relics' as obvious and necessary conditions for the finding of a particular verdict. For if one is to say something like 'if suicide note and/or threats, then suicide' one is exaggerating the 'obviousness' of suicide notes and threats as suicide notes and threats. That is to say, the notes and threats themselves have to be categorized as 'suicidal' before they can attain the status of hard evidence. Notes themselves are frequently less than explicit about the suicidal intent and are not always in a form which can be taken by the officials as a direct 'confession'. The following are examples contained in the records which provided some of the data for Chapter 7:

NOTE 1:   My darling poppet, my ticker isn't what it used to be and it's been getting worse lately.

NOTE 2:   I'm sorry to everyone. I love my mum dad and Ken. Please look after my children

NOTE 3:   You can't very well go so I guess it will have to be me. I don't think I could stay here anyway after today.

NOTE 4:   I should be obliged if the finder of this note will ask the police if I am found drowned to kindly advise Mr Jones [address]. Also my daughter Mrs Shires *After 6 p.m.* [phone number].

NOTE 5:   Dear Ann, I cannot go on it's too depressing. I want you to share out the money equally between you, Bertha, Mavis and Bob can have the car to do what he likes with it.

NOTE 6:   Tell the train driver not to worry. It's my doing not his.

NOTE 7:   Things are getting me down a bit lately, so this evening I am going to commit suicide [extract from letter to girlfriend].

Now there is, it seems, a marked contrast between the degree of explicitness in Notes 1 and 7. The bland statement contained in the last one is somewhat unusual, the others with their references to a future in which the writer will not feature being, according to Shneidman and Farberow (1957), more typical of genuine suicide notes. The point I want to make is that, with the exception of 7 and possibly 6, none of the notes states explicitly that the writer intends to commit suicide. Their status as 'suicide notes', therefore, is something which has to be inferred by the finders. Thus with the exception of 7, given no other information about the settings in which these notes were found, it is possible to imagine non-suicidal situations in which they might have been written. Note 1, for example, might be written from a hospital where the writer was undergoing treatment.[3] Note 2 could be a message from someone about to be admitted to prison, or about to join the Foreign Legion, and Note 4 could be a message from a stunt man, fisherman or lifeboat man prior to a particular journey. The 'go' in Note 3 can only be read in the sense of 'dying' rather than as for example 'going away somewhere else' if taken in conjunction with other special circumstances. Similar inferential work relating features of the situation in which the note is found are required in order to read 'cannot go on' in Note 5 as 'cannot go on living'. And in order to know what it is that the train driver is not to worry about and what it is that is the doing of the author of Note 6, we need to know about the circumstances in which the note was found. Thus, on learning that it was found near a body which had been run over by a train, it becomes easy to see the note as a suicide note.

What I hope is clarified here is that notes are by no means unequivocal, necessary and sufficient cues for enabling a suicide verdict to be registered. Nor should they be seen as 'relics' which point to a suicide irrespective of what other evidence is available in a particular case. Rather they have a reflexive quality in relation to other cues. The identification of a note as a suicide note may certainly make it easier to view other features of the situation as 'suicidal', but it is also the case that it may not be possible to identify a note as a 'suicide note' without reference to those other features of the situation.

Much the same can be said of suicidal threats, except that in some respects, the situation is much more complicated than is the case with notes. Threats and warnings have to be reported by some third party and in recalling and assessing past utterances and actions, all kinds of considerations may enter into the giving of a statement to the coroner's officer. There may, for example, be good reason not to report a remembered warning, for if it went unheeded the witness might feel that he would be seen to be in some way responsible for what had happened (cf. Henslin, 1970). Thus in the coroner's records and newspaper reports examined in the next chapter and at inquests, reports of threats and warnings are regularly accompanied with statements such as 'but I did not think she was serious'. In one case, a witness was able to say this even though he had also reported that the deceased had made numerous previous suicide attempts. The reports of threats and warnings, then, are open to all kinds of interpretive work by the witnesses, the details of which are never and can never be available to an observer. More generally, retrospective assignations of past utterances and actions to the status of 'suicide threats' are done at a point when the deceased may be strongly suspected of having committed suicide. In the light of such knowledge, witnesses may redefine utterances and actions previously regarded as unnoticeable or insignificant as 'suicidal', so that *now*, in the light of the evidence which has become available, they can be seen for what they 'really were in the first place and were all along' – i.e. suicide threats. These assignations, once made, can then be used as evidence to provide support for a verdict of suicide.

Now it may seem that I am saying on the one hand that notes and threats are important cues in aiding the coroners to define a death as a suicide and on the other that they are not correctly to be viewed as cues at all, given that they are themselves defined as 'suicidal' with reference to other cues. As other 'cues' are to be considered later in this chapter, I shall attempt here to clarify the analysis I am proposing. The first version referred to above, namely that certain 'relics', 'facts' or other items of evidence are used in support of a suicide verdict, can be viewed as a members' version of how suicides get categorized as such. Thus the coroners' legal guide referred to the need for 'adequate evidence', while coroners and coroners' officers regularly refer (when asked) to the collection of 'facts'. One coroner's officer, for example, described the division of labour between himself and the coroner by saying: 'My job is just to collect the facts and his is to make the decision.' Another, in similar vein, said, 'The coroner must come to a decision – and it's a very important decision that he makes and you must supply him with all the evidence – this is your job – you must give him as much evidence as possible.' What is being presented, then, is a depiction of a very orderly, straightforward process in which facts are gathered which provide the basis for a decision about 'what really happened'. I have suggested above, however, that even facts which seem the 'hardest' or most unequivocal of all, such as suicide notes and threats, are constituted as such by means of interpretive work on the part of witnesses and officials. In Garfinkel's terms, the 'remains' have to be 'read' and it is only after they have been 'read' that they can be constituted, recognized and used as 'suicidal remains' or, more generally, as evidence or 'facts'. To propose this is not to say that there is anything 'wrong', 'misguided' or 'misleading' about the depiction of the process in terms of the straightforward gathering of facts. Nor is it to claim that there is some irretrievable, irreparable inconsistency between the two versions. Rather it is to highlight a crucial part of the answer to the question of how deaths get categorized as suicides. For to say that interpretive work is necessary for the facts to be constituted as facts is not to make any claims that they are not then regarded as such by the officials and others concerned. In other words, once constituted as 'facts', suicide notes and threats, as well as other features to be discussed below, are treated, used and analysed as facts by members 'for all practical purposes'. That and how coroners and their officers are engaged in the analysis of such facts will hopefully become clearer in the remaining sections of this chapter.

6.3 MODE OF DYING

Particular ways of dying may be viewed as almost certain indicators of suicide or accidental death. Deaths on the road, as either driver or pedestrian, for example, are very unlikely to lead an investigation to a suicide verdict, even though some suicidologists have pointed to such deaths as a possible source of error in suicide statistics (e.g. Ford and Moseley, 1963). Indeed so seldom are road deaths recorded as suicide that they are not included as a sub-classification of suicides in the Registrar-General's mortality statistics. In the same way, there is no provision for a sub-category of accidents 'by hanging', which is consistent with the views expressed to me by coroners and their officers which suggest that they see hanging as an almost certain indicator of a suicidal death. Such a view was also expressed in the international comparison of the official recording processes discussed in Chapter 3, where the equation between 'hanging' and 'suicide' was invoked to support the claim that the certification procedures in one country were especially unproblematic: 'Certification of the type of death usually presents no difficulties, as the most frequently used means of suicide in Czechoslovakia is hanging' (Prokupek, 1968, p. 32). Similarly, when probing in an area of interest to be discussed further below, I received a reply from a coroner's officer which implied the importance of mode of death for imputing suicide:

M.A.: if there are no obvious reasons why somebody should have committed suicide is this likely to make you think that perhaps it isn't suicide?

C.O.: Possibly – um – a suicide really is pretty well-defined. You have a variety of types – you know – they're quite obvious – you have the drowning, the gassing, somebody hanging themselves, cutting the throat, overdose of tablets – something of this nature . . . it's pretty well-defined.

This exchange is, of course, open to a number of interpretations. It could be argued, for instance, that his claims about the clarity with which suicide is defined is offered in order to 'ward off' a line of questioning which he wished to avoid. That the assertion that suicide is 'pretty well-defined' is followed by the 'you have a variety of types, you know' and 'they're quite obvious' could be interpreted as playing for time in the sense that, having asserted that suicide is well-defined, he then realized that the matter is more complicated than that, and hesitates prior to formulating a typology which has the appearance of clarity. I do not propose following up any of these issues here, but want merely to note that this attempt to define suicide in some 'clear' way involved him in listing modes of death, the implication of which is that there is an equation being made between particular modes of death and suicide. In other words, mode of death is being invoked as a 'clear' indicator of suicide.

As was suggested above, death by hanging is the mode of death which is probably most likely to be seen as an indicator of suicide. Why this should be so can be easily understood by reference to Garfinkel's comments on the search procedures involving a consideration of what sequence of events a particular corpse can be seen to fit in with. Thus in the case of persons found hanging, the two main options are suicide and homicide, it being rather difficult to die accidentally by hanging. With respect to homicide, hanging would normally be regarded as a rather unusual method for an assailant to choose given the availability of numerous other methods which are a good deal easier to effect. Alternatives to viewing a hanged corpse as the end result of a suicidal sequence, then, are likely to 'stretch' the imagination, and hence in most cases, the finding of a 'hanging' will prompt the search for other evidence that a suicide has taken place.

But though hanging may provide an almost certain indicator that a suicide has taken place, there are some situations in which the death may be categorized otherwise. One coroner told me, for example, that it was important to check that there were no 'kinky' magazines near the body and that the body was fully dressed. He explained that some people engaged in a form of masochistic masturbation which involved inducing a state of semi-asphyxiation either by the use of ropes or by placing the head in a plastic bag. On occasions, this 'went wrong' and the individual died. In such cases, he said, 'accidental death' would be an appropriate verdict. In another case encountered in the present research, a thirteen-year-old boy was found hanging from the chain in a school lavatory. In support of a verdict of accidental death, a number of points were made at the inquest. First it was suggested that he was too young to have been able to formulate suicidal intent, second that the method used was highly unlikely to have resulted in death and third that he had recently seen a film which contained several hangings. It was possible, therefore, that the boy had been merely 'experimenting' or 'playing around' and had died 'by mistake'. In a further case which will be discussed again below, an open verdict was brought in on a youth who had been found hanging, apparently on the grounds that there was evidence to show that he had been planning a climbing holiday and might have been practising. These examples have been introduced to show that it is not impossible for deaths by hanging to be seen as something other than the last phase in a suicidal episode. What is noticeable is that the coroner presented his account of the cases of masochistic masturbation as unusual, exceptional cases of hanging, while the second case involved the elaboration of the reason why the death was *not* a suicide. Thus the availability of non-suicidal deaths by

hanging does not mean that it cannot be viewed as a crucially important factor, for in cases where a hanging is defined as something
other than a suicide, arguments have to be presented to show why a
mode of death, which is normally 'obviously' suicidal, is *not so* in the
particular examples cited.

The only other mode of dying which, like hanging, may on its own be
seen as a definite indicator of suicide is death resulting from breathing
in the exhaust fumes of a car via a tube connected from the exhaust pipe
to the inside of the car. Here the body is usually found in the driver's
seat of the car, the ignition is switched on, the petrol tank is empty and
a tube from the exhaust pipe enters the car through a small opening in
the window. As with hanging, it is difficult for an observer to imagine
how a person could possibly die in this manner either by homicide or by
accident. The former would presumably require some means for forcing
the victim to remain seated in the car which would be evident from
either the examination of the scene or the post-mortem on the body,
while it is difficult to conceive of how a pipe could be accidently connected to the exhaust pipe and led into a car. Thus of the seventeen
cases of this type of death in my files, only one resulted in a verdict
other than suicide. As in the case of the exceptional hangings, certain
features of that case posed the possibility of an accidental death. No
tube had been connected to the exhaust pipe. The man concerned was
found slumped at the wheel in his garage after he had been out
drinking. The garage door had been closed and the engine left running.
The high level of alcohol found in his blood at the post-mortem showed
that there was a possibility that, having arrived home drunk, he had
passed out in the driver's seat before turning off the engine, and hence
had died accidentally. Two factors, however, seemed suggestive of
suicide. First, he was shown to be in financial difficulties and had been
depressed prior to his death, and second, it was not clear how the garage door had come to be shut. The coroner returned an open verdict.

A central part of my thesis here is that the mode of death provides the
investigators with guidance as to what further evidence should be
sought, and in many cases provides a preliminary categorization which
is increasingly confirmed as the enquiries continue. Thus I have
suggested that deaths from hanging and car fumes, such as those
referred to above, will only exceptionally raise doubts that the
appropriate categorization should be something other than a suicide.
The same tends to hold also with respect to certain forms of accidental
death, and particularly those on the roads. Such deaths are typically
described as 'accidents' from the moment they are reported to the announcement of the verdict. While doing participant observation with
the coroner's officer, for example, a relatively regular occurrence was
that the telephone would ring, and, after the conversation was over, I
would ask him what had happened. His replies obviously varied in

detail but included statements like, 'It's another road accident', and 'Someone's been knocked down by a car'. His descriptions were, in other words, phrased in such a way as to indicate that 'another accidental death had occurred'. In one such case, I accompanied him to the mortuary to inspect the body of an old lady, the news of whose death had come through while I was present on a previous day. He told me at that time: 'A poor old dear has been knocked down by a bus at Xtown.' Knowing that Xtown was some miles away, I asked if he would have to go there to make enquiries. He replied: 'No, it's a pretty straightforward case, so I can leave it to their boys to do the necessary at that end. They've already located the next-of-kin, so it's just a matter of inspecting the body when it arrives and getting it identified.' On arrival at the local mortuary, he found which shelf the body was on, opened the refrigerated cabinet and slid out the body. It was covered with a white sheet, which he pulled to one side to allow an examination. I asked him what he was looking for, to which he replied 'Oh, nothing special in her case. It's obvious what happened.' He peeled back a plaster on her head, pointed to the wound it had covered, and said 'Looks like a fractured skull to me, but we'll have to wait for the P-M for the details.' He replaced the body in the cupboard and the whole inspection had taken less than three minutes. The 'obvious' accident remained an 'obvious' accident throughout the investigation and a verdict of 'accidental death' was brought in at the inquest.

In an interview with another coroner's officer, this procedure of arriving at a preliminary conclusion which directs the subsequent investigations also emerged clearly. An extended quotation is presented below because some of his remarks have a relevance for points to be considered later in the chapter:

M.A.: What sort of things – I mean how do you learn what sort of things to look for?

C.O.: Well, initially, of course, what one does is you go along to the house of the deceased or wherever the body lies – it could be a mortuary – and one examines the body and looks for marks of violence, injection marks and so on. But, of course, the thing to remember is to – er – you're conditioned by the circumstances of the death. If it's just a chap who's lived for eighty years and just fallen down and the doctor refuses to issue a death certificate, you've got a pretty well preconceived idea that the man's just fallen down and the doctor's unwilling to certify the cause of death – he might not have seen him for two or three months, you see. So what you're looking for are in fact marks of violence and this only comes in road accidents, suicides, murders and related types of death.

M.A.: Er – what sort of things – er – what sort of things lead you to look

for further sorts of evidence? In other words you said in the case of
an old person – um – you would assume that he had just dropped
dead. I mean do you in fact form an opinion on most deaths fairly
soon?

C.O.: Yes – you get the information on the deaths from the coroner or
from a doctor, then you inform the coroner – er – the doctor –
you'll see a doctor at the scene possibly – he'll tell you what's
happened, that he's not seen the patient for a long time. He thinks
he's suffered from a heart attack – um – he's got a weak heart or
bad stomach or he's got some sort of industrial disease, but he's
not quite sure. Or alternatively the circumstances of the finding of
the body might lead you to make further enquiries. You'll interview the relatives, you'll form an opinion from them just about
what's happened to cause the death. Was the deceased suffering
from an illness or was he depressed, which would cause him to
commit suicide? Or the other circumstances – it could have been
an accident – falling downstairs, for example. You get sort of
antecedent or background history from the relatives or from the
doctor which helps you in your enquiries.

M.A.: You say that you would be interested in whether someone had
been depressed because this would cause them to commit suicide.
Would you be interested to find out if someone who had been
killed in a road accident had been depressed?

C.O.: Possibly – um – I can see what you're trying to get at in fact. If one
man in a car hit a brick wall or a tree and was killed – was this a
means of his committing suicide? Initially I would say that you'd
think he just lost control of the vehicle and just crashed into the
wall. But it's a sudden death and, as I said earlier, one has to
begin enquiries, you've got to interview the relatives in all sudden
deaths irrespective of how they're caused and it would be in the
interview with the relative that the evidence of depression or
whatever would come out and this would then lead your enquiries
or direct your enquiries towards a certain end.

In these exchanges, an interesting change in emphasis can be noted. To
begin with, he tells us that a 'pretty well preconceived idea' emerges at
the stage of finding the body. An affirmative answer is given when he is
asked if an early opinion is formed in most cases. On the basis of this,
he says, further enquiries will be made, and 'typical' instances of
possibly relevant material are provided. When these were taken up in
my third question to suggest that relevant evidence might not be sought
because it was being assumed that the death was an accident, he begins
by admitting that the situation suggested would 'initially' suggest an
obvious accident. In defence against the possible criticism implied in
the question, he then assures us that any 'suicidal' evidence would

nevertheless emerge in the course of the routine enquiries. One interpretation of these replies, then, would be that initially he provides an oversimplified picture in which an instant opinion is formed on finding the body. This is then modified to provide for the enquiries to be led or directed by the initial scene, a version which allows for the possibility of a starting opinion to be changed by the results of the subsequent enquiries. In the light of his earlier remarks, his final view that the relevant evidence to support a suicide would 'emerge' seems somewhat optimistic, as presumably the enquiries would be unlikely to include questions which would reveal such evidence, and hence appropriate evidence might very well not emerge. What is important about these exchanges in the present context is that they suggest that the mode of death is a crucial initial pointer both to the likely eventual verdict and to the kinds of further evidence it might seem relevant to collect.

The discussion so far may seem to suggest that in general the mode of death points fairly clearly towards a particular verdict. To this point, however, we have been dealing with the extremes where suicide on the one hand and accident on the other seem more or less 'obvious' given the mode of death. More frequently, the mode of death on its own is more ambiguous, and other factors are required to support the particular verdict which emerges at the end of the enquiries. Thus, although the coroner's officer quoted earlier referred to gassings, drug overdoses and drownings as clearly defined 'types' of suicides, each of these methods was more usually portrayed to me as more or less equivocal by coroners whom I met. With respect to drug overdoses, for example, normally non-lethal doses can prove dangerous when taken after or in conjunction with alcohol or other drugs, and frequently verdicts other than suicide are brought in when such evidence is revealed by the post-mortem. One coroner pointed out that some people, and particularly the elderly, may take too many tablets by mistake or through absent-mindedness. In deciding between accident or suicide, he said:

> My real problem is when someone has taken less than ten barbituates. That's when I have to be on the lookout for special evidence. If he takes more than ten, I can be almost sure that it was a suicide.

Not surprisingly, this particular coroner had had medical as well as legal training and therefore had the kind of knowledge which would enable that kind of inference to be made. An almost identical rule-of-thumb is cited by Stengel and Farberow from their international survey of death certification procedures:

> One of the respondents, an English Coroner who is medically

qualified, stated that if the deceased had taken more than three times the therapeutic dose, this to him suggested suicide [Stengel and Farberow, 1967, p. 11].

Indeed so similar is this that it seems possible that we were in this case sharing the same informant.

One coroner also pointed out the potential for gassings to occur by accident. Again, old people were presented as likely victims owing to absent-mindedness and the deterioration of the senses of smell and hearing. Thus gas cookers could be left on unlit, or after spillage had extinguished the flame, so that the old person could easily be overcome by the fumes without realizing what was happening. The accidental potential of gas was recognized also by the routine investigation procedures used in the area where I did participant observation with the coroner's officer, which required checks to be made by a gas fitter in all cases of death by gassing. One of these fitters told me that, in all the cases he had dealt with, it was 'obvious' what had happened without his being consulted and that in the vast majority of the cases they were suicides. When I asked him why he thought he should be required to make the checks, he said that he supposed they had to be sure that the death did not result from a leak for which the gas board might be held responsible.

Possibly the most 'equivocal' of all modes of death is drowning, and all the coroners and coroners' officers I have spoken to have commented on the difficulties it poses. The case cited in the previous section where the officer was unsure because he was unable to find a note was a drowning. Similarly when I asked another officer about the most difficult case he had had to deal with, he described a drowning. At one inquest I attended on a woman who had been found in a canal, questioning of police officers on the location of the body, the depth at that point, the state of the tow path, the presence or absence of 'signs of slipping' and the like took up more time than the questioning on any other topic.[4] The large number of drownings reported to the Dublin coroner were also cited by McCarthy and Walsh (1966) as a reason for the high rate of under-reporting of suicides to which they refer in their study of suicide in Dublin. Why deaths by drowning are likely to be regarded as equivocal can be understood in the same way as those more 'definite' modes of death such as hanging. For just as it is difficult to imagine ways in which people might end up hanged other than as a result of their own actions, it is very easy to envisage persons slipping, falling or even being pushed into the water from which their body is ultimately retrieved. The consequent difficulty in conducting the investigation and arriving at a definite verdict may be one of the reasons for a practice reported to me by a policeman who worked on one bank of a tidal river, which also marked the border between two police forces. According to him, it was not uncommon for policemen finding a body washed up on their side of the river to push it back into the water so that the tide would wash it up on the other side 'so that the other force would have to deal with it'. The other force, however, presumably with similar thoughts in mind used to do the same thing, so that a body might float backwards and forwards several times before it was finally taken in and investigated. Coroners, too, have what I described in my earlier analysis as 'idiosyncratic rules-of-thumb' (Atkinson, 1971) for dealing with drownings. The one I referred to there was mentioned by a coroner in a holiday area where drownings featured quite regularly:

> A thing I look for in a drowning is whether or not the clothes are left folded. If they are found neatly folded on the beach, it usually points to a suicide.

Since then, however, a coroner's officer whose work is in no way connected with the above coroner presented a similar theme, which suggests that the earlier view of it as unusual was somewhat mistaken: '. . . they take all their clothes off, fold them neatly, and jump into the river and leave a little note, or leave a note at home somewhere.' The way in which these and other circumstances surrounding the death are taken to point to a suicide will be considered further in the following section. From the present section, I hope it has become clear that the modes of death vary with respect to the degree of equivocality they present. There are relatively 'clear-cut' suicidal modes of dying such as hanging and relatively 'clear-cut' accidental modes such as dying in a road accident and, between the two, are a series of more equivocal modes.

6.4 LOCATION AND CIRCUMSTANCES OF DEATH

In the previous section, it became difficult to talk exclusively about mode of death without reference to other circumstances surrounding the death. In saying 'you're conditioned by the circumstances of the death', the coroner's officer seemed to be saying more than simply that it was the mode of death that was involved and that it was on the basis of an assessment of the whole scene that enquiries were directed. In my earlier treatment of these features of the situation, I wrote as follows:

> an overdose taken in the middle of a wood would probably be more likely to lead to a suicide verdict than one taken in bed, the journey to the remote place being seen as an indicator of intent. Similarly, a shooting accident is more likely to be defined as such if it takes place in a man's gun room or on a formally designated shoot than if it

takes place in a deserted lay-by. In addition to the actual location of the death, other circumstances surrounding it may be seen as highly relevant. In cases of gassing, for example, coroners may look for evidence that the deceased took special precautions to prevent the escape of gas, perhaps by blocking up windows and doors with rugs. In cases of poisoning, he will want to know about the possibility of drinking the poison by accident, as can easily happen in the case of weed-killer and similar poisons. Similarly in cases where tablets are involved, it may be considered relevant to know whether they had been hoarded, stolen or borrowed, or were normally prescribed to the deceased.

The logic of inferring suicidal intent on the basis of this kind of evidence would appear to be based on the belief, which is certainly not confined to coroners, that if someone wants to kill himself he will make a proper job of it. Thus actions like those described above are presumably seen as steps which were specifically taken to ensure the probability of death occurring before the discovery of the act. The implication of this is that suicide is regarded as being almost by definition a solitary act, which is not normally carried out in public [Atkinson, 1971, pp. 179–80].

Although I do not wish to alter these observations substantially, they do somewhat oversimplify the problems involved in analysing the scene of a death. In particular, they may imply that it is simply a matter of making inferences about suicidal intent from an analysis of the location and circumstances of the death. This is certainly done, but it is not all that is done, as I hope will become clear in the following examples of reconstructed exchanges between a coroner and witnesses at an inquest.

The particular case is that of a woman who had been found drowned in a canal. Before the extracts that follow, it had already been established that she had suffered from depression for a number of years and that she had made at least one previous suicide attempt. The witness at this point in the proceedings is the twenty-year-old son of the deceased woman.

Inquest Extract 1

CORONER: . . . you said she was a non-swimmer and was afraid of water?

WITNESS: Yes.

CORONER: She wouldn't normally have to go down there would she? I mean she wasn't used to going down to this place, was she?

WITNESS: I don't know.

CORONER: It's right off the beaten track as far as the hospital's concerned.

WITNESS: Yes.

CORONER: She wouldn't normally have to go there. Certain times of day it's quite busy but at other times it's very quiet . . . and from the other statements here it looks as though she'd been there quite a time before she went in, so it looks as though she intended to do it, doesn't it?

WITNESS: It does, yes.

One of the things which seems to be going on prior to the coroner's final remark, in which intent is imputed, is that the woman's being near the canal at all is being portrayed as unusual or odd. To begin with, she was a 'non-swimmer' who was 'afraid of water'. Then, using his special knowledge of the locality, the coroner proposes that the woman would 'not normally have to go down there', a statement which depends for its sense on the hearer knowing about, for example, the distance of the canal from the particular mental hospital in which the woman was being treated. Thus the witness, who is a native of a town some thirty miles away from the one where the death occurred and where the inquest was being held, does not share that local knowledge and replies that he doesn't know. The coroner then proceeds to elaborate his analysis further for the benefit of the witness by noting that the place is 'right off the beaten track as far as the hospital is concerned', and then by repeating his observation that the woman would not 'normally' have to go there. He then alludes to the variable crowdedness of the place, an issue which is as we shall see taken up further with a later witness. Alluding again to evidence yet to be heard about the length of time she was believed to have been by the canal before 'going in', the coroner then observes that she 'intended to do it', a conclusion with which the witness seems prepared to agree. Now although this procedure of inferring intent on the basis of an analysis of the scene of the death is in keeping with our earlier published analysis, it may be noted also that the coroner arrives at that inference only after depicting a scene which is somewhat odd or unusual with respect to the particular person concerned. Having asserted that there is something strange about the woman being there at all, the need for some account of what she could have been doing there is also pointed to. Had the place been one which she passed regularly, then presumably she may, on this one occasion, have slipped into the water so that an accidental death would provide an adequate and consistent answer to the problem of how she died. But the claim that it was not a part of her routine activities to go to or pass by this particular place raises the possibility that she had some special (as opposed to routine) reason for going there on that day. Given that the conclusion to her visit was death by drowning, the imputation of intent to commit suicide emerges as a 'reasonable' way of accounting for her presence at the canal. We may note that the fact of her death is particularly important in arriving at this particular account of what she was doing in this place where she had no 'normal' reason to be. Had she not died, for example, 'going for a walk', 'feeding the ducks', or 'watching the boats' might have been considered adequate grounds for her being there. These possibilities, however, were not only never raised during the inquest, but it could also be argued that they are ruled out by sequences like that cited above in which the very presence of a mental hospital patient at that particular place is depicted as odd.

What I am suggesting here, then, is that it is not just a matter of inferring suicidal intent on the basis of an analysis of the scene, but that such analyses are also directed towards ruling out other possible ways of making sense of the particular setting. This process is, I would argue, to be found at all inquests, and can be exemplified further by reference to the case discussed above. When the pathologist came to the stand, his report on the post-mortem showed that the woman had alcohol in her bloodstream, a finding which might add credence to an accidental account of her death, given our commonsense knowledge of the effects of alcohol on steadiness of walking, and hence on the dangers of walking by a canal while drunk. It would seem important to establish, therefore, precisely how much alcohol she had drunk prior to her death in order to assess how drunk she may have been. The pathologist replied that it was the equivalent of two whiskies, an amount which he described as 'moderate'. The coroner then asked for his opinion on the cause of death, to which the reply was that 'death was due to drowning'. Although this may seem a remarkably 'obvious' answer to a rather pointless question, it is crucial in the process of ruling out alternative verdicts, as is evidenced in the exchange which follows:

Inquest Extract 2

CORONER: Would you say that the deceased was a reasonably healthy person?
WITNESS: Yes – physically.
CORONER: Yes, now about these depressions and things. Could that come on suddenly and overpower her?
WITNESS: I would give that opinion, sir, yes.
CORONER: Yes. [Long pause while he read through the papers in front of him.] And could you find any evidence that she might have dizzy or blackout turns?
WITNESS: No, not from my examination.
CORONER: Thank you. [Witness stands down.]

Thus it is 'established' that the deceased was physically healthy. The expert witness testifies that the post-mortem yielded no evidence that she had been suffering from any illness which might have led to her death, or to her suddenly passing out on the tow-path. The death, then, was due to 'drowning' and there was no physical reason why she should have fallen into the canal. Her depressions, however, could 'suddenly overpower her', a view which is given the added weight of being confirmed by a medical expert. Slowly, then, we can see the alternatives being ruled out, evidence being presented to show that the intake of alcohol had not been excessive, and hence an accident involving stumbling or tripping into the canal made less likely, and further medical evidence which gives no support to a verdict of death by natural causes.

The process of ruling out alternatives to a suicidal verdict and of analysing the location and circumstances of the death continue in considerable detail when the police officer who took the body from the water comes to the stand. Thus the possibility of homicide is considered and put aside:

Inquest Extract 3

> CORONER: Were there any marks on the body?
> WITNESS: No, sir.
>
> ....
>
> CORONER: And you were satisfied that there were no signs of other suspicious circumstances or foul play?
> WITNESS: No, there were no signs of violence.
> CORONER: No signs of a struggle either?
> WITNESS: No, sir.

Precisely what such signs might consist of is not touched on, but what is important is that someone with the *professional expertise* to recognize such signs had they been present (i.e. a policeman) testifies that they were absent. The location of the death is then subjected to an extended discussion:

Inquest Extract 4

> CORONER: ... with regard to this place, it is quite busy at times when they're going home from Jones's and the factory. It's a short cut over Trap Lane isn't it?
> WITNESS: I use it pretty often going home, but I wouldn't say it was busy – except perhaps around quarter past four when the children are going home from school.
> CORONER: But at *this* time it would be fairly deserted wouldn't it?
> WITNESS: Oh, yes, at this time it's free, yes.

CORONER: I mean there wouldn't be many people about.
WITNESS: No, sir.

Here then, the coroner is continuing his depiction of the place as a deserted one, even though the responses of the policeman suggest that there may be some doubt about the matter. The relevance of this line of questioning seems likely to be based on the belief referred to earlier that people do not normally commit suicide in a public way. Thus a scene is being set where the woman could have jumped in without anyone seeing and without possibility of immediate rescue. The 'jumping in', however, has yet to be firmly established, though the pathologist's statement has already lessened the plausibility of a conclusion to the effect that she collapsed or slipped in. The sequence proceeds to this topic:

Inquest Extract 5

CORONER: Did you examine the area where the body was found?
WITNESS: Yes, sir. Both where it was found and along the banks both ways.
CORONER: And did you find anything that might be traceable to her?
WITNESS: Under the railway bridge about 100 yards south there were a number of cigarette ends, matches and on the stone slabs which border the tow-path were footprints corresponding near enough to the shoes that the deceased had been wearing. It had been raining quite heavily, sir.
CORONER: And were there any signs of slipping in?
WITNESS: No sir. You could see quite clearly defined footprints.

Although no forensic evidence linking either the footprints or the cigarettes to the deceased was presented, the inference that the woman was under the bridge *and* that she jumped in from there seems to be quickly arrived at. There were no signs of slipping and clearly defined footprints are suggestive of an 'instant' rather than a 'sliding' departure from the bank (i.e. jumping in). The evidence about the cigarettes was also the only material presented which provided grounds for the coroner's earlier observation to the deceased's son that his mother had been there 'for some time'. And being under a railway bridge on a tow-path in the pouring rain, smoking cigarettes provides a further depiction of a strange scene which needs to be accounted for in some way. The presence of the rain also increases the weakness of any claims that she was 'just going for a walk'. Furthermore, by showing her to have spent some time under the bridge, she is depicted as doing something which it is commonly believed suicides do prior to the act, that is, weighing up the situation before finally taking the plunge in the manner of Hamlet's celebrated soliloquy. The accidental possibilities, however, are explored a little further:

Inquest Extract 6

CORONER: How deep is the water there?

WITNESS: I didn't actually measure it, but I'd say that it's about three feet at the side.

CORONER: So if you'd fallen, it would be fairly easy to get out, would it?

WITNESS: If you'd fallen in accidentally, yes sir. The surface of the water was only about ten inches below the stone slabs on the bank.

CORONER: So you could have stood up in the water?

WITNESS: Yes sir.

So even if she had fallen in accidentally, it would apparently have been easy enough for her to get out – *if* she had wanted to. That she had not got out and that there were no signs of her having attempted to do so, therefore, points to something other than an accident. It is inferred, in short, that she intended to die.

I have concentrated on this one case at some length in order to illustrate how the location and circumstances of a death are analysed at an inquest. The coroner's problem can be seen as one of considering which of the categorizations available to him renders understandable or intelligible a set of circumstances which would otherwise not be immediately 'clear'. The alternatives are considered with reference to common-sense knowledge of the locality, of 'normal' scenes and 'normal practices', and to professional assessments of various 'signs', including the pathologist's report on the post-mortem and the police assessments of the presence or absence of particular 'signs' at the scene of the death. Death from 'Natural Causes', 'Homicide' and 'Accident' can be shown to be inappropriate categorizations by reference to selected features of the setting and, once this has been done, it is only a short step to a verdict of suicide.

It should not be thought, however, that suicide verdicts are always, or indeed ever, arrived at solely by reference to an analysis of the location and circumstances of the death. In the above, for example, the designation of the place as an 'odd' place for the deceased to have been in in the 'normal' run of things was dependent on knowledge about her status as a mental hospital patient and on an analysis of the kinds of places such a person is typically to be found. In other words, the force of much of the coroner's inferential work in this case was dependent on and added to by analysis of particular features of the deceased's

biography. It is to a consideration of this that the section which follows
is directed.

6.5 THE BIOGRAPHY OF THE DECEASED

One of the factors assessed in the Los Angeles Psychological Autopsies
referred to earlier is the mental condition of the deceased prior to death.
The importance of this kind of assessment in leading the coroner
towards a verdict of suicide was first brought to my attention by a coroner while he was showing me some of his records. On the first page of
these was a section with the printed title 'Brief Circumstances of
Death'. These consist usually of a resumé of the evidence contained in
the more detailed statements of other witnesses included in the records
for each case, and are prepared by the coroner's officer in charge of the
investigation. Before reporting on the coroner's comments on one of
these, some examples and preliminary comments on them may serve to
underline their significance in the process of leading to a verdict of
suicide.[5]

Coroner's Record Extract 1

> About 3.10 p.m. on Tuesday, 2nd May, 1967, the deceased, John
> Frederick Smith, 59 years, Coalman, of 17, North Parade, Xtown,
> was found hanging in an open lean-to shed in Wilson's coal-yard,
> Albert Street, Xtown.
>   In September, 1966, the deceased was away from work for three
> weeks with heart trouble and in November, 1966, he was away from
> work for 5 weeks with bronchitis. Since this last illness, he had lost
> weight for no apparent reason and had been worried about his abili-
> ty to continue working as a coalman during the winter. About 1 p.m.
> on Tuesday 2nd May, while driving his coal lorry, he was involved in
> a road accident. Although the accident was slight, afterwards he
> appeared worried and depressed.
>   About 2 p.m. on Thursday, 4th May, 1967, I was present when Dr
> J. B. Burt conducted a post-mortem examination of the body at the
> Xshire County Hospital, Xtown, with the result that the cause of
> death was hanging.
> 7th May, 1967   OFFICER'S SIGNATURE

Coroner's Record Extract 2

> Deceased had suffered from a heart complaint for some four years. In
> 1962 he was told to reduce his smoking, drinking and to keep to a
> diet which had been given him. He did this for some time and reduc-

ed his weight, but gradually dropped back into his old routine. At that time he had a small myocardial infarct and was probably heading for a longer one.

He was a hard-working man and contrary to advice would not rest. He did not take a holiday. He found that rest interfered with his work. His heart trouble returned, he worried because this prevented him working and he was drinking alcohol more than he should. His work deteriorated to such an extent that he was told by his employer, in no uncertain terms, about this. He was told to take a holiday, but refused.

On Friday, 9th October, 1968, he had a headache and arrived at work at about 10.45 a.m. He was told by his employer that he was not working as he should, he appeared ill and had been drinking too much. He was told to take two weeks holiday and sort himself out. He left in the firm's car about 1.30 p.m. driving erratically and did not return. Later the same day he was reported as missing to Xtown police. Late that night the car was found in a lane at Woodley Farm, Gateford. During the early hours of 10th October, 1968, his body was found in a ditch close to the car in long grass. He had a wound in his head and an automatic pistol was found near by. He was examined by C.I.D. officers and Drs Broadbent and Jones.

About 10.30 a.m. on 10th October, 1968, a post-mortem examination was carried out by Dr Jones at St. Swithen's Hospital, Fordly. He was of the opinion that this was a self-inflicted wound. Cause of death: (a) Cerebral concussion and laceration (b) Gun-shot wound of the head.

14th October, 1968   OFFICER'S SIGNATURE

On these two 'Brief Circumstances of Death' reports, a number of observations seem pertinent. First, the reports were written after all the other statements and evidence had been collected, some five days after the occurrence of the deaths in each case. Second, the reports are necessarily selective in the evidence to which they refer. Third, the reports refer not only to the 'Circumstances of Death' but to past features of the deceased persons' biographies and to the events which occurred just prior to their deaths. Fourth, a common feature of the biographical remarks is that the deceased persons both had 'troubles' of some sort. Fifth, both go a long way towards predicting, in advance of reading the statements of the other witnesses, a suicidal verdict. This is particularly so with Extract 2, where the pathologist is quoted as being of the opinion that the death was 'self-inflicted'. With reference to the 'Brief Circumstances of Death' sections, the coroner who was showing me his records observed that they were most important and that he always gave them special attention. Their importance in guiding him towards a particular verdict can easily be appreciated when it is remembered that these sections provide the coroner with his introduction to the case. He will have been notified of the death prior to receiving the reports from the coroner's officer, but the degree of detail at that early stage is usually fairly minimal. Before reading the more detailed statements of witnesses, then, he starts his examination of the evidence with the kinds of précis presented above. It seems very likely, then, that his reading of the later evidence will in large measure be influenced by these preliminary 'potted' accounts of the deaths and the biographies of the deceased.

The particular summary that he read through with me went as follows:

Coroner's Record Extract 3

The deceased man has suffered from no physical illness, but has always been prone to fits of depression. His mother took her own life when he was six years old and, after remarriage, his father left the country. As a boy, the deceased lived with twelve different families.

He made the Army his career. He served in a number of countries before leaving the Army in June 1967. He failed to settle into civilian life, in spite of having a good job. Frequently he went missing from home, for periods varying from one day to one week. He underwent a ten-week period of hospital treatment late in 1969, and benefited from this but he had recently refused to re-enter a hospital as suggested by his doctor.

On Monday, 31st March, 1970, he became restless. He left for work at 7.55 a.m. the following morning and did not return home again. He was at work on the morning of that date, but failed to return after lunch. The deceased was seen in the Xtown area by a close friend on three occasions during the days that followed, and on Sunday, 6th May, 1970, he thought he had succeeded in persuading the deceased to return to his work and home. About 12 noon on Monday, 7th May, 1970, Mr Barley, a farmer at Burston, saw a car parked near a barn on his land, from a distance. When the car was still behind the barn at 3.00 p.m. that day he walked across the field to investigate.

He found a Volkswagen car, with the engine running at idling speed, filled with smoke. The deceased was sitting in the driver's seat, slumped against the door. On opening the car, Mr Barley found it to be filled with fumes. He pulled the deceased from the car and tried to revive him without success. He then called the police and ambulance. The deceased was taken from the farm to the Xtown hospital, where he was seen on arrival at 8.30 p.m. by Dr Dean. He found he was dead. The fuel tank of the car still contained two or three gallons of petrol. A length of plastic tubing was attached to the exhaust pipe of the car by Sellotape, and inserted through the passenger's window. On the front passenger's seat of the car was a note reading 'God Bless Mary and Ann'.

Date   OFFICER'S SIGNATURE

On reading of the man's disturbed childhood following the suicide of his mother, the coroner remarked, 'That's highly significant.' On learning of his Army career and the difficulties of settling to civilian life, the coroner offered a series of generalizations about the typicality of such a career, noting that it was surprising how many ex-servicemen ended up by committing suicide. As we read through the later sections, it became increasingly clear that some very extraordinary evidence would be needed to show this to be anything other than a suicide. As we came to the end, the coroner observed: 'There's a classic pattern for you – broken home, escape to the services, nervous breakdown, unsettled at work, no family ties – what could be clearer?'

Now it is of some interest to note that in his concluding remarks, the coroner made no reference to the 'circumstances of death' but commented only on biographical parts of the account. What seems to be indicated is that notions of typical 'suicidal biographies' and 'precipitating circumstances' are important in establishing that a death was unequivocally a suicide. Out of the thousands of possible events, stories and so on which could be told about the life of any person, only certain items are selected by the witnesses and the coroner's officer who writes up the report. In commenting that Extract 3 was a 'classic pattern', the coroner can be seen as endorsing the 'relevance' of his officer's selection for the purpose in hand. If it were not the case that such items were deemed relevant to a consideration of a possibly suicidal death, then presumably the coroner might have made comments like, 'What's all this stuff about his childhood doing here'? or, 'Why do my officers always have to present so much superfluous evidence which has no relevance for the task in hand?' On no occasion, however, have I heard a coroner make such comments, and that they seem to agree with their officers as to what is relevant gives support to the proposition that there is extensive agreement as to the importance not only of biographical evidence, but of particular sorts of biographical evidence in enabling a decision to be reached. Considerable overlap in the features selected for inclusion can be seen in the three examples given above, worries about health and work being alluded to in all of them. These, coupled with specific items such as a recent road accident, a drink problem, a row with the boss, a suicide in the family, a disturbed childhood and mental illness, can be characterized in a general way as 'troubles'. Similarly, the following first sentences taken from 'Brief Circumstances of Death' reports introduce the case not with evidence on the 'circumstances of the death' as such, but on features of the deceased's biography:

Coroner's Record Extract 4

The deceased was a diabetic, a hypochondriac, he had a record of mental disorder and was undergoing regular treatment as an out-patient at St Lucy's Hospital, Xtown under Dr Franks. . . .

Coroner's Record Extract 5

The deceased man suffered from a mental disease from 1948 and spent some time in Xtown mental hospital where he had made several attempts to take his own life. . . .

Coroner's Record Extract 6

The deceased John Smith was an informal patient at Xtown mental hospital and was allowed home at weekends. . . .

Coroner's Record Extract 7

The deceased was of good health. He was a bachelor who liked living on his own. . . .

With the exception of Extract 7, then, all the above begin not just with references to 'troubles', but with reference to a specific trouble, namely mental illness. But although 'troubles' are not explicitly mentioned in Extract 7, there is at least a hint that there may have been something odd about this man's biography in the second sentence. Why, that is, should it be deemed reportable news that the man was 'a bachelor who liked living on his own', when none of the reports I have read refer to a 'married man who liked living with a woman'? That no such statements were found is, of course, not surprising, as the 'who . . .' clause is normally taken as being implicit in the announcement of marital status. By the same logic, bachelors may be reasonably expected to be womanizers, anti-woman, or pro-women and lonely. Extract 7, then, can be read as a warning against inferring either of these 'normal expectations' about this particular unmarried man; given that 'anybody knows' that most people do not live alone and that many of those that do are prone to loneliness, the news that this man actually 'likes living on his own' is not only news worthy of announcing, but also suggests that there may be something unusual about his biography which will be revealed in the rest of the report.

Searching through a person's biography is also a notable feature at inquests which result in verdicts of suicide. Compared with the often very limited enquiries made at inquests on deaths which are ultimately categorized as accidents or natural causes, the probing into the deceased's past life can become immensely detailed. At the inquest already referred to, for example, questioning of the son of the deceased was focused almost exclusively on biographical details of his mother's life. Some of these, such as date and place of birth and maiden name, statutorily have to be given on oath for the purposes of matching birth and death certificates at Somerset House.[6] Thus at the start of the questioning of the deceased's son, the coroner is reading details from statements already given to his officer which are then confirmed by the witness. A point of some interest, then, is whether there is anything 'special' about the point at which the coroner asks the first open-ended question which requires more than simply a 'yes' or 'no' answer:

Inquest Extract 7

CORONER: ... you came to the Localtown General Infirmary and identified the body lying there as that of your mother?
WITNESS: **Yes**
CORONER: Full name Amy Smith, formerly Amy Jones and she was a widow aged 48, born 19th March, 1923, at Docktown?
WITNESS: Yes.
CORONER: And she formerly resided with you at 30 Honeysuckle Avenue, Blakeston?
WITNESS: Yes.
CORONER: From which she became a patient at the Dale Hospital here. She enjoyed good health apart from minor ailments until 1968?
WITNESS: Yes.
CORONER: Then what happened?
WITNESS: She had an upset with my dad and she took some pills.

The 'Then what happened?' question is the first question in the whole exchange between the coroner and the witness that requires the witness to say anything more than 'yes' or 'no'. That the coroner is not only able to ask it at this point but also receives an immediate and precise reply about a previous suicide attempt suggests that he and the witness were both familiar with the story and with the significance of the particular point in it that had been reached. The final question and answer would also seem reasonable at that point to a local observer who would know that the 'Dale Hospital' is in fact a mental hospital. Given this information, it can be seen that the coroner's penultimate question has posed a puzzle which is in need of clarification, so that the final question to the witness can be seen as a request for that clarification. The puzzle posed in the penultimate remarks from the coroner is that the woman had been a patient in a mental hospital yet had enjoyed good health until 1968. What was it, then, that changed her health to such a degree that she was admitted to the hospital in question? It is, further-more, not just that someone whose erstwhile 'good health' had come to an end had been constructed to that point, but there is a further bio-graphical puzzle to be answered: namely, that until the news of her entry into the mental hospital, the details of her life depict a thoroughly 'normal' biography. Though it may not appear immediately obvious, the very presence of routine 'face-sheet' type data is constitutive of a 'normal person'. To have had no maiden name would have been to cast doubts on her morals and the legitimacy of the witness. To have no clearly specifiable date of birth is to have doubtful origins (gypsy, bastard, etc.) and 'no fixed abode' is a legend normally reserved for dis-reputable criminals. The news of her status as a mental hospital patient, then, is the first question-mark in an otherwise 'normal' biography. How her 'normal' biography came to contain this unusual feature as well as how her 'normal health' became less than normal are both relevant questions at this point in the inquest, and both receive an answer in the final statement of the witness.

From that point onwards, the coroner's main interest in the exchange with this witness was in how his mother 'got worse'. Having established that the suicide attempt led to a first admission to mental hospital, the exchange continued:

Inquest Extract 8

CORONER: . . . afterwards she became quite a highly strung person?
WITNESS: Yes.
CORONER: More so than before?
WITNESS: Well . . . er . . .
CORONER: And then your father died on 20th July last year?
WITNESS: Yes.
CORONER: And she became worse then and was quite distressed from time to time?
WITNESS: Yes.

Thus the witness initially seems reluctant to admit that his mother became 'more highly strung than before', in that he offers only a hesi-tant reply to the coroner's second question. After the news of his father's death, however, it may have seemed odd had he denied that his mother 'became worse and was quite distressed from time to time', and that state of affairs is at this point confirmed by the witness. The cor-oner goes on to discuss two further admissions to the mental hospital, one of which included the administration of E.C.T. He then continues the line of questioning designed to discover whether she 'got worse' or not:

Inquest Extract 9

CORONER: And what was her condition then, better or worse?

WITNESS: I should say about the same.

CORONER: Mmm – (pause) – and you thought there were some personal problems. Do you know what sort they were, health or finance or . . .'

WITNESS: I'm not sure – money problems perhaps.

CORONER: And she seemed to be letting everything get on top of her and unable to cope . . . and then this year she attempted to take her life again by cutting her wrists?

WITNESS: Yes – but it wasn't a serious attempt.

CORONER: Why do you think she did that then?

WITNESS: Well, she'd been drinking, she was a bit upset.

CORONER: I see – did she get worse when she'd been drinking?

Here again, then, the coroner receives an indecisive reply when he asks if she got better or worse, and the 'Mmm – (pause)' seems to indicate that he has been stopped in that line of questioning. By raising the issue of other personal problems, however, further evidence of her deteriorating condition might be revealed, but again he receives a vague reply, which is followed by his generalizing about her inability 'to cope'. That she made another suicide attempt can then be seen as further definite evidence that she really was 'getting worse', and it is noticeable here that the son attempts to define the event as non-serious. When pressed for a reason for his belief that it was not serious, he mentions drinking, which then provides the coroner with further grounds for inferring that she became worse after drinking, a line of reasoning which, as we have already seen, had a relevance for the later analysis of her condition just before death. On two further occasions in the questioning the coroner observes that she 'was getting worse', and this theme can be seen as preparing the ground for viewing a suicidal death as a logical, and perhaps the only logical, outcome of a gradual process of mental deterioration. Were this not the case, then the coroner's second and third questions in the following extract would appear unreasonable and outrageous in the extreme:

Inquest Extract 10

CORONER: And then you were told by the police that your mother had been found drowned at Localtown?

WITNESS: Yes.

CORONER: Did that surprise you?
WITNESS: It shocked me.
CORONER: And why was that?
WITNESS: I didn't think she'd do a thing like that.

Given that sudden deaths are by definition unexpected deaths, to ask a person if they were surprised at the news of such a death seems to be asking the obvious, and it is easy to imagine such a question in other settings arousing angry answers such as, 'wouldn't you be surprised if your mother was found drowned?'[7] Similarly, to probe further by asking why he was shocked might easily provoke answers like, 'Do you really need to ask that question?' or, 'What's so unusual about being shocked by the death of one's mother?' The questions, however, not only invoke 'reasonable' replies, but also receive a reply which involves the recognition by the witness that in this case there were grounds *other than* the 'normal' grounds for being shocked at his mother's death. His 'shock' is not simply that which would constitute a 'normal' reaction to a sudden bereavement in the family, but is a reaction to a particular type of death, namely a suicide. In other words, the son has apparently already 'read' his mother's drowning as a 'suicide', and hence hears and answers the coroner's questions about if and why he was surprised as referring to surprise about the suicide rather than surprise about her death. In these terms, it is arguable that the coroner's question gains its sense and its appropriateness at that point only because the mother had been shown to have a biography which could easily be imagined to be a typically 'suicidal biography'. Thus, if someone can be shown to have such a biography, then it is not only reasonable to conclude that if it ends with death it is a suicide, but it is also reasonable to expect that that type of death might have been expected by any person familiar with the suicidal biography. The suicide, then, may not be a surprise, so that it is perfectly in order to ask whether indeed it did come as a surprise.

6.6 CONCLUSIONS AND IMPLICATIONS

In this chapter, I have attempted to provide some of the arguments and ideas put forward in my earlier published analysis with additional empirical backing and to add some new analyses of the data presented. As I have pointed out in certain places in the chapter, the new data indicate the need to qualify and partially revise some of my earlier remarks. But although the evidence gives added support to the view that coroners and their officers are engaged in analysing features of the deaths and of the biographies of the deceased according to a variety of taken-for-granted assumptions about what constitutes a 'typical suicide', a 'typical suicidal biography', and so on, it also points to the danger of treating items such as 'Suicide Notes', 'Modes of Dying', 'Circumstances of Death' and 'Biographical Factors' as somehow having a separate or independent relevance. Thus features of a particular death may come to be viewed as indicative of suicide only in the light of biographical data which are regarded as indicative of a possible suicide and vice versa. The division of this chapter into sections then is to be viewed as an attempt to order an argument rather than as an attempt to depict separate and independent procedures in which coroners and their officers are involved.

As the additional data presented here seem in general to be supportive of the conclusions arrived at earlier on the basis of much less empirical research, extracts from the 'original' concluding section are presented below.[8] I shall then make some further comments on the implications of these conclusions in introducing the research reported in Chapter 7. The extracts from my original conclusions begin with a consideration of the significance of coroners' analyses of the biographical circumstances of the deceased (Atkinson, 1971):

> Just as they have ideas about what modes of dying are typically suicidal, so also do coroners have ideas about the kinds of circumstances which lead people to commit suicide. I would argue further that, together with the kinds of cues discussed earlier, these are used to build up an explanatory model of how each death occurred. Thus, for a suicide verdict to be recorded, no part of the model must be inconsistent with the coroner's ideas about factors which are typically associated with suicide. Two further examples of cases which fail to meet the requirements of logical consistency may help to clarify what I mean:
>
>> CASE 1: A widow aged eighty-five was found gassed in the kitchen of her cottage, where she had lived alone since the death of her husband. Rugs and towels had been stuffed under the door and around the window casements. At the inquest, the few people who knew her testified that she always seemed to be a very happy and cheerful person, and the coroner recorded an open verdict on the grounds that there was no evidence to show how the gas taps had been turned on.
>
> Here, the case appears initially as a clear-cut suicide: a lonely old widow gasses herself taking special precautions to prevent the escape of gas. The evidence that she was apparently perfectly happy, however, must have raised enough doubt in the coroner's mind to lead him away from a suicidal verdict, as happiness is inconsistent with suicidal intent. Putting this another way, one could say that the

evidence about her happiness prevented him from explaining satisfactorily why she should have committed suicide. The same thing also seems to apply in this next case:

> CASE 2: A seventeen-year-old schoolboy who normally went out shopping with his parents at a certain time on a particular day refused to do so on the day he died, and was thus left alone in the house. When his parents returned, they found him hanging from the banisters on the landing. During the previous two years he had been under regular psychiatric treatment for depression, and was known to be currently worried about what he would do when he left school. At the inquest, a witness testified that he and the boy had been planning a climbing holiday together in the near future, and that a book on climbing had been found open on the deceased's bed at the time of the death. An open verdict was recorded.

Here again, everything initially pointed to a suicide. The method used, the fact that steps had been taken to minimize the chances of intervention, the recurrent depressions and the present worries. The additional evidence, however, raised the possibility of an alternative explanation: he could have been practising climbing and hanged himself accidentally. That the coroners in these two cases had doubts is evidenced by the fact that open verdicts were recorded, as coroners on the whole tend to avoid open verdicts whenever possible. In other words, the evidence in both was not sufficiently consistent to enable them to build up a tenable model of either a suicidal or accidental death. In contrast to this, the following case . . . raised few problems for the coroner:

> CASE 3: A sixty-three-old man was found gassed by his wife on her return from shopping. He had suffered from bronchitis for the past fourteen years and had been half-paralysed for the last three. His wife testified that he had recently been very depressed, and that, on several occasion, he had threatened to take his own life. A verdict of suicide was recorded.

Thus the man's death could easily be explained: ill health had led to depression, which had led to suicide. In addition he had actually verbalized his intentions shortly before he died.

The discussion of the criteria used in inferring intent draws attention to a number of important issues. In the first place, it shows that there are certain cues which are likely to suggest that a particular verdict is the probable one or that other *types* of evidence are needed. In the case of a death resulting from a car crash, for example, it is highly unlikely that much will be made of the deceased's family history. Whether or not the dead man had experienced a broken home in childhood or details about his current personal financial situation will probably never be considered. In other words, this particular mode of death would not lead those concerned with the official categorization of deaths to look for evidence of this kind. Conversely, if a man dies by hanging, this may be taken as a cue that it would be appropriate to look for evidence such as this.

A second general conclusion is that the process of investigating sudden deaths involves the coroner in a process of *explanation*. If the cues available allow him to construct an explanatory model which seems to fit a particular type of death, then the verdict will categorize that death accordingly. Thus, if he cannot adequately explain why a person should have committed suicide, then another verdict will be recorded. In relation to this, two additional points can be made. First, it was noted earlier that the coroners' general brief is to explain residual deaths which have not been adequately explained by other personnel in the system for registering deaths. This kind of explanation, however, only requires him to pin a label to each death which refers to the *cause of death*. Thus he is required to say that these deaths were caused by accidents, while those were caused by suicide. What I am saying here, however, is that, at least in the case of suicide, he is involved in a more complex form of explanation because the legal need to establish intent necessitates the search for a motive or reason why the deceased should have taken his own life. Explicitly, then, he has to explain all the deaths referred to him, while, in the case of suicides, he is implicitly bound to explain the suicide. The second and related point is that coroners are not the only people who do this. Jack Douglas (1967, p. 229) has noted: '. . . an *official* categorization of the cause of death is as much the end result of an *argument* as such a categorization by any other member of society'. The implication of this is that, in talking about different kinds of death, people in society at large are also involved in processes, which, although less sophisticated than those of the officials, are very similar in kind. That this is so is supported by an examination I carried out of fifty consecutive local newspaper reports of suicide. In all but six of these, the reporters were at pains to explain why the individual had committed suicide, and, in many cases, suggested explanations appeared in the headlines to the stories. Examples of this are as follows: 'Depressed Man Gasses Himself', 'Homesick Woman Commits Suicide' and 'Man who Thought he had Cancer Kills Himself'.

The implictions of this kind of analysis for suicide research which depends on the correlational work with data derived from coroners' records are clearly very serious. By showing relationships between variables like marital status, mental illness, alcoholism, economic disaster and so on with suicide, it is arguable that all the researchers are doing is to make explicit the explanations used implicitly by coroners in their everyday work. Indeed, the evidence cited above is at least suggestive of the hypothesis that the cues which coroners use as indicators of suicidal intent bear a very close resemblance to the variables cited by experts in their attempts to explain suicide. Furthermore, in the light of what was said above, it also seems likely that there will be some correspondence between these *expert* explanations and those employed by the proverbial 'average man'.

The argument as to whether or not the experts' explanations of suicide are any more than formalized versions of the informal ones used by coroners is further complicated by the possibility of feedback from the researchers to the coroners. The coroners I have met certainly seem interested in suicide, and the volume of published research which is based on their records would suggest that they are very willing to assist in the cause of research. The Los Angeles coroner has contributed to the literature on suicide, and, as was noted earlier, has formal links with the Los Angeles Suicide Prevention Center, while, at the most recent International Conference for Suicide Prevention, at least one English coroner was present. It therefore seems reasonable to assume that some coroners are well informed about some of the results of research into suicide, and, if this is the case, it seems unlikely that their decisions at inquests will be totally unaffected by this knowledge. It is possible, for example, that acquaintance with research results might lead them to feel surer about the kinds of cues used in inferring intent, or it may even suggest new ones.

It should now be clear that the orientation [here] owes much to that presented by Douglas in *The Social Meanings of Suicide*, and that what has been said supports many of his contentions. . . . Yet his critique of the validity of official statistics led him to a position where he rejected their usefulness both for the traditional kinds of correlational study and for the analysis of the social meanings of suicide which is the alternative he offers. The logic of the present discussion, however, suggests that data obtainable from coroners is of central significance in examining the social meanings of suicide. Not only do coroners, to an admittedly unknown extent, share the prevalent definitions of suicide in a society at any one time, but they are also in a position to reaffirm these definitions publicly and even perhaps to introduce new ones. By defining certain deaths as suicides, they are in effect saying to others in the society: 'These kinds of deaths are suicides, these are the kinds of situations in which people commit suicide and these are the types of people who commit suicide.' Given the fact that coroners' courts in England and Wales are public and that inquests provide a steady flow of copy for local and occasionally national news media, the role of coroners in maintaining and sometimes changing shared definitions of suicidal situations attains a crucial importance, for they can be seen as defining for their society what kind of behaviour constitutes suicide at a particular point in time. Thus if we are to determine the shared meanings of suicide prevalent in a society, an analysis of the kinds of decisions being made by coroners and their counterparts must take a predominant place in our enquiries.

Yet this is not to suggest that once this is done, suicidal behaviour will suddenly be explained, but rather that it will not be explained without analysing the kind of decisions coroners make and without attempting to understand the role they play in relation to society as a whole. Clearly this is easier said than done, and Figure 6.6.1 is presented in an attempt to clarify the way in which shared definitions of suicidal situations are transmitted in a social system. It is entitled a 'dynamic' model because it attempts to account for changes over time. The shared definitions of suicidal situations prevalent in a society at any one time (A) will also be shared, to a greater or lesser extent, by the coroners (B), the individuals who indulge in suicidal behaviour (C), the researchers (D), and those employed by the media of mass communication (E). That the definitions of each of these people will have direct and indirect effects on the definitions of the others is indicated by the arrows. Without actually articulating this model formally, I have tried to show how it holds for the case of student suicides in another paper (Atkinson,

Figure 6.6.1 *A dynamic model of the transmission of shared definitions of suicide through a social system*

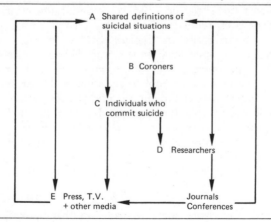

1969). I argue there that there is evidence to show that there is a shared definition of students as a group of people who are particularly prone to suicide. The more students there are who share this definition (and my evidence suggested that they do share such a view of themselves), the more likely are they to contemplate a suicidal solution to a problem. The more coroners there are who are aware of this view of students as being especially suicide-prone, the more likely will it be that they will look for evidence of a suicide when a student dies. The more suicide verdicts the coroners bring in on student deaths, the more papers on the subject will experts write. Both the verdicts and the academic papers may then be transmitted to the rest of society via the media, with the result that the definition of students as special suicide risks will become more firmly established and more widely shared.

It will be noted that this model both leaves out and suggests more relationships than it is possible to discuss in detail here. Ignored, for example, is the role of literature, the arts and religion in propagating definitions of suicidal behaviour, and one only has to look at the Bible, Shakespeare, films and television to see that suicide is a common theme in all these areas. Similarly, the model suggests that the shared definitions themselves have a marked effect on suicidal behaviour, as those who actually attempt and commit suicide are unlikely to be ignorant of the meanings commonly associated with suicide. In the case of student suicides, for example, it is relatively easy to see how the relationship holds. Thus they may be more likely to contemplate a suicidal solution precisely because they are aware of the shared definition of students as a group which is particularly suicide-prone. With regard to other forms of suicide, however, it is not so easy to determine the precise relationship between these shared definitions and actual behaviour, and further research is needed before this situation will be changed. Some relevant evidence has however been reported recently by Jerome Motto (1969), who analysed suicide rates in Detroit before, during and after a nine-month newspaper strike in that city. While he stresses the need for caution in interpreting such results, he did find two very noticeable changes which took place during the strike. First there was a very substantial decline in the officially recorded suicide rate of women below the age of thirty-five, and second, for the first time ever recorded, the rate at which men committed suicide by swallowing pills exceeded that of women. In other words, even over such a short period, the removal of only one source of definitions of suicidal situations had a very marked effect on the rate of officially reported suicide.

It will be noticed from the remainder of this book that the conclusions proposed above were the closest we came to making sense of and developing some of Douglas's recommendations about studying the social meanings of suicide. Thus in his terms, it could possibly be argued that the analysis had succeeded in following his suggestion that one should start with 'individual meanings' and move to the analysis of 'general shared patterns of meanings' (Douglas, 1967, p. 242). It seems doubtful, however, that there are any grounds for such optimism, for how such a 'leap' had been made and whether or not it was or even could be warranted by reference to the data analysed was not specified. And, as will be noted at the start of the following chapter, the implications for further research were far from obvious.

Chapter 7

Common-Sense Theorizing about Suicide

7.1 INTRODUCTION

Though the apparent use of common-sense theories of suicide by officials in arriving at a verdict of suicide seemed to be an important finding of the research reported in the previous chapter, it can be argued, particularly with reference to the more recently gathered data, that too much of a distinction was made between that and the analysis of the circumstances immediately surrounding the death. Thus the focus in the conclusion was more on the theorizing and its significance, while the relationship between that activity and the analysis of the death was under-emphasized and not explored to the full. This topic will be taken up again later and, for the present, I want to deal with another problem posed by that earlier conclusion with special reference to its implications for further research. The remainder of the chapter proceeds with a report on research which was done in an attempt to follow up those preliminary conclusions.

What seems most notable in retrospect about the position reached at the end of Chapter 6 is that, from an initial concern with the problem of *how* some deaths get categorized as suicides which had explicitly put problems of suicide causation to one side, we ended up with a deterministic, or at least implicitly deterministic, model of the suicide process. By presenting the 'Dynamic Model of the Transmission of Shared Definitions of Suicide Through a Social System', a line of argument was put forward very similar to those normally associated with deviance amplification theories,[1] which claimed to account for how at least some suicides come about. In terms of the analyses of the various responses to the problems posed by data derived from official sources discussed in Chapter 3, a position had been arrived at which was very close to what was characterized in that earlier section as the 'interactionist revisionist' response, where conventional interpretations of official statistics were denied and replaced by an alternative interpretation (cf. Chapter 3.3, above). The methodological problem of how such an interpretation could be warranted, or indeed whether it could be warranted at all, then, posed itself in serious and pressing form. That is, there appeared to be no clear methodological procedures available which would confirm or otherwise the 'dynamic model' as anything more than plausible speculation about a general societal process, and hence no obvious lines along which the research should proceed.

Fortunately, the 'dynamic model' was not the only point of interest to have emerged from the preliminary enquiries, for those and the later work reported on in the previous chapter had suggested that the officials responsible for registering deaths were engaged in theorizing about suicide in a way which appeared to be very similar to the way in which 'experts' such as sociologists and psychiatrists theorized about suicide. It seemed likely, furthermore, given the heavy reliance of these latter on data generated by the former, that not only could that similarity be accounted for, but also that a new and difficult problem might be before us. For if coroners and their officers were using common-sense sociological and psychiatric knowledge in deciding whether or not a death was a suicide, what then was the status of that corpus of 'expert' knowledge, and what was the relationship between that and those of the officials? It was a fascination with this aspect of the findings reported in Chapter 6 that led to the studies to be reported on below, which involved searches in various places for instances of common-sense theorizing in an attempt to see whether or not the claim that there was a convergence between the expert and common-sense theories could be sustained in the face of more extensive empirical investigation.

7.2 'VARIABLES' RELATED TO SUICIDE AND TYPES OF EVIDENCE IN CORONER'S RECORDS OF SEVENTY SUICIDES AND SEVENTY ACCIDENTS [2]

The willingness of one coroner to make his records available to me provided the opportunity both to examine the materials typically used by suicide researchers in their studies of suicide and to conduct such a study myself. Indeed the methodology used for this part of the research was deliberately modelled on that normally used by other suicide researchers with the original intent of showing how they could yield data which could be interpreted in quite different ways. A major difference between this and other studies, however, was that I included equal numbers of suicides *and* accidents in the sample. Before elaborating on the methods used and the interests addressed, however, some remarks about the special features of the system within which this particular coroner worked are in order.

The coroner was a full-timer, trained in both medicine and law. His interest in the work, he said, was aroused mainly by his view that accurate death certification had an important part to play in medical research, a factor which was probably reflected in his routine use of post-mortem examinations in almost every case referred to him.[3] The area for which he was responsible was a heavily populated county in the South of England, and, as he covered a large geographical area, his records were compiled by a large number of different local officers. The sample of records studied here, then, were compiled and written by a number of different coroners' officers working in different parts of the county. No attempt was made to control for this in the study, as the main focus was on the types of evidence reported on. The officers did, however, use standardized forms, which meant that there was a high degree of consistency in the reporting of 'face-sheet' type data and certain other sorts of evidence. Each set of records presented to the coroner before an inquest consists of the following minimum details: a pathologist's report on the post-mortem examination; a statement by the last person to have seen the deceased alive; statements by the first person to find the body and by the person who identifies the body; a statement by the coroner's officer himself. The records begin with 'face-sheet data' and the 'Circumstances of Death' summaries discussed in Chapter 6.

The analysis presented in the previous chapter, which suggested that certain types of 'cues' lead coroners and their officers to look for specific sorts of evidence in the light of their common-sense theories of suicide, suggested that marked differences might be found between the *types* of evidence present in the records relating to deaths which resulted in verdicts of suicide and accident. A coding schedule was therefore devised which would enable the two samples of records to be coded and compared. The 'types' of evidence looked for were deliberately selected as being those regularly found in conventional statistical analyses of suicide.[4] A novel feature of the way the coding was carried out was that a check was made on whether a particular type of evidence was mentioned or not. If, for example, it was noted in a statement that 'no suicide threats had been made', then it would be coded as 'an included negative reference', which meant that the *absence* of that particular piece of evidence had been mentioned in the record. Unlike conventional statistical analyses, then, which code items only when they were reported as being *positively present*, the present study provided for comparisons to be made between *no mention* and *some mention* of the particular type of evidence. The logic of doing this was based on the finding reported in the previous chapter that the absence of certain types of evidence may be deemed to be significant enough to be commented on by a coroner's officer.

The sample sizes (seventy *suicides* and seventy *accidents*) were determined more by pragmatic and biographical circumstances than by any elaborate sampling procedures. To generate samples of even seventy of each requires the researcher to go through many times more records than that, for only one in thirty of the deaths referred to coroners finally result in a suicide verdict and only one in six in verdicts of accidental death. This meant that some 2000 records had to be sifted through in order to assemble the seventy suicides in the present sample. They were drawn from the first 'batch' of records delivered to me by the coroner and were as many as would fit into the boot of his car. My move from the South-East to the North-West of England shortly after this delivery meant that no further batches were received and hence that the sample size was fixed at the seventy plus seventy figure made possible by that first delivery. The deaths had been referred to the coroner over a period of about ten months in 1967, and all the suicides in the batch were coded along with the accidental death occurring on the nearest date to each suicide. The coding of the records was conducted in accordance with the 'normal' practices associated with such methods, and no special claims can be made that the kinds of problems elaborated by Cicourel (1964) and Garfinkel (1967a) were resolved or overcome. Thus the categories in the coding schedule were 'imposed' by the observer and coded by reference to unspecified common-sense understandings of the statements contained in the records. The only check introduced was of the sort typically used in studies involving this type of coding procedure, namely that a second coder went through the records and, where a difference of opinion emerged, an 'appropriate' code was agreed on the basis of discussion between us. In none of the small number of instances where this was necessary did it prove impossible to arrive at an agreed decision. The rationale for adopting conventional solutions to the coding problem in spite of known difficulties was that the study was explicitly intended to follow the methodology conventionally used in suicide research which obtains its data from records of this sort.

The distribution by sex, age and marital status of the two samples is presented in Table 7.2.1, from which it can be seen that men stand a far greater chance of dying both by accident and by suicide than is the case for women. Indeed, the male-female difference for the suicide sample is relatively large compared with some recent studies of suicide rates in which it has been suggested that the ratio between the two has been closing up as a result of an increasing female suicide rate.[5] Had these records been analysed with the sole purpose of testing such trends, then, the marked difference between the numbers of men and women in the suicide sample would have been a worthy topic for comment and comparison with other studies. Similarly, the age distribution of the suicides shows the usual steady increase with increasing age, which would presumably be even more marked had the rates per 100,000 been computed for each age-group. The sudden increase during 'middle age' might also merit special comment in the context of a conventional wisdom of suicidology that suicide is one of the most important single causes of death among the middle-aged. Results such as these, then, could be presented as providing yet further support for these trends.

TABLE 7.2.1   *Sex, age and marital status of seventy accidents and seventy suicides*

		Verdict	
		Accident	Suicide
SEX:	Male	48	44
	Female	22	26
	TOTAL	70	70
AGE:	10–19	19	5
	20–20	4	3
	30–39	7	4
	40–49	6	15
	50–59	4	16
	60+	30	27
	TOTAL	70	70
MARITAL STATUS:			
	Married	27	39
	Single	29	17
	Widowed	13	8
	Separated/Divorced	1	6
	TOTAL	70	70

With regard to the small number of suicides in the youngest age-group, it is worth noting that it is also a 'fact' of suicidology that suicide among the very young is an extremely rare occurrence.[6] It can be argued further that this view has parallels in common-sense knowledge about suicide in that suicide may well be commonly defined as an essentially adult form of action associated with adult problems. Thus the discussion of the case of the thirteen-year-old boy in the previous chapter suggested that the coroner had doubts about its being logically possible for a child of that age to commit suicide. Indeed, given that the law officially denies the possibility of 'criminal' intent before a certain age, it is not beyond the bounds of possibility that it may also be technically impossible for a verdict of suicide to be brought in on deaths of very young children. Whether or not this is so, however, the kind of problem which seemed to be posed in the case cited in the previous chapter suggests that coroners may look harder for evidence to support some other verdict in those cases where it initially appears that a child may have committed suicide. And if this is so, of course, statistical findings based on coroners' records are bound to reflect a very low incidence of suicide among the young.

Though the number of suicides who were married was higher than the number of accidental deaths with that marital status, the finding should not be taken as a possible refutation of Durkheimian theory, for the higher proportion of single people who died by accident is a reflection of the greater number of persons under twenty in that sample. Furthermore, had the study been carried out in order to explore Durkheimian theory, the discrepancy would not have become a topic for comment, as the comparable figures for accidental deaths would not have been collected. What would have been an important topic for comment, however, would have been the high proportion (44 per cent) of the suicides who were either single, widowed, divorced or separated, and, as was noted with reference to the age distributions, the differences would be even more marked if the rates per 100,000 for each category had been computed. As far as the 'face-sheet' data presented in Table 7.2.1 are concerned, then, it would have been easy to have written a report of the research as having been 'consistent with' or 'supportive of' some of the most important relationships analysed by Durkheim and many subsequent suicide researchers.

Similar claims 'supportive of' many other finding in the literature of suicidology could be made by focusing only on the statistics presented in one of the columns of Table 7.2.2, namely the 'Evidence present: Positive' column. On that basis, we could show that '20 per cent of the suicides had work problems, 20 per cent had marital problems, 33 per cent had emotional problems, 48 per cent had been taking prescribed drugs, 80 per cent had been depressed, 17 per cent had made previous suicide attempts, 21 per cent had made threats or given warnings and 29 per cent had left suicide notes'. We could then have made the analysis more sophisticated by presenting cross-tabulations and engaging in a variety of statistical tests of relationships between the many variables available from the coding schedule. The sample of accidents could have been used as a 'control group', which would have further underlined the 'significance' of the findings by showing the same 'variables' to be much less prevalent in that sample. In short, the data collected for this part of the study could very easily have been used in such a way as to prepare a 'scientific' paper which (apart from the precise numerical findings) would have been almost identical with what has become the standardized way of doing analyses of suicide from data derived from coroners' records.

As has already been indicated, however, the main aim of collecting the data was to examine further the question of how far the presence of

TABLE 7.2.2   *Types of evidence present in cases resulting in verdicts of suicide and accidental death*

Type of evidence	'Accidents'			'Suicides'		
	No evidence present	Evidence Present		No evidence present	Evidence present	
		Positive	Negative		Positive	Negative
Work problems	66	2	2	54	14	2
Financial problems	68	–	2	59	5	6
Marital problems	65	1	4	53	14	3
Emotional problems	59	5	6	45	23	2
History of heavy drinking	64	5	1	63	4	3
History of Drug-taking*	64	6	–	36	34	–
History of mental illness	59	7	4	33	32	5
Depression	59	3	8	8	56	6
Social isolation	64	1	5	61	5	4
Previous suicide attempts	69	1	–	55	12	3
Other suicides in family	69	1	–	65	4	1
Suicide threats, warnings, etc.	68	1	1	34	15	21
Criminal history	69	1	–	67	3	–
Childhood unhappiness	70	–	–	67	3	–
Homosexuality	70	–	–	69	1	–
Suicide note	69	–	1	31	20	19
History of drug addiction	69	1	–	69	1	–

* 'Drug-traking' here means that the person had been taking prescribed drugs during a period prior to death, and is to be distinguished from 'History of drug addict!ion' which appears last on the list.

particular kinds of evidence in the statements presented to coroners is a factor in the decision-making process. Thus it was argued earlier that coroners are unlikely to bring in a verdict of suicide if the evidence is inconsistent with their common-sense assumptions as to what constitutes a typical suicide. If that argument is correct, then one would expect to find that the topics raised in the statements would differ considerably according to verdict. Similarly, if the contention that the common-sense theories of suicide used by coroners and their officers are very similar to those elaborated by expert suicidologists is correct, then one would expect to find many more references to the kinds of 'variables' stressed in academic studies among the records resulting in suicide verdicts than among those resulting in verdicts of accidental death. If we take it that the 'Types of evidence' listed in Table 7.2.2 are a fairly representative sample of the kinds of 'variable' regularly focused on by suicidologists, a preliminary glance at the table is enough to suggest that there are indeed marked differences between the two samples in terms of the frequency with which the variables are referred to. Thus Table 7.2.3 gives the aggregated totals and shows that the selected variables were mentioned 331 times in the records which led to a suicide verdict, compared with 69 times in the records which resulted in verdicts of accidental death.

TABLE 7.2.3   *'Positive' and 'negative' evidence presented and verdicts*

	Accidents	Suicides
Total items of 'positive' evidence presented	35	256
Total items of 'negative' evidence presented	34	75
OVERALL TOTAL	69	331

A number of individual comparisons are also of interest. Thus mental illness and depression are among the most frequently referred-to of all the items of evidence in the 'suicide' sample, which is consistent with the earlier suggestion that testimonies saying that the deceased was 'happy' may avert a suicide verdict even when other indicators are present. Similarly, the first five items in Table 7.2.2 can be loosely regarded as 'troubles' of the sort which might be deemed to lead someone to suicide. With regard to more explicit indicators of intent, the high frequency with which references were found to the fact that the deceased had *not* made threats or had *not* left a note tends to give support to the earlier suggestion that these are crucially important for arriving at a suicide verdict. Thus not only are references to them confined almost exclusively to the 'suicide' sample, but they are also the items most frequently noted as being not present. The implication of this is that the coroners' officers who write up the statements consider the *absence* of suicide notes and threats to be sufficiently important to report that absence in cases where other evidence is suggestive of a suicide verdict.

Now it can be argued that these findings are in general supportive of the arguments in the previous chapter which suggested that coroners and their officers are not only engaged in theorizing about suicide, but also that those theories closely approximate those of the experts. One could go on examining more of the data, such as that on mode of death, to argue the case further.[7] I do not, however, wish to do this, as to do so is to ignore what is one of the central difficulties to have emerged in the course of this research, namely that the same data can be subjected to completely different interpretations. Thus one can claim, as was shown earlier, that these data support the theories of Durkheim and other suicidologists and hence that the variables listed in Table 7.2.2 'really are' causal factors which somehow or other lead to suicide. Or one can claim that they are 'seen to be' causal factors by the officials who, having ascertained their presence in a particular case, record the death as a suicide. Which interpretation is 'correct', whether indeed there is one interpretation which is 'the correct' one, or what procedures might be adopted in order to arrive at such a conclusion is unclear, however. Nor does it seem that there are any such procedures available from elsewhere in sociology which might enable an assessment of the rival interpretations to be made.[8]

7.3 THEORIZING ABOUT SUICIDE IN NEWSPAPER REPORTS

At the end of Chapter 6, a study of newspaper reports was referred to. The aim of that had initially been to attempt to follow up the 'deviance amplification' theme by seeing if reports in a local newspaper revealed any special patterns of suicidal behaviour from which it might be inferred that there was some kind of 'media influence' at work in defining suicidal situations and hence influencing the types of suicides which took place in the particular town in question.[9] Not surprisingly, perhaps, it proved almost impossible to come up with any such finding, but what did emerge as particularly striking was the tendency for newspaper reports to contain possible explanations of suicides both in the text of the reports and in the headlines. As the original study had been conducted at the British Museum Newspaper Library at Colindale, I had not more than abbreviated notes about the stories examined and hence further analysis of this new theme, which did not become apparent until that first study had been completed, was not possible. Subsequently, then, I set about collecting a file of newspaper cuttings, all taken from the same local newspaper over a period of five years. A local library collection of back numbers formed the source of the materials, and photo-copies were taken of every report of a suicide until the collection numbered 100.[10] The aims of the exercise were twofold. First, I wanted to check on the earlier claim that possible explanations were found in the headlines and the text, and second, I wanted to look more closely at the form of the explanation contained in the stories in order to see how closely they compared with the explanations proposed by expert suicidologists.

The problem in such an exercise is that there are no widely recognized procedures for identifying possible explanations or even for guaranteeing agreement between persons as to what constitutes an explanation.[11] For present purposes, therefore, I shall present some of the data, namely the headlines, in full so that the reader can assess how far my interpretations seem adequate. It should be noted first what is being meant when I say that explanations are present or implied in the stories. Thus I am not claiming that the authors of the accounts are offering some general theory of suicide in the manner of a suicicologist or that they are necessarily asserting that X is the cause of a particular suicide. What I am saying is that some casual account of the suicide. whether it takes the form of showing what 'troubles' the deceased had prior to death, ascribing some possible motive to the deceased or whatever, is at least implied in many of the reports and headlines. Thus few headlines make as explicit a causal link as 'Domestic trouble led to suicide' (No 46), but many imply such a link by referring to 'depression', 'worries' or particular events in the lives of the deceased. The newspaper headlines which seem to be theorizing in this sense are marked with an asterisk in the list below:

Headlines to Newspaper Stories of Suicide[12]

*1 Tragedy of two widows – Could not face anniversary of tragedy
*2 'Lost' after death of husband
*3 'No one will ever know the agonies of mind'
4 Gas tragedy inquest – Widow and son made death pact
*5 'Depressed' wife took overdose of drugs
6 Man who planned visit to Australia took his own life
*7 Drowned man was depressed
8 Gaton woman took overdose of capsules – inquest told
9 Man found dead in car – inquest told
10 Widow (56) took her own life

*11 Man had 'illusions of persecution' – coroner told
12 Teacher left notes before taking her life – coroner told
*13 Coroner is told reason for man's depression
*14 Shotgun death – Man had been depressed
15 City man's death by sleeping tablets
16 Wife returned to find husband hanging
17 Dead woman had 36 self-inflicted wounds – police
18 Cheerful man who never complained is found gassed
19 Male nurse found dead on railway left note for wife
20 Man killed on railway had left note – inquest told
21 Student dies in town centre
*22 Housewife was depressed – Took own life
23 Woman drowned while taking dog for walk
*24 'Upset' girl took an overdose of sleeping tablets
*25 Woman had visions – coroner told
*26 Man found hanging had been depressed
27 Woman took fatal overdose then told police
28 Left home to go shopping, found drowned in canal
29 Woman found drowned after visit from doctor
30 Children found man hanging
31 Former nurse 'took life' by falling from roof – inquest verdict
32 Gas tragedy inquest
*33 Woman found drowned did not want to enter hospital – coroner told
*34 Depressed at brother's death, took own life
35 'Happy' youth took his life with pipe to car exhaust
*36 Inquest hears of butcher's incessant pain
37 Inquest told – Woman took overdose after watching Churchill's funeral
38 Woman found with head in oven had taken overdose
39 Mental hospital patient found hanging after Christmas at home
40 Man dead in chair had plastic bag on his head
41 Localtown woman took overdose of tablets
*42 'Upset by marriage break-up' – City verdict of 'took own life'
*43 Man dead in car had nervous trouble
*44 Depressed widow cut her wrists in bath
45 Man filled caravan with gas – inquest told
*46 Domestic trouble led to suicide
*47 Drowning tragedy – Man 'couldn't get used to retirement'
48 Patient hanged himself with piece of string
*49 Mother found son dead in bedroom – Radio engineer electrocuted himself. 'Balance of mind was disturbed' verdict
*50 Wife found hanging in pantry had been depressed – inquest told
51 Man in sea killed himself
*52 Man who poisoned himself had felt frustrated – coroner told

53 Inquest told – Pole hanged himself after quit notice and rates demand

54 Man killed himself by fall from window

55 Inquest – Girl found her father gassed

56 Found wife dead in kitchen

*57 Director found hanged – Had been depressed

58 Bible student found hanged in old chapel

59 Pathologist at inquest tells coroner – Pensioner was dead before explosion wrecked bungalow

*60 Woman 'could not face long years ahead' – Found drowned in canal

61 Left note in bottle – Found dead

62 Line Bank tragedy – Driver saw man lie on rails in front of train

63 Man 'took own life' verdict

64 Woman died from tablets overdose – Local town man's inquest evidence of friendship

*65 Widow was lonely and depressed

*66 Found dead with pen and pad in hands – Glendale widow 'couldn't live without husband' – wrote 'empty years ahead frighten me'

*67 Xtown Inn tragedy – 'We cannot pay debts,' said note — Not true on evidence says coroner

68 Woman found in garden took 70 aspirins

69 Woman cut herself with glass

70 Gas tragedy inquest

*71 Localtown councillor shot himself while balance of mind was disturbed – inquest verdict

*72 'Nervous' Balton woman found drowned in river

*73 Inquest story of check on drugs at hospital – Husband says wife told him of affair with another man – Mother of four took overdose of tablets

*74 Aged man worried about going into hospital, gassed himself

75 Localtown inquest – Widow tells how brother held gun to his mouth

*76 60 ft drop into river – Mental patient 'took own life' – inquest verdict

*77 Drowned man 'had complex'

78 Sister finds farmer hanging in barn

79 Man dead in gas-filled kitchen

*80 Vicar, former grammar school captain, found shot in garage of home – Mind disturbed through ill-health – says coroner

81 Woman died from overdose of sleeping tablets

82 Mother, 26, found dead in kitchen

*83 Mother of two drank acid while depressed

84 Xtown gassing tragedy inquest

85 Farmer found dead, shotgun beside him – coroner told

86 Woman took overdose of tablets – coroner told
87 Drowned woman left a note
*88 Man found gassed became depressed after retiring
89 Man found drowned 'well looked after at old people's home' says coroner – Son tells of complaint
*90 Coroner on 'terrible experience' of brother and sister – Drowned man had 40lb. car jack tied to ankle – Wife had taken own life two months ago
91 Inquest told – Book with essay on suicide near body on railway – was marked at that chapter
92 Bookmaker took his own life – inquest verdict
*93 'Depressed' Director gassed himself with car exhaust fumes – Inquest told of health worries
*94 Inquest story of man's depression after wife's death
95 Widow tells coroner – Man found gassed had made previous suicide attempts
*96 Man found gassed 'could not stand worsening pains'
*97 Licensee gassed himself with car fumes – Left note revealing discrepancy in savings fund, coroner reveals
98 Joiner found dead in car took own life said coroner
*99 Shrapnel victim who felt 'Buzzes' took his own life
*100 Engagement was broken – Temperamental young man gassed himself.

Of the particular grounds for the suicide implied in these headlines, a considerable number can be regarded as involving 'lay psychiatric theorizing' in the sense that they refer to 'variables' which have been among the most widely used in psychiatric studies of suicide. Thus there are frequent references to 'depression' (Nos 5, 7, 13, 14, 22, 26, 34, 44, 50, 57, 65, 83, 88, 93, 94) and there are references to 'unbalanced' states of minds, hallucinations and other phenomena which might be taken as indicating insanity (Nos 11, 25, 43, 49, 71, 72, 76, 77, 80). In these cases it can be argued that the state of mind of the deceased is being invoked as a possible cause of the suicide, a procedure which is the normal form of theorizing found in psychiatric studies of suicide. In others, a more Durkheimian or sociological emphasis can be noted in references to loneliness, impending loneliness, marital and family break-ups and the 'anomie' of retirement (e.g. Nos 1, 2, 34, 42, 47, 65, 66, 88). On the basis of the headlines alone, then, it can be argued that there are instances of common-sense psychiatric and sociological theorizing about suicide which do indeed reflect themes which have had predominance in the specialist studies by expert suicidologists.

This is not, of course, to say that all the headlines contain instances of such theorizing, or indeed that all the possible causal links that are implied can be neatly depicted as 'psychiatric' or 'sociological'. Some of the others, however, do reflect findings reported in statistical studies, worries about health and finance being two examples (Nos 33, 36, 53, 67, 74, 80, 93, 96, 97, 99). In others it is less immediately obvious that the feature of the deceased's life referred to in the headlines are possible causes. Ones like 'Man who planned to visit Australia took his own life' (6), 'Woman drowned while taking dog for walk' (23), 'Woman found drowned after visit from doctor' (29) and 'Woman took overdose after watching Churchill's funeral' (37) pose something of a mystery, which presumably is to be resolved in the texts which follow. The deaths in these cases are located at particular points in the biographies of the dead persons, but the particulars mentioned are not ones which, like depression and loneliness, for example, can be easily associated with suicide.

Two headlines are of special interest in the light of the discussion in the previous chapter where it was suggested that evidence of happiness can cast serious doubt on a proposed suicide verdict. Thus 'Cheerful man who never complained is found gassed' (18) and ' "Happy" youth took his life with pipe to car exhaust' (35) may seem to suggest that our earlier contention was false or at least exaggerated. Both cases, however, can also be taken as further confirmatory evidence of the importance of the officials' analyses of the circumstances of the death in leading to a particular verdict, for both died in ways which are not easily imaginable as anything other than suicides. The 'youth' used the 'pipe to car exhaust' method referred to in the previous chapter as an almost definite indicator of a suicide, and the 'Cheerful man' was found 'in his kitchen with a plastic bag over his face and a tube from the gas cooker tied in it. . . .' In the report on this latter case, it emerges also that the 'cheerfulness' may well have been only a temporary state, that he had suffered from a depression serious enough to merit medical attention and that the thing he had 'never complained' about was his health:

> The Localtown Coroner reported a verdict that Mr Joseph Smith (62), hospital porter, of Redlance Road, Localtown, had taken his own life by gas poisoning.
>
> Mrs Spriggs said that she and her husband returned from holiday on Tuesday last week.
>
> She saw her father at lunchtime the following day and he seemed to be quite cheerful.
>
> He had been doing quite a bit of overtime at the hospital and he found it too much, she added.
>
> She thought that was why he had not been sleeping too well. Mrs Spriggs said her father had never threatened to do anything to himself.
>
> Since her father's death she had seen his doctor who had told her

that her father had been seriously depressed.

Mr Reginald Jones, storeman, of Redland Avenue, Localtown, said he had known Mr Smith for 20 years as their gardens were back to back.

'He has never complained to me about his health,' said Mr Jones. 'The last time I saw him was in his garden at about 7 p.m. on Wednesday when we had a chat and a joke about gardens.'

Thus the headline singled out the daughter's assessment of him as having been 'quite cheerful' and the neighbour's observation that 'he never complained to me about his health', while the story itself reveals that he had been finding overtime working 'too much', he had 'not been sleeping too well', and he had 'been seriously depressed'. And in addition to those troubles from his biography which could be seen as consistent with his having committed suicide, 'suicide' seemed to be the most appropriate and possibly the only category available for making sense of the circumstances in which he was found dead:

'He had a plastic bag over his face and a tube in it from the cooker,' said P.C. Brown. 'His head was resting on a pillow and he was holding the bag closed by pressing his left hand to his chest. The tube was tied in the bag at the top.'

P.C. Brown said the tube belonged to the gas cooker lighter.

The case of the 'happy' youth is somewhat more complex as, although evidence was presented suggesting that he had been having troubles with his girlfriend, statements from witnesses and indeed the coroner himself seem to indicate that these were not important enough to have led to his suicide. The story begins with the contradiction between a 'definitely suicidal' mode of death and apparently 'happy' biographical circumstances:

A 19 year old Localtown youth who was found dead in a car which had a piece of hose pipe leading from the exhaust to the interior was 'as happy as the day is long' said his mother at an inquest on Thursday.

The Coroner received a verdict that the youth, Robert Andrews, car salesman, of Elder Street, Localtown, took his own life and added: 'There was no doubt that he intended to take his life but there was no evidence to show the condition of his mind at the time.'

This latter statement is somewhat strange in view of the fact that much of the relatively long report which follows deals with an apparently stormy love affair the deceased had been having. What is interesting is that in other cases, such evidence would be taken seriously and used as an indicator of intent. Here, however, the witnesses seem at pains to make out that the affair had not been a serious one. His brother describes a row between the two of them as a 'tiff', and his mother described his relationship with the girl thus:

> they were just good pals. He had only been calling on her recently and when I asked him if she had given him the push, he replied 'perhaps I have given her the push'. He had a habit of making a joke of things, she said.

A lifelong friend of the deceased had:

> For the last two years met him regularly at the Black Bear Inn. After being together on the Tuesday of the week he died, Robert [the deceased] had told him he had met his girlfriend in town, but she had not stopped with him for long. He thought he would ring her up and if she would not come out he would get drunk. Next day Robert told him that when he had phoned his girlfriend she had put the phone down. He was not really depressed, but was a little quieter than usual. . . .

Thus he tended to make a joke of things and, after unspecified troubles with his girlfriend, he was 'not really depressed'. What we seem to have here, then, is an apparent agreement between the witnesses and the coroner that the troubles with the girlfriend were not 'serious' enough to have featured in a possible theory as to why the deceased may have committed suicide. In other words, the process of theorizing may lead to the rejection of possible causal links as well as their acceptance. Another instance where a particular worry was reported but was rejected by the coroner as a serious indicator of the deceased's state of mind was the following:

> Recording a verdict at a Localtown inquest yesterday that a 22 year old bricklayer who was found hanging in a partly constructed bungalow on the Valley Estate, took his own life, the coroner added: 'I am satisfied that the balance of his mind was disturbed in some way and for some reason which we cannot say.'
> The man . . . was said by his father . . . with whom he lived, to have been worried because his feet smelled.

From the coroner's observation that we cannot say what it was that disturbed the balance of his mind, we can infer that the source of worry referred to by the deceased's father is ruled out of the reckoning as a possible grounds for suicide: people do not on the whole commit suicide because of worries about smelly feet and hence something else must have led to the disturbed balance of mind. The inability to specify that something else, however, does not prevent a suicide verdict, for the mode of death (hanging) was sufficiently unequivocal to provide for such a decision.

But though the process of theorizing may lead to the rejection of certain possible explanations and thence to an almost total reliance on the analysis of the circumstances of the death to give the basis for the verdict, the examples discussed so far are somewhat exceptional. Much more typical of the newspaper reports are stories in which the suicide is presented as the logical outcome of some particular troubles or some specified states of mind. Indeed, in the vast majority of cases the reader is left with a fairly clear view not only *that* the death was a suicide, but also of *why* the suicide took place. Quite frequently the coroner offers a theory in the very wording of his verdict (the numbers in brackets in the following extracts refer to the headline above the report from which they are taken):

(23) The coroner said that he had no hesitation in saying she took her life while the balance of her mind was upset owing to ill health. . . .

(79) The coroner recorded a verdict that [the deceased] took his own life and said that he thought this was due to his nervous complaint.

(84) The coroner recorded a verdict that death was due to coal-gas poisoning while the balance of [the deceased's] mind was temporarily disturbed owing to ill health.

(85) A verdict that death was caused by a gun-shot wound, self-inflicted during a period of depression due to illness was recorded. . . .

(93) [the deceased] took his own life while the balance of his mind was disturbed by depression about his health and that of his brother.

(96) The coroner recorded a verdict that [the deceased] took his own life while the balance of his mind was disturbed which was, he said, as a result of his deteriorating physical condition. . . .

(40) The coroner recorded a verdict that death was due to respiratory obstruction and that [the deceased] had contributed to his own death by putting a plastic bag on his head while the balance of his mind was disturbed by depression caused by the condition of his health.

In these cases, then, the suicide is depicted as being the result of an un-balanced mind which is in turn the result of a particular cause. That the particular cause is in each case something to do with ill-health or worry about ill-health is of special interest in a number of ways. In the first place, the examples were selected as instances where the coroner explicitly provided some account for the 'unbalanced mind', and not because 'ill-health' was what was invoked. Further inspection of this set of 100 reports revealed no cases in which such an addition was made where 'ill-health' or some similar reference was not specified as the fac-tor lying behind the unbalanced mind. This suggests, and it can be no more than a suggestion given the limitations of the present data, that it is only in such cases that the coroner feels sufficiently confident about specifying why the balance of the mind was disturbed at the same time as giving his verdict. And that confidence might in turn be a reflection of a view of 'worries about ill-health' as offering both an easily under-standable and non-controversial account of how a suicide comes to take place. Thus to do the same thing with 'family troubles' or 'emotional problems', for example, would require a greater degree of interpreta-tion of the evidence by the coroner as well as pose the possibility of argument from persons to whom some responsibility for the suicide might seem to be implied by such a designation. Evidence of 'ill-health', of worries about it, however, have the advantage of being tied personal-ly and exclusively to the deceased: no one else is involved and no blame is due to them. Nor is the deceased discredited, as a concern about ill-health is not necessarily to be regarded as a source of shame.

The association between ill-health and suicide is not confined to the examples given above, but is a common theme in the evidence presented by witnesses in many of the reports. That such an association is made in a common-sense way is of some interest in the light of 'ex-pert' studies of suicide, for a good deal has been made of that connec-tion in the writings of suicidologists. Post-mortem examinations, for ex-ample, reveal a higher incidence of serious physical ailments among suicides than among 'control' samples,[13] and other studies have made much of the finding that large proportions of persons who commit suicide have visited a doctor shortly before their deaths,[14] and some others have invoked 'hypochondria' or 'hypochondrial delusions' as 'causes' of suicide (e.g. Batchelor and Napier, 1953). That this is so, then, provides support for the view that there is a degree of convergence between common-sense and expert reasoning about the possible con-nection between ill-health or worries about ill-health and suicide.

Statements about the relationship between mental illness and suicide which forms so central a part in much of the psychiatric research on suicide[15] also appear regularly in the newspaper reports, as one might expect from a perusal of the headlines alone. Thus in the first of the ex-tracts below, a juryman has apparently enquired about the mental state

of the deceased and receives a 'diagnostic' reply from the witness, a
nurse at a mental hospital. In the others, careers of mental illness are
portrayed which are similar to the 'recurrent bouts' and 'steadily
getting worse' themes of the inquest case discussed in the previous
chapter:

> (69) In reply to a juryman, she said that [the deceased] showed no
> real signs of any deep depression. Her mental condition on ad-
> mittance was one of agitation with anxiety, but no depression.

> (41) [Witness] said that his wife had always been a nervous person
> and her mental health had been very bad for about 10 years.
> She had been treated for epilepsy and had suffered convulsions.
> She had been a patient at the [mental hospital] on several oc-
> casions and had had an operation to relieve pressure on the
> brain.

> (39) [Witness] said that her husband had had a mental breakdown,
> triggered off by family troubles, and was admitted to hospital in
> October. He was discharged in November, but on December
> 19th he became ill again and returned to [the mental hospital]
> for further treatment. He came home for Christmas, but on 28
> December when he was due to return to hospital he was ex-
> tremely depressed.

> (15) As a result of his depression, he attended the [mental hospital]
> clinic as an out-patient but did not stay in the hospital. He got
> better but gradually became depressed again. He was seen by a
> doctor and given electrical treatment for about a week. . . .

These are typical of the many references in the reports to the mental
hospital admissions, discharges and treatment of persons who subsequently commit suicide. Thus, just as the expert studies by psychiatrists seek to establish causal connections between mental illness
and specific sorts of mental illness and suicides, so also is that topic
singled out for extensive treatment in these reports, so that the suicides
emerge as a logical conclusion to a career of increasingly severe mental
illness.

Other 'trends' reported by expert researchers also seem to be regarded as relevant by witnesses and by the reporters who single out certain
of their statements for inclusion in the newspaper reports. The
tendency to report the absence of threats noted in the analysis of the
records in the previous section is also apparent from the reports.
Sometimes witnesses state that the deceased did make threats and
sometimes that they did not, and that the presence or absence of a

threat is deemed significant enough for comment implies that there is a general awareness at the common-sense level that suicides are likely to have made some kind of threat or may have been expected to do so:

(54) On August 10 he came home for a few hours and complained of being shut up, but did not threaten to take his own life in set terms. . . .

(63) She told the coroner that last year, before going to the mental hospital he had threatened to do something to himself. . . .

(93) . . . she said her husband [the deceased] had worried all his life about his health, and as far as she knew there was no cause for it. He had never threatened to take his own life.

(69) He was satisfied that she was receiving good treatment and made no suggestion to him that she might take her life or do anything to herself.

(70) He often talked about 'doing away with himself', but they did not take him seriously. . . .

(72) After an attack of influenza she became worse and complained about her general health . . . he never heard her threaten to take her life.

(74) [The deceased] was worried about going into hospital but had never mentioned taking his own life.

(75) He said that he objected to going to the 'work-house' and that he would rather do away with himself.

(78) Normally he was of good spirit and never threatened to take his life.

(81) She never threatened to do anything to herself, but she said many times that she wished she could die.

(96) Her husband had never threatened to do anything to himself though he had said he could not go on any longer.

In so far as the making and reporting of such statements reveal a taken for granted awareness that 'threats' are probable antecedents of suicidal events, it seems strange indeed that expert suicidologists should depict the frequency with which threats are made as a 'finding'.

Another 'finding' from the works of experts is that suicides frequently appear to get better just prior to the suicidal act, [16] and this too emerges as a theme in many of the reports studied:

(33) On the Sunday before she was found in the canal, she seemed to be better. . . .

(81) On the Thursday she seemed better than usual and went into town alone, something she had not done for quite a long time. That night she had a beaker of milk prior to going to bed at 10 o'clock. She appeared quite normal. [Found dead next morning.]

(81) She had recently been tired and depressed but when he saw her on Thursday she seemed brighter. The next day he was told his mother had been found unconscious in bed. . . .

(86) She had been very depressed and run down and constantly under the care of a doctor. Her health had then improved, but then on November 10 . . .

(95) On the Monday he seemed more cheerful than usual. She went out at 3.05 p.m. to go shopping . . . on returning home at 4.45 p.m. there was a strong smell of gas . . .

These accounts stand in contrast to those which depict the suicide as marking a logical and almost expected end to a career of mental illness, for they depict the suicide as unexpected, in spite of the fact that it might have been expected had it occurred some days earlier. Thus they are similar to the others in so far as some kind of ebb and flow of a mental illness is depicted, but different in the way in which the end of the story is presented. A case could possibly be made for seeing these as 'guilt-neutralization techniques' in the sense elaborated by Henslin (1970), for if the person 'appeared better' or 'more normal' just prior to death, then the witness who made that assessment cannot reasonably be held responsible for not having done something to prevent the suicide taking place. On present evidence, however, that must remain conjecture, and the main point to be noted is that trends are depicted in these common-sense versions of suicidal episodes which can be found presented as 'findings' in the literature of suicidology.

The final bunch of extracts are of perhaps greatest interest to the sociologist, for in them we find witnesses offering interpretations of the 'troubles' of the deceased in terms of social integration. As will be seen, the most common of these lay Durkheimian theories makes a connection between 'domestic integration', or rather the lack of it, and suicide.

What is perhaps of even greater interest than the fact that such theorizing is done is the way in which these 'sociological factors' are placed in relation to the 'psychological factors'. In the extracts above where the coroner proposed a reason for the balance of the mind having been disturbed, his theoretical reasoning seemed to have a temporal structure something like this (where ⟶ means 'leads to'):

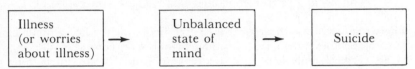

Thus the 'psychological state' (i.e. unbalanced state of mind) seems to be invoked as an 'intervening variable', *stemming from* something else and *leading to* suicide. In the extracts which follow, the 'psychological state' maintains its structural position just prior to the suicide and can be seen as stemming from, in Durkheim's terms, a 'low degree of domestic integration':

(34) A niece of [the deceased] said that since the death of her brother, for whom she kept house, [the deceased] had been depressed but was reluctant to have medical treatment.

(41) A Localtown woman who took an overdose of sleeping pills was said to have been depressed over a brother's illness and to have been lonely ever since he went into hospital.

(10) Her brother-in-law said that her husband had died two years ago and that she had become increasingly depressed ever since.

(8) [The witness] said that her sister [the deceased] had enjoyed good health. Her husband had been killed in the 1939–45 war and from then on she had been depressed from time to time and never really recovered from the loss, she said.

(13) A Localtown process worker who was found dead in the gas-filled kitchen of his home on Monday of last week had suffered from periods of depression ever since his wife had left him in October, it was stated at an inquest on Friday.

(65) Evidence that she had been lonely and depressed since the death of her husband in January was given at an inquest . . .

(77) The deceased was said to have had an inferiority complex and to have had no friends.

(66) ... her husband had died 12 months ago. She had been very upset since the death of her husband but she seemed to have been getting over it recently. ... In one of the notes she had written 'I cannot live this new life without Percy ...'

(88) Since the deceased had retired, he had visited him at his home and he had often complained that nobody ever called ...'

The structure of the theoretical interpretation which is being made in some of the above, then, is very similar to that in the coroner's additions to his verdicts, only here it is 'depression' which is the 'intervening variable' and 'lack of domestic integration' which leads to it:

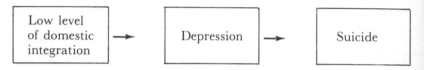

Though the data presented in this section provides support for the view that there is a convergence between common-sense and expert theorizing about suicide, the particular structure of common-sense theorizing proposed above suggests that there may be at least one important difference between the nature of the two sorts of theorizing. For while sociologists and suicidologists have spent a good deal of time worrying about the differences between 'sociological' and 'psychological' modes of explanation, the common-sense theorists seem to manage such difficulties with straightforward and uninhibited ease. For them, it seems, 'social' or 'medical' factors lead to a particular state of mind which in turn leads to suicide. Unlike the experts, they do not concentrate exclusively on one kind of factor or attempt to claim that one is more important than the other, but combine the two in a way which nowhere seems to pose difficulties either for them or for their audiences. This 'mixing' of the sociological with the psychological emerged also when I explicitly asked a coroner's officer to theorize about suicide:

M.A.: In the light of your quite long experience of this work, did you come to any sorts of conclusions about the kinds of reasons why people commit suicide? Did you come up with any theories of suicide?

C.O.: Well, I did, but they're entirely personal and – um – I think basically it's the inability of the individual to come to grips with a situation. *He finds himself totally isolated from his fellows, from his family, from his friends.* ... He can't see any way out of his dilemma and the only path open to him is through suicide, *generally brought about by or preceded by acute depression* [my emphases].

So in his 'entirely personal' theories, the coroner's officer included the central theoretical propositions of two of the major disciplines which comprise suicidology, the social isolation thesis from sociology and the depression thesis from psychiatry. And, as I have suggested is the case with the 'theories' found in newspaper reports, the sociological factor is depicted as occurring prior to the psychological factor in the causal chain leading to suicide.

7.4 COMMON-SENSE THEORIZING: SOME PRELIMINARY CONCLUSIONS

In this chapter, the earlier suggestion that coroners and their officers are engaged in theorizing about suicide and that their theories bear a close similarity to those of expert suicidologists has been examined further with reference to different empirical materials. In general, the evidence seems to provide added support for that contention and hence for the serious questions raised about the status of theories of suicide proposed by suicidologists. The evidence also shows that it is not just coroners and coroners' officers who theorize about suicide but that witnesses and, by implication, newspaper reporters engage in similar practices. More particularly, the findings reported in Section 7.2 show marked differences in the topics referred to in evidence between the records which resulted in suicide verdicts and those which resulted in verdicts of accidental death, and it was suggested that the former group were characterized by a concern for types of evidence which are in many cases the same as the variables so often manipulated in statistical studies of suicide. The analysis of the newspaper reports in Section 7.3 showed that such reports tell the reader not only *that* particular deaths were suicides but also give a version of *why* the suicides took place. In addressing the *why* issue, causal relationships and other trends are referred to which seem in large measure identical to those contained in the writings of experts. Given the reliance of suicidologists on data derived from official sources and on other evidence obtained from witnesses to suicidal events, it is easy to understand how it is that the experts 'discover' findings and construct theories which are already known and used by ordinary members of society. This problem, which is inherent in almost all research into suicide, has been well summarized by Blum and McHugh (1971, p. 107):

> He killed himself because he was depressed or he left the party because he was bored – both are observers' ways of saying that killing oneself is a method of doing depression or that prematurely leaving the party is a way of doing boredom . . . something cannot be cited as a cause of an event if this 'something' is involved (or presupposed) in the very description of the event . . .

Thus our analysis so far suggests that *all or most of the 'causes' cited by suicidologists are indeed 'involved in the very description' of suicide* – to the extent that even such mundane 'factual' reports as are found in the columns of local newspapers bristle with theoretical interpretations and possible explanations of the suicides they report.

From the point of view of the ongoing research, findings and conclusions such as these seemed to pose more problems than they solved. Certainly they provided the basis for far-reaching criticisms to be made of the way most suicide research had been done and also by implication, of much other sociological research. But in terms of our research problem of how deaths get categorized as suicides and the more practical problem of 'what to do next', a solution did not seem immediately obvious. Or, rather, the solution which did seem obvious seemed too obvious and too final. That is to say, the theorizing of coroners, their officers and others could be seen simply as a way of making sense of potentially senseless and disorganized occurrences in society. That sudden deaths confront persons with a disordered situation which needs further and special clarification is given institutionalized recognition by the existence of special provisions for processing them and of special categories which are used for describing 'what actually happened'. Those responsible for deciding that then have to bring their knowledge to bear on particular cases in order to analyse 'how this death could have happened'. If a suicide seems to be indicated by the analysis of the circumstances surrounding the death, then to declare a 'suicide' would be to imply that it had somehow come 'out of the blue' and hence leave a degree of mystery surrounding the case. If the analysis of the circumstances of the death leaves more than one possible category as a possible verdict, further work is needed to rule out alternatives and hence impose order on the still disorderly situation. In either case, the disorganization can be resolved by considering how far a proposed categorization is consistent with the biographical history of the deceased. Thus it is not simply a case of asking whether a particular death could have been a suicide, but of asking whether that particular person could have committed suicide, or in other words of assessing how far 'suicide' would be a possibly 'appropriate' end to a particular person's biography. And it is in doing that that different theories are considered and assessed in relation to particular cases. The importance of this practice for the social organization of sudden death is that it provides for the construction of a plausible story of how and why the death occurred without which uncertainty and disorder would prevail. The abiding concern of coroners' officers to achieve order out of chaos is exemplified in the following statement by a coroner's officer whom I interrupted as he was writing up statements in preparation for an inquest. He began to talk about the problem of translating the disordered bits and pieces of evidence obtained from interviews with witnesses. I had asked him if he had ever used a tape-recorder, but he replied that he did not like them because the verbatim version of an interview was always too 'muddled' and 'disjointed', and hence of little practical use when it came to writing up the statements. He went on:

> Normally I don't think I could really take a story, even from you now, so that every word you said would be in story-book form, it would be impossible. I've got to try interviewing some people, they don't know what I want so I've got to ask them . . . the way these statements have been taken is question, answer – er – question then answer. Sometimes you get, particularly some elderly women, and they bloody go on and on, so I've got to interrupt them. But I must admit, in this very one I've got here – um – she was rambling on a bit, back and forwards, and he, I was taking the statement off him and she was chipping in. You get two sides of the tale then. And you think, 'Well now, how do I play this?' So rather than taking two statements – you're only going to end up with two negative statements, one against the other. So you bring it all into like a proper perspective, as you think it is. It's a nice, well to me it's a nice story-book finish. Sometimes I get mixed up. I've read it through myself and then I'll suddenly scrap it and say, 'Well, that's no flippin' good,' and start again.

Precisely how he assesses what counts as a good 'story-book finish' is not specified by the coroner's officer, but it seems clear from the analysis so far that this entails the quest for a plausible account of how the deceased came to die in the way that it is proposed he did die. *The 'theorizing' which we have observed, then, can be viewed as providing for the social organization of sudden deaths by rendering otherwise disordered and potentially senseless events ordered and sensible.* Our observations also suggest, however, that expert suicidologists, whether they be professional sociologists, psychiatrists or whatever, are engaged in similar practices.

These conclusions point to two important questions both for the present research and for any future related research which might be envisaged: (1) Is there anything else that can be said about the social organization of sudden death (and hence about how some deaths get categorized as suicides) other than that it is accomplished by consulting and constructing common-sense theories which provide for how particular deaths occurred? (2) Can it be claimed that expert theories accomplish anything more than, or different from, that which is accomplished by common-sense theories? A negative answer to the first question would seem to indicate not only that our research has reached a final conclusion but also that there is no obvious further research to be done,[17] while a negative answer to the second would seem to suggest the pointlessness of the sociological enterprise as it has been generally conceived: in other words, it would involve a guilty plea to the frequently made charge that sociology's findings are 'mere common-sense'. The next chapter, therefore, consideres the claims of ethnomethodology to provide a solution to this dilemna.

Chapter 8

Ethnomethodology and the Problem of Categorization

8.1 INTRODUCTION

In the latter stages of the research, my attention became increasingly focused on the work of ethnomethodologists.[1] This interest was increased by the persistent failure to find any positive assistance from other types of sociology in solving the problem of what to do next in the light of the research findings, or indeed of what sort of conclusion could be drawn on the basis of them other than that proposed at the end of the last chapter. Their writings had considered in depth the relationship between common-sense and professional sociological theorizing and, although their conclusions yielded a negative answer to the second question posed at the end of Chapter 7, they had worked from that conclusion to new ways of doing analysis which were offered as a positive alternative to the existing procedures available in sociology. This seemed to open up the possibility that there was indeed more that could be said about the social organization of sudden death, and hence that an affirmative response to the first of the questions posed at the end of the last chapter was available. My preference would have been for devoting this last section of the book to some preliminary attempts at an ethnomethodological analysis of some of the empirical materials already discussed. The controversial nature of ethnomethodology within sociology, however, and the misunderstandings which seem to persist about its claims indicate the need for at least a brief survey of the central programmatic assumptions involved. These, then, provide the focus for Section 8.2, which is followed by a brief consideration of the work done on suicide by Garfinkel (1967a; 1967b) and Sacks (1966; 1972) and its relevance for the present research.

8.2 THE GENERAL CLAIMS OF ETHNOMETHODOLOGY [2]

Ethnomethodology grew out of a concern for the kinds of problems which have provided the focus for much of the methodological discussion in this book. That is, underlying the issues considered in Part I was the problem of the nature of social reality and of how it is to be appropriately studied. In the discussion of data derived from official sources, it was seen how various alternatives to the Durkheimian view of social facts as entities with an existence external to the subjective experiences of members of society had been proposed by sociologists, and that the sociology of deviance in particular had been involved in a shift towards the analysis of the symbolic nature of social interaction and the attempt to 'understand' or 'appreciate' the actor's orientation to action. Attempts to come to terms with the problems of meaning and intersubjectivity have also featured in much recent sociological theorizing, and it was seen for example how Douglas had attempted to shift the focus of suicide research towards what he claims is a Weberian approach to the study of social reality. Ethnomethodologists have made far more ambitious claims about their analyses, and have proposed more positive solutions to these perennial and worrying concerns of sociology, than any of the alternative sociological attempts to solve them. Thus their analysis of the intersubjective character of social reality not only implies a rejection of rival analyses, but has led to the development of alternative ways of conducting empirical research[3] which, while very different from the practices of other sociologists, nevertheless retain a central interest in the original concern of sociology with the problem of social order.

At the heart of sociology's problem are two competing and mutually exclusive theories of social reality which have been characterized by Garfinkel as the 'correspondence' and 'congruence' theory respectively.[4] The correspondence theory seeks to maintain a distinction between the subjectively *perceived* object of the world and the concrete object, such that an analysis may differentiate between what '*appears*' to be the case and what '*really is*' the case. In other words, there is held to be a reality 'out there' in the world which is separate and distinct from the reality which is perceived and intersubjectively constructed by members.[5] According to this view, the sociologists' problem is to somehow cut through, or get behind, appearances in order to render some version of how it 'really' is in the world which corresponds with, or approximately corresponds with, the concrete objective reality that is held to be out there in the world. By contrast, the congruence theory proposes that the perceived object that is 'out there in the world' is the concrete object that is there and that the two terms are synonymous and interchangeable. That the subjective experiencing of an object in the world may involve doubt, ambiguity or uncertainty does not necessitate the revision of such a proposition, for these may be and often are features of the experienced object, in that what is being experienced is some doubtful, ambiguous or uncertain object. If, for example, one is woken by an unidentified bump in the night, the object in the world is an unidentified bump in the night. Subsequently it may be discovered that it was a child falling out of bed, a burglar dropping his jemmy or one of an infinite range of possibilities, in which case the object in the world will be reconstituted as whatever it turned out to be. And what it turned out to be will then become the object that it had been originally and all along and is now until further notice and for all practical purposes. The point of this example is that it is tempting to conclude that the first subjective perception of the object as an 'unidentified bump in the night' was, in its failure to correspond with what was later found to be 'really' going on, 'wrong' or 'mistaken'. Such a conclusion, however, involves an acceptance of the correspondence theory of reality in its attempt to sustain and use a distinction between a subjectively perceived object and a 'real' object for analytic purposes. The point that is missed (or denied) is that the first perceived object in the world (the unidentified bump) was, at the time and for all practical purposes no less, no worse, or less valid an object in the world than the second perceived object (e.g. 'child falling out of bed'). Indeed treating it as *the* 'real' object is presumably what led to the investigations which resulted in the reconstitution of the object as 'child falling out of bed'. That it was so reconstituted, furthermore, is no guarantee against later revision, and, without such a guarantee, there seems to be no way in which the second perceived object can be claimed to be of a different order to the first. Thus treating 'child falling out of bed' as the objective reality in the world might lead parents to 'show concern', 'act comfortingly', and the like. Were such activities then followed by a sly grin from the child, the object in the world would no doubt be reconstituted as another object (e.g. 'prank', 'naughtiness', etc.). According to the congruence theory, then, there are only multiple realities, which cannot in any absolute or independent sense be distinguished from or contrasted with some proposed concrete objective reality (cf. Schutz, 1968).

Just as the correspondence theorist, by maintaining a distinction between perceived objects and concrete objects in the world, is attempting to discover 'what is actually going on', so also does it appear that, in perceiving an object in the world, the parent in the above example was involved in a search for an answer to the question 'What is actually going on?' That the possible answers were in the form of descriptions ('child falling out of bed', etc.) points to a further correspondence which is asserted by both members and professional theorists, namely that between what is observed and what is said to be actually going on or, in other words, between the description and the events or objects in the world. The problem of 'literal description' that is involved here is one which has been treated at length by Garfinkel and Sacks, who use their analyses both to highlight an insoluble problem for conventional sociology and to elaborate the distinctiveness of the ethnomethodological alternative.[6] In doing so, they also draw attention to the fundamental similarity between sociological theorizing about society and that by lay members, which emerged as one of the most problematic features of our own findings reported above. Thus in an early paper, Sacks (1963, p. 10) made the following observation:

> It is the case that the sole difference between the writings of sociologists and the talk about society by anyone else turns on the concern of sociologists with a single methodological problem which sociologists have 'discovered'. I shall call this problem 'the etcetera problem'. . . . How is the scientific requirement of literal description to be achieved in the face of the fact, widely recognized by researchers, that a description even of a particular 'concrete object' can never be complete? That is, how is a description to be warranted when, however long or intensive it may be, it may nonetheless be indefinitely extended? We call this 'the etcetera problem' to note: To any description of a concrete object (or event, or course of action, or etc.), however long, the researcher must add an etcetera clause to permit the description to be brought to a close.

In his subsequent discussion of the 'etcetera problem', Sacks notes that for a correspondence between a description and some object to be arrived at, the description would have to be complete. Given that all that can be done is an incomplete description, the possibilities exist that such descriptions may be read as an irony, a metaphor, a sketch, or whatever. If one accepts the et cetera problem:

> one cannot establish correspondence by just reading the description and looking at the object; one must produce besides the description some appendix which establishes a reconciliation of the two [Sacks, 1963, p. 12].

According to Sacks, sociological theory, including the classical works of Durkheim, Weber and Marx involves the attempt to arrive at a 'principled resolution' of such problems and it is only in that concern that professional sociological theorizing differs from that of anyone else.

Garfinkel (1967a, pp. 24–34) deals with the problem of literal description with reference to some of his 'experiments', and develops his analysis to elaborate the character and distinctiveness of the ethnomethodological solution to the problem. The task set was for students to report mundane conversations by writing what was actually said on the left-hand side of a sheet of paper and to elaborate on the right-hand side what they and their partners understood they were talking about. The contents of the right-hand side of the reports provided Garfinkel with the possibility of requiring further explication, further clarity and accuracy and, as he increasingly asked for these, the students complained not only at the laboriousness of having to write more and more, but also that the more they wrote, the greater the amount of possibly relevant questions became: 'The very way of accomplishing the task multiplied its features' (ibid, p. 26). The students also came to the conclusion that the task of providing a literal description by attempting to achieve a correspondence between what was said and what was talked about was 'in principle' impossible. Given such results, Garfinkel proceeds to ask what was it that he had asked them to do which they found so difficult and, in answering this, he outlines the character of the topic for sociological analysis. To begin with, we are asked to drop certain assumptions, including the correspondence theory of reality:

> suppose we drop the assumption that in order to describe a usage as a feature of a community of understandings we must know at the outset what the substantive common understandings consist of. With it, drop the assumption's accompanying theory of signs, according to which a 'sign' and 'referent' are respectively properties of something said and something talked about, and which in this fashion proposes sign and referent to be related as corresponding contents. By dropping such a theory of signs we drop as well, thereby, the possibility that an invoked shared agreement on substantive matters explain a usage [ibid., p. 28].

Once done, argues Garfinkel, *what* was talked about can no longer be distinguished from *how* they were talking, so that a complete explanation of what they were talking about would consist of describing *how* the parties had been speaking. Thus were it claimed that persons were talking ironically, jokingly or whatever, a method for hearing what was said in the particular way invoked would have to be provided. The severe difficulties encountered by the students resulted from the fact that Garfinkel had asked them to formulate the method that the speakers had used as rules of procedure to be followed in order to see what they had said. He goes on to conclude:

> To recognise *what* is said *means* to recognise how a person is speaking. . . . For the conduct of their everyday affairs, persons take for granted that what is said will be made out according to methods that the parties use to make out what they are saying for its clear, consistent, coherent, understandable, or planful character, i.e., as subject to some rule's jurisdiction – in a word, rational. To see the 'sense' of what is said is to accord to what was said its character 'as a rule'. *'Shared agreement' refers to various social methods for accomplishing the member's recognition that something was said-according-to-a-rule and not the*

demonstrable matching of substantive matters. The appropriate image of a common understanding is therefore an operation rather than a common intersection of overlapping sets [ibid., p. 30; Garfinkel's italics].

Encapsuled here are two of the central notions of ethnomethodology, first that members have methods for resolving the ambiguities of social reality which render that which is potentially senseless 'rational' and 'accountable' for all practical purposes, and second that the order which is understood and agreed by members is an 'operation' or an 'ongoing accomplishment' of members. Accordingly, members and sociologists:

can treat a common understanding as a shared agreement on substantive matters by taking for granted that what is said will be made out in accordance with methods that need not be specified, which is to say that they need only be specified on 'special' occasions [ibid.].

By ignoring the 'operational structure' of common understandings, the professional sociologist is involved in using common-sense knowledge in exactly the same ways that members of society do in deciding what is really going on or what is really being talked about. Common-sense knowledge of social structures is both a topic and a resource of such enquiries, and this failure to distinguish between common-sense knowledge and command of the natural language as topics and resources for doing sociology has been elaborated at length in the more programmatic writings of the ethnomethodologists (e.g. Zimmerman and Pollner, 1971). The alternative offered by Garfinkel (1967a) is that sociology must give exclusive priority to the study of the methods of concerted actions and methods of common understanding. As the accomplishment of these involves mastery of the natural language, sociologists are invited to treat the use of the natural language as the discipline's problematic topic rather than to continue to use their own command of it as an unexplicated resource in their analyses. Put at its simplest, then, ethnomethodology recommends and involves the study of members' methods for accomplishing social order as its central topic.

One response to this conclusion is to note that it is all very well to make such programmatic claims, but Garfinkel and his colleagues do not provide any clear instructions for how to do ethnomethodological studies or what they might look like. Such a complaint, however, reveals a profound misunderstanding of the distinction between the correspondence and congruence theories of reality outlined above, and, in particular seems to stem from a persistent adherence to the correspondence version. That is, if one accepts that there are severe and insoluble difficulties involved in attempting to warrant a correspondence between a particular object in the world and a possible description (such as those faced by Garfinkel's students referred to above), then it follows that similar difficulties will be faced in any attempt to achieve a correspondence between a particular description of what ethnomethodologists do and the work that they do. In order to discover what kind of studies they do and, perhaps more importantly in the present context, how to do them, there appears to be no substitute for looking at studies and attempting to do such studies. In other words, to complain that ethnomethodology fails to tell us what kind of study is indicated by their programmatics is to complain that they are accepting the logic of their own programmatics, namely that the task of formulating a literal description of some object in the world (which in this case would be 'ethnomethodological work') with that concrete object itself is an infinite and impossible task. Thus the reluctance of some and perhaps most ethnomethodologists to engage in programmatic debate together with their apparently obsessional claim that a more appropriate focus for discussion is their ongoing work, which tend to be viewed by other sociologists as 'bloody-mindedness', 'sectarianism', or plain 'cowardice', can be seen as being wholly consistent with a determined refusal to accept the assumptions of the correspondence theory. It is also probably no coincidence that Garfinkel's *Studies in Ethnomethodology* are indeed 'studies' and not mere programmatics and that Sacks, who was almost certainly the most sophisticated and prolific exponent of ethnomethodological analyses to date, seldom engaged in programmatic debate.

Other responses to the general claims of ethnomethodology are that it diverts (or subverts?) sociology away from macro-structural concerns to the details of micro-analyses (e.g. Gouldner, 1970; Taylor, Walton and Young, 1973; Worsley, 1974), that the programmatics are not news (e.g. Goldthorpe, 1973), that there is a convergence between ethnomethodology and other 'labelling theory' (e.g. Denzin, 1971), and that its programmatics are mistaken anyway (e.g. Goldthorpe, 1973). Rather than present a detailed account and critique of each of these, I want to suggest that they all involve an apparent misunderstanding or refusal to worry about the problem of indexicality and its repair. On indexical expressions, Garfinkel (1967, p. 29) writes as follows:

Husserl spoke of expressions whose sense cannot be decided by an auditor without his necessarily knowing or assuming something about the biography and purposes of the user of the expression, the circumstances of the utterance, the previous course of the conversation, or the particular relationship of actual or potential interaction that exists between the expressor and the auditor. Russell observed that descriptions involving them apply on each occasion of their use to only one thing, but to different things on different occasions. Such expressions, wrote Goodman, are used to make une-

quivocal statements that nevertheless seem to change in truth
value. . . . The list can be extended indefinitely.

Now though the implication of this is that social interaction is an
awesomely complex and delicate matter, members of society have, as
was indicated earlier, methods for coping with the indexical particulars
with which they are continually faced. That is, in perceiving what they
see or hear as an object in the world, they are involved in substituting
an objective for an indexical expression. The warrant for this claim is
that were it not so, we would never be able to make sense of what was
going on, and hence social life would not be possible. In the same way,
all professional sociology is held to be engaged in the same exercise:

> The indexical properties of natural language assure to the
> technology of sociological inquiries, lay and professional, the follow-
> ing unavoidable and irremediable practice as their earmark:
> Wherever and by whomever practical sociological reasoning is done,
> it seeks to remedy the indexical properties of practical discourse; it
> does so in the interests of demonstrating the rational accountability
> of everyday activities; and it does so in order that its assessments be
> warranted by methodic observation and report of situated, socially
> organized particulars of everyday activities, which of course include
> particulars of natural language [Garfinkel and Sacks, 1970, p. 339].

With respect to the second of the two questions with which the previous
chapter ended ('Can it be claimed that expert theories accomplish
anything more than, or different from, that which is accomplished by
common-sense theories?'), we seem to have here a very clear negative
answer. In addition, we have the promise of a positive answer to the
question which preceded it ('Is there anything else that can be said
about the social organization of sudden death other than that it is accomplished by consulting and constructing common-sense theories
which provide for how particular deaths occurred?'), for members'
procedures for repairing indexical expressions are to be focused on as
the *topic* of enquiry (cf Zimmerman and Pollner, 1971). I draw attention
to this optimistic response to the pessimism on which the last chapter
ended in the present context in order to contrast this response to the
problem of indexicality with that of Douglas (1967) in *The Social
Meanings of Suicide* (and by implication to that of others who have shown
deep concern about the problem of studying 'social meanings'). Thus,
having located the immense variation and ambiguity in social meanings
as a critical resource for use against Durkheimian positivism, he
proposes that the empirical solution lies in the doing of detailed studies
of the contexts in which suicidal meanings are invoked. As was noted in
Chapter 3, similar recommendations are to be found in the writings of

other sociologists such as Becker (1963), Matza (1969) and Polsky (1971). What such policies seem to be proposing is that sociologists must improve their descriptions by chasing up more and more and ever more of the details of the various contexts on which social life is lived in the hope that somehow or other 'subjective meanings', 'versions of the world', and the like, can be spotted and reported. In other words, the enterprise that seems to be recommended is one in which the observer is to root out as many of the indexical particulars as he can, such that the longer the list, the better is the description deemed to be. In exhortations to do the kind of observations that might permit such 'findings', furthermore, the would-be researcher is typically invited to learn the natural language of the particular language community he is studying, not so much so that he can provide for *how* members of the community see things and hear things in the way that they hear them, but rather so that he can *use* the natural language as a resource for hearing and seeing as they do. What are then reported are members' repairs of indexical expressions and not the way in which such work is accomplished. Here, then seems to be an important distinction between the concerns of ethnomethodology on the one hand, and symbolic interactionism and phenomenological orientations to sociology on the other. If it is accepted, then any claims of these latter groups to the effect that there is nothing new about ethnomethodology, or that they are essentially interested in doing the same kind of work, can be seen as resting on a misunderstanding of the ethnomethodological formulation of the problem of indexicality. Ethnomethodologists are not interested in the endless elaboration of indexical particulars or in the simple reportage of repairs that members do, but are concerned with the discovery of members' methods for repairing indexical particulars.

A further sort of misunderstanding of the ethnomethodological interest in indexicality is the view expressed by Douglas (1971, pp. 40–3) and taken up elsewhere (e.g. Goldthorpe, 1973) that expressions and situations vary with respect to the degree of indexicality. Thus, because some situations are apparently 'clearer' than others, it is held that it may still be legitimate to do constructive analyses on those topics. The ethnomethodologists, according to this view, have exaggerated the ambiguous and intangible nature of social reality by making out that everything in the world is 'awesomely' indexical. One eminent British sociologist, for example, has suggested to me that the problem of indexicality could in most circumstances be overcome by careful piloting of questionnaires. By claiming that there are degrees of indexicality which thereby affect the appropriateness or otherwise of conventional sociological procedures, all that is being observed is that in many aspects of social life indexicalities pose unnoticed practical problems for members in that they are able to repair them in a routine and unnoticed way. That this can be done in such an unproblematic manner, far from undermining ethnomethodological claims, highlights the methodic character of the interpretive rules and procedures which enable members to accomplish the substitution of objective for indexical expressions. In other words, the suggestion that there are degrees of indexicality and that the claims of ethnomethodology are in some way invalidated thereby is to take it that indexicality is important to ethnomethodologists only in the way that it has always been an important problem for philosophers and sociologists, namely in that indexical expressions are 'nuisances', 'awkward for formal discourse', and so on (Garfinkel, 1967a, p. 5). Ethnomethodologists do not, however, claim to have discovered the problem, as is indicated by Garfinkel's references to philosophers as a resource in elaborating what is involved in the notion of indexicality, but they do claim to have formulated the problem of how members repair indexical expressions in such a way as to provide for empirical analyses to be undertaken.

Another source of concern to sociologists is the view that ethnomethodology is obsessively concerned with 'micro' analyses of social phenomena and hence threatens to divert the central concerns of sociology away from what are claimed to be its central interest in 'macro-structural' matters. At its most patronizing, this position regards the attractions of ethnomethodology as 'understandable', given the sorry state of Western sociology, or as a way of 'dropping out', but as nevertheless misguided (e.g. Gouldner, 1970; Worsley, 1974). A related line of argument has it that the stress of ethnomethodologists on the indexical character of social interaction permits of no generalizations to be made beyond particular situations. With regard to the former position, it may be noted first that it rests on the assertion that not only is there something about the *essence* of sociology which demands an emphasis on macro-structural matters such that any other sort of study may be regarded as 'suspect', but also that ethnomethodology falls clearly into the class of micro study to be regarded as suspect. If it is granted, however, that studies concerned with and directed towards sociology's original interest in social order may be exempted from such criticisms, it is difficult to see how ethnomethodology can be construed as an attempt to divert sociology from its main course, as its practitioners would claim that it is precisely to that problem that their interests have been diverted. Garfinkel's early work, for example, was done under no less a student of social order than Parsons and, in his own words, he subsequently 'acted for many years as Parsons' agent on the West Coast'.[7] In a more explicit statement of indebtedness to him than is usually to be found in his work, he observed:

> Parsons' work, particularly, remains awesome for the penetrating depth and unfailing precision of its practical sociological reasoning

on the constituent tasks of the problem of social order and its solutions [Garfinkel, 1967a, p. ix].

But, as is implicit in this, ethnomethodologists would in no sense claim to be 'Parsonians' and the essential difference between their interest in social order and more conventional sociological concerns is referred to here by Garfinkel. That is, macro concerns with the problem of social order are seen as involving 'practical sociological reasoning', just as social order is accomplished by members via the same procedure. The difference, then, lies in the formulation of the problem and the nature of the solutions thereby indicated. For the ethnomethodologists, the problem is not to produce generalizations which impose an order on the world, or which allegedly explain a particular order that is claimed to be there. Rather it involves seeing social order as a members' accomplishment and the task of analysis as the discovery of members' methods for accomplishing that order. That this formulation equates the kind of general theorizing engaged in by sociologists with the theorizing of members, that the two sorts of theory are seen to be in competition with each other, and that there are no widely agreed methodic procedures for warranting the professional theories as 'better', or 'more accurate', or whatever, than those of members are matters which do not seem to have been adequately responded to by ethnomethodology's macro critics. In general, then, we may note that the interest in the repair of indexical expressions as a means of accomplishing social order seems to have been ignored or misunderstood by critics who construe the interest in indexicality as merely an interest in the details of 'micro' settings.

The related line of argument referred to above that the phenomenon of indexicality must inevitably permit no generality in the findings of ethnomethodologists seems similarly to rest on a misunderstanding of the interest in indexicality. It probably also results from a reading only of the more programmatic ethnomethodological writings to the exclusion of the more detailed empirical analyses. Thus, as has been repeatedly noted above, the ethnomethodological interest is not simply in elaborating the indexical particulars of social settings, but in locating formal properties, or formal structures of practical action (Garfinkel and Sacks, 1970). Sacks's work on Membership Categorization Devices (see, e.g., Sacks, 1972a, 1972b), for example, appears to have immense generality, as do many of his other conclusions based on the analysis of natural conversations. Similarly, Schegloff's (1972) analysis of the way members do place formulations would seem to be very general in its applicability. We may note that these studies, though based on talk between American speakers of English, have so far attracted no criticisms, complaints or charges of invalidity from English-speaking speakers of English, which, given normal sociological stresses on the differences between cultures, may be seen as a compliment to the degree of generality arrived at in such studies. Having said that, however, it must of course be admitted that the kind of generality aimed at by ethnomethodologists is very different from that normally recommended in sociology. That is, the interest is not in doing generalized descriptions of society or in arriving at general theories which explain this or that, but rather in locating and describing methodic procedures used by members in providing for and reproduceably providing for any particular social order. It is not, then, that ethnomethodologists are uninterested in arriving at conclusions which have no generality beyond the particular piece of data being analysed, but that the kind of generality aimed for is very different from that which has provided the traditional directive for sociology.

Having attempted to outline the general claims of ethnomethodology and to clarify them by reference to some of the objections which have been raised against them, I want now to refer briefly to the attractions of those claims in the context of the present research, before going on to look at the work by Garfinkel and Sacks on suicidal data. As was noted at the end of the last chapter, the findings of our research had left us with serious problems. That is, what we seemed to have discovered was that there was very little difference between lay and expert theories of suicide, a finding which posed serious difficulties in terms both of the kind of conclusion which was indicated and of the question 'What to do next?' It seemed that there was little provision in sociology for what to make of such findings other than to attempt to force them into some kind of quasi-deterministic model of the sort presented in the 'Dynamic Model of the Transmission of Shared Definitions of Suicide Through a Social System' in Section 6.6 above.[8] In contrast with other sociologists, however, the ethnomethodologists had treated the problem of the relationship between lay and expert theorizing at length and were uninhibited in concluding that *both* were members' methods for accomplishing order by the substitution of objective for indexical expressions. Such a formulation, then, had the attraction for the present research that it provided a method for making sense of, and hence accomplishing some kind of order out of, the bewildering puzzlement which initially accompanied the findings. That they had used that formulation to develop alternative modes of empirical analysis held out the further promise that the answers to our questions at the end of Chapter 7 could be other than the pessimistic responses which at first seemed to be indicated. One unfortunate feature of this realization was that it came too late to allow a start to be made on more detailed attempts at such analysis that what has been reported so far.

Another somewhat disconcerting feature to emerge from these observations is that they suggest that, in terms of our general conclusions, we had discovered no more than what was already well-known to the ethnomethodologists. That this had been done probably arose from the fact that some of their writings had been unwittingly used as an important resource in formulating our research problem. Thus it had been suggested in the discussion of problems associated with data derived from official sources in Chapter 3 that the works of Cicourel (1968) and Sudnow (1965) in this area seemed to be the most satisfactory, and they, it was to emerge later, were not the straightforward interactionists they are often depicted as being.[9] Subsequently the 'discovery' in Chapter 5 that official definitions were not arrived at in the idealized way that had been anticipated led to the formulation of the research's central empirical interest in the problem of *how* some deaths get categorized as suicides. By so doing, the problem had again 'unwittingly' been formulated in a way very similar to that in which it might have been done by an ethnomethodologist, as is evidenced by comparing it with the following more explicitly ethnomethodological formulation by Sacks (1963, p. 8):

> The crucial difficulty with Durkheim's *Suicide* is not that he employs official statistics, but that he adopts for sociology the problem of practical theory. 'Suicide' is a category of the natural language. It leads to a variety of practical problems, such as, for example, explaining particular suicides or explaining the variety of suicide rates. To say that Durkheim's error was to use official records rather than for example studying the variation in the reporting of suicides is to suppose that it is obvious that events occur which sociologists should consider 'really suicide,' . . . *An investigation of how it is that a decision that a suicide occurred is assembled, and an investigation of how an object must be conceived in order to talk of it as 'committing suicide, these are the preliminary problems for sociology* [my emphasis].

Thus the kind of research reported on in Chapters 5–7 was very close to the sort recommended by Sacks in the underlined passage above.[10] Sacks furthermore continued his above remarks to anticipate the situation to which those studies now seem to have led:

> *Having produced procedural descriptions of the assembly of a suicide classification it may turn out that it is the category and the methodology for applying it that constitutes the interesting sociological problems.* We may not choose to conceive persons as 'possible suicides'. We may choose rather to investigate how the notion of person is used in the assessments of the range of each other's behaviours [ibid., p. 8].

By proposing that ethnomethodology promises an answer, and possibly the only answer, to the problems we were left with at the end of Chapter 7, then, the underlined part of this extract from Sacks provides a summary of what indeed the problem has turned out to be. There is also a sense in which the stress on the importance of analysing the biographies of deceased persons in our earlier analysis marks a beginning of an investigation of 'how the notion of person is used in the assessments of the range of each other's behaviours'.

8.3 SUICIDE IN STUDIES BY ETHNOMETHODOLOGISTS

Although suicide has featured in the writings of both Garfinkel and Sacks, it would be misleading and incorrect to view their works as studies *of* suicide in any conventional sense. Thus both address other and more general analytic issues by reference to empirical materials collected at the Los Angeles Suicide Prevention Center. That this is the case is, of course, not surprising, for it would be surprising indeed, given what has been said so far about ethnomethodology, had they treated phenomena collected together in the natural language category 'suicide' as the topic for research.

The central analytic issues addressed by Garfinkel (1967a; 1967b) with reference to 'Some Features in the Work of the Los Angeles Suicide Prevention Center' are the nature of practical sociological reasoning and reflexivity, two fundamental notions in the logic of ethnomethodological enquiry. His aim, then, is to show how the repair of indexicality is accomplished via procedures of practical sociological reasoning and how that work, and by extension all other such work, by members is unavoidably reflexive in character. The attraction of the 'psychological autopsies' done by members of the S.P.C. staff is that it provides an extreme and obvious case where the task in hand is to cope with and clarify some highly equivocal situations, namely deaths referred to them as 'equivocal' by the Los Angeles coroner. The nature and manner of practical sociological reasoning is perhaps best summed up in the passage from Garfinkel already quoted earlier in this book at the beginning of Chapter 6, and indeed much of our analysis in that and the subsequent chapter was illustrative of the way in which officials and others do this in the process of arriving at the decision that a death was a suicide. The puzzlement with which the finding that there was an apparent convergence between practical sociological reasoning (or in the terms used earlier 'common-sense theorizing') and professional sociological reasoning confronted us stemmed partly from an imperfect understanding of Garfinkel's analysis of the repair of indexical expressions as a members' practical problem and accomplishment, and more importantly from a failure to recognize the import of the reflexive character of that enterprise. That is, an understanding of reflexivity provides for an understanding of how it was that the officials were doing the kind of thing we described in the way that they were doing it.

Garfinkel illustrates reflexivity with reference to two main features in the work of the Suicide Prevention Center (hereafter referred to as the S.P.C.), first with reference to the organized character of the work that they do, and second with reference to the particular problem of investigating equivocal deaths. It must be stressed, however, that this is not to suggest that he is engaged in elaborating two kinds of problem or that these are the only kinds of situation in which reflexivity is a pervading phenomenon. With reference to his first illustration, Garfinkel is concerned to show that and how the organizational arrangements for doing the work of the S.P.C. are simultaneously taken for granted and not commented on, yet at the same time are continually being made visible by the work that the Centre is doing. Put another way, the rational character of members' actions is made recognizable and observable by members seeing what they are doing and what others are doing as being consistent with or falling under the auspices of some rule, set of rules or description of what it is that they are supposed to be doing (Garfinkel, 1967b, p. 172). That the grounds for doing what they are doing are constitutive features of what they are doing is summarized by Garfinkel (ibid., p. 182) in the following way:

> With respect to the problematic character of practical actions and the practical adequacy of their inquiries members take for granted that a member must at the outset 'know' the settings in which he is to operate if his practices are to serve as measures to bring particular, located features of these settings to recognizable account. They treat as the most passing matter of fact that members' accounts of every sort in all their logical modes, with all of their uses and for every method of their assembly, are constituent features of the settings that they make observable. SPC members know, require, count on, and make use of this reflexivity to produce, accomplish, recognize, or demonstrate the scientific adequacy for all practical purposes of their procedures and findings.

In short, the accounts or grounds for particular activities are not distinct from those activities but are situationally embedded in the activities to which they relate.

This 'essential reflexivity of accounts' is perhaps even more clearly manifested in the production of clear, rational accounts for what were initially seen as 'equivocal deaths'. The point that Garfinkel is at pains to make here is that the accounts of a particular death as this or that type of death are constitutive features of the death. Thus the 'remains' and 'relics' which are 'read' in arriving at an account which is 'rational for all practical purposes' are not just already there, but are all that are there. And in that they provide grounds for warranting the death as this or that type of death, the accounts of the death are essentially reflexive.

The 'relics' suggest a proposed categorization and the proposed categorization is checked by reference to the relics. Thus we saw, for example, in Chapter 6, Section 2 how suicide notes were constituted as suicide notes, rather than some other sort of note, by reference to the apparent mode of death, and how the mode of death could also be constituted as that mode of death by reference to the suicide note. The relevance of that reflexivity for the work of coroners, however, tended to be overlooked in our examination of the other kinds of 'relic' which seemed relevant in arriving at a categorization of suicide. Thus with reference to such procedures, Garfinkel notes that coroners and S.P.C. staff:

> have to start with *this* much; *this* sight; *this* note; *this* collection of whatever is at hand. And *whatever* is there is good enough in the sense that whatever is there not only *will* do but does. One makes whatever is there do. By this is not meant that an SPC investigator is too easily content or that he does not look for more when he should. What is meant is rather that the 'whatever' it is that he has to deal with is what will be used to find out, to make decidable the way in which that society operated to produce *that* picture, to have *that* scene as its end result. In this way the remains on the slab serve not only as a precedent but as a goal of SPC inquiries. *Whatsoever* SPC members are faced with must serve as the precedent by means of which they read the remains in order to see how the society could have operated to have produced what it is that they have 'in the end', 'in the final analysis', and 'in *any* case'. What the inquiry can come to is what the death came to [ibid., p. 177; his italics].

The implications of this extend far beyond the problems faced by S.P.C. members in the categorization of sudden deaths and point to the way in which members generally go about describing or ordering the world. Thus features of an action, utterance, situation or whatever are 'read' for a possible description, which is then checked out by reference to the same features of that action, utterance or situation. An acceptance of such formulations of reflexivity renders intelligible what was originally so puzzling about our findings regarding the activities of coroners and their connection with those of suicidologists. That is, if it is the case that members are continually and in all imaginable settings engaged in this 'monitoring' of descriptions derived from the features of the setting by reference to features of that same setting, [11] then it ceases to be surprising or puzzling that coroners and their officers appeared to be engaged in testing hypotheses, ruling out alternatives, using theories, etc., in the manner of professional suicidologists. For such processes are, according to Garfinkel, invariant and inescapable given the reflexive character of practical sociological reasoning.

In contrast with Garfinkel's illustrative purposes, Sacks (1966; 1972b) is concerned with finding a solution to a specific analytic problem in his study of suicidal telephone calls to a suicide prevention center. The problem is a very general one which is certainly not exclusively associated with suicide:

> The fact that everyone has many more identities than they assume in a given interaction poses for the researcher the problem of how it is that for any given interaction, identities are selected [Sacks, 1972b, p. 31].

The central theoretical task in this work, then, is to arrive at a precise formulation of the selection problem such that specific empirical questions posed by the suicidal telephone conversations can be answered, namely how it is that persons come to categorize themselves as having 'no one to turn to', and how such categorizations are used in organizing the search for help. The ethnomethodological character of such a formulation of the problem can be clearly seen even in an abbreviated version of his problem, in that the members' problem of doing descriptions is taken as problematic, and is further conceived as being inextricably tied to the organized settings of the description's use. In short, reflexivity is central to the way in which Sacks formulates his analytic task, as is evidenced in the following:

> What one ought to seek to build is an apparatus which will provide for how it is that any activities, which members do in such a way as to be recognizable as such to members, are done, and done recognizably [Sacks, 1966, p. 10].

That apparatus, which was first developed in the analysis of the calls to the suicide prevention center is the Membership Categorization Device, which marked the beginnings of Sacks's prolific demonstrations of how to do sociology according to the recommendations of Garfinkel. Sacks introduces his detailed elaboration of what is involved in Membership Categorization Devices as follows:

> My attention shall be exclusively limited to those categories in the language in terms of which *persons* may be classified. For example, the categories: 'male', 'teacher', first baseman', 'professional', 'Negro', etc., are of the sort I shall be dealing with.
>
> Frequently, such 'membership categories' are organized, by persons of the society using them, into what I shall call 'collections of membership categories'. These collections constitute the *natural*

groupings of categories, categories that members of society feel 'go together'. They are not constructed merely as aids to my analysis; whether or not a particular category is a member of a particular collection is, in each and every case, a matter to be decided empirically [ibid., pp. 15–16; his italics].

After detailing the ways in which this formulation needs to be qualified by reference to variations within and between societies and in terms of the degree of fixity in the number of categories which may be included in different collections, Sacks proceeds to specify what he means by a Membership Categorization Device (hereafter referred to as M.C.D. or Device):

> Such natural collections of membership categories – collections such as 'age', 'sex', 'occupation', 'race', 'team', etc. – *plus* whatever rules of application the use of the collection involves, I shall call Membership Categorization Devices, or, in short, Devices, or M.C.D.'s. A Device, then, is a collection and rules for applying that collection to some set of persons [ibid., p. 17].

In a later version of the study, a somewhat more formal specification is given:

> By the term *categorization device* we mean that *collection of membership categories*, containing at least a category, that may be applied to some population, containing at least a Member, so as to provide, by the use of some rules of application, for the pairing of at least a population Member and a categorization device member. A *device* is then a *collection* plus rules of application [Sacks, 1972b, p. 32; his italics].

The relevance of this for his analysis of the suicidal telephone calls is that the callers propose, in making the calls, that they have been engaged in a 'search for help' which has involved looking for help from certain persons to the exclusion of others. The way in which that distinction is made by a caller, or in other words the way in which he categorizes those persons is subsequently shown by Sacks to be crucial in understanding how he comes to see his problem as he does.

The problem of categorizing persons is not particular to the makers of suicidal telephone calls, but is a general one which Sacks (loc. cit.) depicts as the 'problem of the "relevance" of competing ways of categorizing persons'. This is elaborated by reference to the availability of M.C.D.s with different characteristics. Put simply, there are some which can be used on any group of persons however large (e.g. 'sex', 'age', 'race') and some which cannot (e.g. a category from the device 'occupations' cannot be used on a group of children). If all M.C.D.s had this latter quality and were applicable only to limited collections of people, the issue of correct categorization would be that of whether or not the correct category from the device had been applied in a particular case. If on the other hand there are M.C.D.s which can be used in categorize any group of persons of any size, then the problem would not simply be that of finding a Device which exclusively describes the group of persons at hand, but would involve the question of which of several appropriate M.C.D.s should be used.

> The task of categorization would then be more complicated; it would have to involve some principled selection procedure, some special means of deciding the relevance of this as against that Device. The problem of correctness – has the right category been chosen for this particular person? – would be a second order question. The first question – which Device should be used? – would be much more troublesome [Sacks, 1966, p. 18].

Sacks proceeds to note that there are indeed such Devices available to members and it is that availability which makes categorization continually problematic, in that it renders the problem of 'relevance' continually problematic. Examples of these, which he refers to as 'Pn-adequate Devices' are 'sex', 'age', and 'race', so that any member of a society may be placed simultaneously in a category from each Device (ibid., p. 19). The problem facing suicidal persons is subsequently analysed in terms of the simultaneous availability of two Pn-adequate Devices.

That there are always more than one Device that may be used in categorizing persons poses the important problem of convergence in interactional situations. Thus if two people are engaged in categorizing a third, there is always the possibility that different Devices may be used, and this applies even with Devices that are not Pn-adequate. A familiar instance of the problem cited by Sacks is where 'The female person whom the male professor sees as "student", sees the professor as "man" (or vice versa)' (ibid., pp. 20–3). The convergence problem is not just a problem for members, but has a more programmatic relevance for sociology:

> Sociologists frequently treat some categorizations which members have done, for example, 'negro', 'white', 'other', as providing them with materials which are descriptive, that is that may be used, as they stand, for further sociological investigation. Alternatively, sociologists themselves frequently use members' categorization devices to categorize members as one step in doing sociological inquiries, for example, they decide to compare 'males' and 'females' for some purpose, or contrast 'young people' and 'old people' with

respect to some dependent variable. In both cases – whether they use an already categorized population or engage in some categorization themselves – the presumptive warrant for this use is, or would seem to be, that demonstrable correctness of the categorization may properly be established by some such procedure as looking to see whether the person(s) so categorized was properly so categorized, i.e. by, for example, observing that the member categorized as Negro is, in fact, a negro. Having decided the correctness of the categorization they proceed to employ it in doing their further researches.

While these types of procedures seem to be adequate, seem to employ a 'correspondence' notion of the correctness of a categorization, the fact that there are at least two devices always available, operates to prevent the use of their warrant [ibid., p. 23].

In other words, the correctness of a description cannot be established in any once and for all 'objective' way so long as two persons can point to a third person and apply different descriptors. This is not to say that members do not have organized ways of recognizing and agreeing on descriptions, but rather that sociologists have failed to take the way in which categorizations are accomplished as the topic for research. It is also to note that the determination of what in any given case is an appropriate description is reflexively tied to the circumstances of its use. Thus central in Sack's detailed analysis of the problem is the way in which the relevance of a particular device is located in the situations of its use. The search for help, for example, involves the use of M.C.D.s the categories of which are 'category-bound' to the activity of helping. In arriving at the decision that they have no one to turn to, the telephone callers monitor their search by reference to one M.C.D. (R) which includes categories of persons with special obligations to provide help to the particular individual concerned, and another (K) whose category members have professional obligations to provide help. Elsewhere in a briefer and simpler form and with reference to an apparently trivial piece of data comprising a couple of sentences, he has provided an extremely rigorous and elegant demonstration of how, via the use of M.C.D.s and the notion of category-bound activities, members are able to do recognizable descriptions and to achieve a convergence in recognizing them as correct (Sacks, 1972a).[12]

It may be that in time, Sacks's preliminary works will come to be regarded as 'too good to be true' in the same way as it was noted has been observed of Durkheim's theory of suicide. For the present, however, the impressiveness of his demonstrations and the systematic rigour with which they are formulated appear as quite exceptional within the context of the kinds of ambiguous and vague generalizations so typical of most sociology. To date, his work seems to have attracted little detailed attention from sociologists other than ethnomethodologists, and there has certainly yet to be a systematic attempt to seriously question or dismiss the details of his analysis. For ethnomethodologists, his work has provided a crucial resource which has inspired further detailed empirical studies which, again unusually for sociology, have been cumulative in character rather than merely repetitive, critical or dismissive. From the point of view of the present research interests, his work was clearly immensely relevant, given his detailed and systematic formulations of the fundamental problem of categorizations which we had increasingly had to confront, but the discovery of his works came too late for any of the implications to be followed up in any detail. The discovery did, however, come soon enough to assist in seeing some of the faults of conventional solutions of the problem of categorization as formulated by Douglas with reference to suicide and by labelling theorists more generally. Thus, the breakthrough of the latter was to see the importance of labelling and categorizing in the social world, though their studies seemed to provide only for the doing of more and more studies of instances where persons could be seen to be engaged in labelling. In so far as the problem of how categorizations were done was regarded as a problem, the answer was seen to reside in the results of some vaguely defined process of negotiation which was always won by the most powerful person or group involved. The breakthrough of the ethnomethodologists, then, was to take the problem of *how* members' categorizations are accomplished as a central and fundamental problem in studying social order, and to show how such a complex task may be begun.

8.4 CONCLUDING REMARKS

In the light of this view that members' methods for categorizing persons, things, activities, etc., are to be regarded as a central topic in the analysis of social order, and not merely as a small step on the way to producing 'better' or 'different' explanations, some brief remarks seem in order about the implications of such studies for the present and future work addressed to the topic area of suicide. Does it help, for example, to resolve the book's central problematic of how some deaths get categorized as suicides, and how far further research along these lines is or is not a useful exercise?

While it has been suggested that there was a sense in which the research problem remained constant throughout the studies, and that it was one which was potentially amenable to ethnomethodological analysis, it should be noted that the way in which it was formulated can retrospectively be seen to be misleading in two important respects. The first has to do with the decontextualized way in which the question 'How do some deaths get categorized as suicides?' was phrased, as it also implies that some decontextualized solution is available. In other words, once the question had been posed in that way, it was assumed that some generalized description of how deaths get categorized as suicides could be arrived at via the various research strategies adopted. In the light of the above discussion, however, it will hopefully be clear that such an approach retains the problem of how descriptions of events in the world can be warranted with reference to the reported observations, and is less than explicit about the context-bound 'practical purposes' character of members' categorizing procedures.

A second and related issue is that, by focusing on the categorization of suicides, the research question implies that there is something distinctive or special about the way members categorize sudden deaths as compared with the ways in which any other events in the world get categorized. That is, if members' methodic procedures of categorization are taken as a topic for study, then the main focus of any analysis must be on the situated methods themselves rather than on the particular categorization being selected. And it seems unlikely that it can be warrantably demonstrated that there is anything special about the procedures used in arriving at recognizably correct possible descriptions of suicidal deaths as opposed to those used in describing any other describable events in the world. For, while one can elaborate *ad nauseam* the indexical particulars involved in situations where members are engaged in the analysis and categorization of suicidal phenomena, there is no reason to suppose that their methods for arriving at a categorization which is objective, factual and definite for the practical purposes involved in such settings differ from those used in other settings where descriptive problems are being resolved.

Although such a conclusion may seem at first sight to have rather negative and depressing implications for the present work and for any future work on suicide, there is a sense in which it does provide a solution to the original research question, namely that deaths get categorized as suicides in much the same way as anything else gets categorized. This too, with its implication that the topic for analysis is no longer to be suicide, or how it in particular gets categorized, but rather members' methods for categorization, may also initially seem to be equally negative and depressing. But it remains so only as long as one retains the traditional sociological concern for engaging in the members' task of repairing indexicality, and continues to have faith in the capacity of sociologists to generate and warrant descriptions and explanations of social order which are essentially different, better, more accurate, etc., than those of members. Having said that, however, it must also be admitted that making such a transition is by no means easy, as it requires the sociologist to abandon so many of the assumptions which have been central to his discipline for so long. The transition is also complicated by the fear that there is no substitute provided by ethnomethodology, and that the import of the programmatic writings is that the problems associated with indexicality and reflexivity are so overwhelming that nothing more can be said about anything, and that sociological analysis may as well be abandoned altogether. But while it may be possible to retain such a reading of the earlier writings of Cicourel and Garfinkel, it is probably less easy to do so with respect to the later studies of the conversational analysts, and it may be significant that few of the attempted dismissals of ethnomethodology have directly addressed these later analyses. In saying this, I do not include as being directly addressed to such studies claims to the effect that the analysis of greetings sequences, openings and closings of telephone conversations and the like is an essentially trivial concern. For remarks of this sort betray a fundamental misunderstanding of the distinction between topic and resource such that the description of such work as 'trivial' is itself recognizably possibly correct only so long as the topic of such studies is stipulated to be 'greetings', 'telephone conversations', etc., and not that of how people understand and exhibit their understandings of one another. If, however, this latter is regarded as the analytic topic, then it becomes less easy for 'trivial' to pass without question as a possibly recognizably correct or appropriate descriptor of such analyses. For to insist on that would be to confess also that the methods such critical sociologists themselves have for understanding one another, and for attempting to make themselves understood to people outside the profession, are of equally trivial significance.

As far as the continued study of suicide as a topic is concerned, it should be now be clear that ethnomethodology has no glib or easy solution. As a source of data on members' methods of practical reasoning, it is clearly as suitable as any other possible source, and hence may continue to attract ethnomethodologists. Indeed, it may even have a special attraction for those with a particular analytic interest in settings where issues of explanation and description are explicitly problematic for members, given that the accomplishment of a factual description is at the centre of the practical concerns of those associated with the social organization of sudden death. So, just as it was argued at the start of this book that suicide as a topic for empirical research was traditionally of less interest to sociologists than the theoretical and methodological issues raised by Durkheim's *Suicide*, it may now seem that the ethnomethodologists' indifference to suicide as a topic both in past and possible future studies ensures that a similar situation will persist. But hopefully it will also be clear by now that, while there may seem to be close parallels between the way suicide was associated with the establishment of positivistic sociology and has more recently been addressed by Garfinkel and Sacks in establishing ethnomethodology, the similarity is no more than a superficial one.

Notes

NOTES TO CHAPTER 1

1. This occurred at the London School of Economics, where I had registered as a part-time M.Sc. student while on the staff of the Home Office Research Unit.
2. At the Home Office Research Unit, reconviction rates were routinely used to measure the relative effectiveness of different sorts of penal treatment. Though the unreliability and our general ignorance of such figures were well known to us all and frequently commented on, we still continued to use them 'as if' they were accurate measures.
3. This was as part of an application for a research post at the University of Essex. I did not get that particular one but was subsequently offered one as Research Assistant to Professor MacIntyre.
4. I found very quickly that there was a massive literature on suicide. References to nearly 4,000 works on the subject were contained in H. Rost (1927). A further 2,000 which appeared between then and 1958 were listed in N. L. Farberow and E. Schneidman (Eds.) (1961). Since then, at least another 350 studies have been published.
5. J. D. Douglas also started out with similar intent in that he had originally planned to use recent developments in mathematical sociology and model building to add rigour to Durkheim's statistical analysis. See the preface to his *The Social Meanings of Suicide* (Princeton: Princeton University Press, 1967).
6. Reactions to my research when I first started tended to support the view that sociologists were remarkably unworried about official statistics in that it seemed that I was engaged in a very limited technical inquiry which could only lead to the discovery of 'minor' errors in the rates.
7. Though I had read some of these before (e.g. Garfinkel, 1967a; Cicourel, 1968), I had mistakenly viewed them as more examples of labelling theory which were written in a rather obscure style, and used the writings of Schutz as a new resource for such work.

NOTES TO CHAPTER 2

1. See for example the extended use of Durkheim as an example by A. Stinchcombe (1968, pp. 15–28). His choice of Durkheim's work on suicide as an example in his very technical discussion of 'The Logic of Scientific Inference' (Chapter 2), seems particularly curious, given that he had earlier

made the ambitious claim with reference to Durkheim, Marx and Weber that 'Usually we [i.e. contemporary sociologists] can now do better than they did, because the empirical basis for their explanations has been tested and found wanting (pp. 2–3).

2. Selvin (1954), for example, observed that Durkheim's *Suicide* had attracted great interest from theorists but little from methodologists. He proceeded to look at it as an early example of multivariate analysis, as a model of how to relate theory and research, and praises Durkheim for his 'replicative' research method. A more recent and much more technical study which translates Durkheim's theory of suicide into a bewildering array of diagrams and algebraic formulae is R. Bowden (1968), 'A New Look at Correlation Analysis' in H. M. and A. B. Blalock (Eds.), *Methodology in Social Research*, pp. 199–235. What seems curious about this is that the 'New Look' did not involve a newer theory or newer data.

3. This is even the case in a recent introductory sociology text which seeks to introduce students to 'radical' sociology. See M. Coulson and D. Riddell (1970).

4. In particular the status consistency theorists, for a discussion of which see P. Doreian and N. Stockman (1969).

5. Douglas (1967) argues strongly that this indeed was the case, and in places he seems almost to be accusing Durkheim of having committed intellectual fraud in *Suicide*.

6. Thus it can be argued that debates about such issues between philosophers (e.g. Winch, 1958; MacIntyre, 1967) and pleas from sociologists for reorientation to the study of social action along Weberian lines (e.g. Rex, 1961) came very late in the history of sociology. Similarly in the U.S.A., it was not until long after Cooley, Thomas and Mead that symbolic interactionism gained the importance which seems to be indicated by the increasing number of books and readers which have appeared in recent years (e.g. Lindesmith and Strauss, 1949; Rose, 1962; Manis and Meltzer, 1967; Rubington and Weinberg, 1968; Blumer, 1969).

7. The establishment by the SSRC of a Survey Archive and Survey Unit can also be seen as indicating a strong commitment of the SSRC to quantitatively oriented research. More recently, however, there have been signs of a growing interest on the part of the Council in qualitative research methods.

8. This statement is based on the pervading puzzlement I have personally experienced with respect to the notion of 'social fact' since my earliest encounter with sociology. Later experiences as a teacher of students suggest that I am not alone in experiencing such bewilderment.

9. By these I intend the ecological studies associated with Park and Burgess (e.g. R. E. Park et al., 1925) as distinct from the ethnographic studies (e.g. N. Anderson, 1923; C. R. Shaw, 1930; W. F. Whyte, 1943).

10. I am indebted to Alasdair MacIntyre for the 'hole-digging' analogy.

11. One reason why this issue may have been particularly attractive to suicide researchers is that Durkheim's treatment of it in *Suicide* tended towards ambiguity. Thus it may have been seen as one of the few aspects in need of improvement, and hence possibly the only way of coming up with any very different conclusions from those of Durkheim.

12. That I felt obliged to justify the exclusion of such interests from a book on suicide can itself be seen as an indication of the extent to which it is those interests, rather than suicide as a research topic, which have dominated the suicide problem in sociology. In other words, the omission of further discussion of them seemed to be an accountable matter for which grounds had to be given. This implies a recognition that a suicide researcher would normally be expected to direct his work to those interests, and that failure to do so stands in need of some justification.

13. Exempt from this general charge of 'unhelpfulness' is Douglas and others whose work is discussed in Chapter 4. As will be argued there, however, their contributions were not as 'helpful' as was initially envisaged.

NOTES TO CHAPTER 3

1. That so many coroners have been ready to give researchers access to their records is itself a point of some interest, as it would appear that there are considerable differences of opinion among British coroners about the appropriateness of such a practice. When the University of Essex was founded, for example, the County Coroner offered to open his records to any researcher with a serious interest in suicide, and these provide the basis for some of the subsequent analyses in this book. His line was that he regarded his work as important for medical research and that it seemed a waste of resources that such an extensive collection of data as is to be found in his records should remain unexploited by scientists. By contrast, another coroner whom I approached for permission to look at the records refused on the grounds that they contained so much detailed and confidential information about local people that it would be undesirable to risk releasing them. On a national scale, the Coroners' Society, the professional association to which all coroners belong, has found it necessary to institute special procedures for 'vetting' research requests in the face of an immense demand from would-be researchers, and my own experience with these procedures is discussed further in Chapter 5.4 below.

2. This and subsequent remarks on research being conducted by Barraclough at the Medical Research Council Clinical Psychiatry Research Unit at Chichester are based on personal communications from and discussions with Brian Barraclough and other members of the Unit's staff, mainly in 1969.

3. This may seem to be a rather trivial distinction with only minimal heuristic uses. I have two main justifications for wanting to establish the point, however, the first being that a central theme of the book is the problematic character of definitions of suicide. As all the studies derived from official sources are necessarily affected by official definitions, it seems important that the discussion should not be limited only to those which focus on the manipulation of published official statistics. The second justification for the distinction is that ploys such as those used by Breed and Barraclough are often cited in discussions with other suicidologists as 'good' or 'adequate' solutions to any problems there might be. Alternatively, it can be claimed

that studies are not based on official statistics but on official records in a bid to protect such works against any general critical statements made about the uses of official statistics.

4. This observation is limited to 'conscientious researchers' on the grounds that the vast majority of studies of this sort do no more than pay lip service to the problems as a preliminary to getting on to the business of doing analyses. As Kitsuse and Cicourel (1963, p. 133) put it:

   It is evident . . . that inappropriate or not, sociologists, including Merton himself, do make use of the official statistics after a few conventional words of caution concerning the 'unreliability' of such statistics.

5. These observations are based on the research experiences of the author while a member of the staff of the Home Office Research Unit, 1966–67.

6. Notable exceptions where sociologists have addressed the problem of attempted suicide are J. Wilkins and I. Goffman (1966) and (1967). These are discussed further in Chapter 4.2 below.

7. Experts in quantitative methodology (e.g. Selvin, 1957) are exceedingly critical of the cavalier way in which sociologists have been ready to use procedures of statistical inference.

8. This is, of course, the central claim of the ethnomethodologists, whose work is considered in more detail in Chapter 8.

9. This is not to say that there has been no reaction to the studies by Cicourel and others, which pose serious questions for traditional approaches to officially derived data. The point is that the replies avoid dealing with these kinds of issues and focus on the problems discussed in section 3.2.

10. This characterization of the way in which some sociologists have responded to the official statistics problem is, of course, extremely oversimplified and hence may appear exaggerated. I would, however, wish to maintain that it is a locatable theme in certain writings on deviance. In Criminology it is to be found in Chapman (1968) and Quinney (1970). See also the special issue of the journal *Catalyst* (1971) on 'Crime, Law and the State'. The theme is also in evidence in the writings on mental illness by the 'Anti-psychiatrists' (e.g. R. D. Laing, 1967). With respect to these and other areas of deviance, such arguments have been regularly expressed in discussions at the meetings of the National Deviancy Conference (see the *Register of Abstracts 1968–72*, National Deviancy Conference, mimeo, 1973).

    I have chosen to present these concerns in truncated form as my purpose is not to examine this response to the official statistics in detail, but rather to compare it with the responses already characterized as studies of the social organization of rate producing processes and ethnographies respectively.

11. It may be noted that even so vehement an advocate of participant observation as Polsky has to admit that there may be serious problems involved in doing such studies with certain categories of deviants, who are in conflict with official agencies (Polsky, 1967, pp. 115–147).

12. The shorthand term 'revisionist' is adopted here for convenience. 'Interactionist-revisionists' might have been more appropriate though it is rather cumbersome to qualify as a shorthand term. The difference between my use of the term 'revisionist' and that of Sudnow (1965) should also be noted.

13. It is of course difficult to say exactly who comprises the new 'discipline' of

suicidology. What is clear from the bibliographical work conducted during the present work, however, is that sociologists represent only a tiny proportion of the authors of papers and other works on suicide. Very few appear at the conferences organized by the International Association for Suicide Prevention, and the officers of that association are almost exclusively trained in psychology, psychiatry or medicine.

14. A personal communication to Professor Kessel in 1967 failed to obtain any further elaboration. His reason was that enough had already been said by Stengel to endanger the confidentiality of his source of information. A comparative study of the Scottish and English systems of sudden death registration is, however, currently being conducted in Edinburgh under the direction of Dr Norman Kreitman (personal communication, 1971).

15. In addition to those cited in this section, an investigation on behalf of the WHO has been conducted in the Department of Psychiatry at the University of Manchester under the direction of Professor Kessel.

16. Part of this discussion also appears in Atkinson (1973).

17. This was an area I had become interested in independently of Douglas, and on which I was working during the early stages of the present research, shortly before his work began to be published. Just as Douglas's discussion of the problem seems to construe the official statistics problem as one of accuracy, so also was my early work addressed to that issue (e.g. Atkinson, 1968). In that paper I too had suggested that suicide rates may be determined by rates of concealment, which in turn might be determined by social integration. By so doing, however, one is still left with a variant of Durkheimian theory in which it could be claimed that all one has done is to propose that certain other 'intervening variables' are at work. The similarity between that formulation and Durkheim's was first pointed out to me by David Lockwood (personal communication, 1969).

18. For the most part there has been an almost total lack of reference to Douglas's work among suicidologists outside sociology. One psychiatric researcher told me he could not make sense of the book and that he was telling colleagues that it was not worth taking the trouble to read it on those grounds. Of the sociological suicide researchers cited below, none has devoted more than a page to a consideration of Douglas's thesis.

NOTES TO CHAPTER 4

1. As was noted in the previous chapter, there have been no studies and indeed would be great difficulties involved in doing such studies, which attempt to study suicide by means of participant observation, an important methodological weapon in the hands of adherents to the sequential approach. It is also the case that one of the studies considered below shows no familiarity whatsoever with the works of Becker, Lemert or any other proponent of the sequential approach, but nevertheless has some important things to say about the role of labelling in the suicide process (A. L. Kobler and E. Stotland, 1964).

2. This discussion is based on a paper (Atkinson, 1968) which represented an early attempt in the present study to move from the literature to empirical

research. It led to a number of false starts, and some of the reasons for this have already been dealt with in the previous chapter where I suggest that the paper misconstrues the problem of official statistics. There are also a number of other serious mistakes in it which will become evident in later parts of the book. Lest it seem that I am giving my own work too much attention, I should point out that I am informed that it is or has been used fairly widely for teaching purposes, and that requests for permission to reprint it have been and are still being received (e.g. Giddens, 1971). This wider circulation of it seems to make the identification of its errors all the more important.

3. This observation is based on my own experiences of trying to obtain access to a mental hospital situation in which it might have been possible to follow up the kind of study done by Kobler and Stotland. One of the biggest problems a sociologist has in this field is accounting for his interest in mental hospitals and in suicide. Psychiatrists and nurses typically have only a hazy conception of what sociologists do and, in so far as they have any idea, it tends to exclude mental illness and hospitals from what they take to be the proper interests of sociologists. Additionally, the kind of detailed analysis which I was interested in doing is likely to lead to the invocation of medical ethics and the guarding of confidentiality of patients. Without any other official sponsorship other than being a member of a University department, it is almost impossible to overcome such difficulties unless one is lucky enough to gain the confidence of some influential person in the hospital. With sponsorship, the task is much easier, as I was to discover in some related research I did which was financed by the SSRC (SSRC Grant HR/1491: 'Community Reactions to Deviance'). The sociological literature on mental illness and medical sociology from the U.S.A. would suggest that the situation is more favourable in that country than in Britain, though Julius Roth considers that even there it is becoming more difficult for sociologists to gain such access (personal communication, 1971). One reason for this may be that such access can lead to 'exposures' and critical analyses such as that by Goffman (1961). If doctors wish to avoid the adverse attention such works may bring them, it is not difficult to understand why they are likely to continue to guard their domain of interest from sociologists.

4. This observation is again based partly on early attempts to start a study like that referred to in the previous note. It is also a general criticism which can be levelled against much of labelling theory. That is, there seems to have been a good deal more attention given to the fact of labelling and *that* it gets done by certain persons to others rather than in *how* the ascriptions get done and *how* the categories of deviance being used are assembled in the first place. For a much neglected discussion of this and related issues see Sacks (1963).

5. Patients diagnosed as suffering from depressive illnesses, for example, are often treated as out-patients, admission to the hospital possibly resulting subsequently from a suicidal attempt. In other words, one of the criteria which may be used by hospital staff to categorize patients as suicidal is a previous, and particularly a recent, suicide attempt. For these patients at least, the interactions which take place following admission may be of

minor significance as far as their subsequent actions are concerned compared with those prior to admission.

6. 'Community Reactions to Deviance', SSRC Grant HR/1491.

7. Large numbers of people ask my opinion of this adage on learning of my research interest in suicide. Further evidence of its widespread use in our culture is given by Stengel's (1964) discussion of it. He regards its use as widespread enough to argue against it and to counsel its more public debunking.

8. Estimates of the ratio between completed and attempted suicides vary widely. Stengel (1964, p. 103) says, with respect to England and Wales, 'only a minority of suicidal acts, one in six or eight, have a fatal outcome'. He does not, however, say anything about how such a figure was or could possibly be arrived at. There is no official register of suicide attempts, it is not known how many are dealt with by General Practitioners without referring them to hospitals, and there is presumably not even any way in which it could be known how many never get as far as a doctor. In short, if accuracy is taken as an important problem the difficulties connected with the official statistics on *completed* suicides would shade into insignificance compared with those which would be involved in attempting to arrive at an accurate count of non-fatal suicidal acts.

9. One of the ambiguities in Firth's study, about which he is quite explicit, is whether the actions he refers to are to be regarded as 'suicidal' or as 'risk-taking'. This is a distinction in which there has been a good deal of interest on the part of non-sociological suicide researchers, and again is one which sociologists have almost totally ignored.

10. As was noted in Chapter 3, this observation can be extended into a more general critique of interactionist alternatives to 'positivist' studies of deviance. Thus the latter are typically accused of being deterministic (e.g. by Matza, 1964) and yet what is offered as an alternative is still directed to accounting for particular patterns of deviance. For a recent discussion of this tension between deterministic and voluntaristic theories, see Coulter (1973).

11. This was one of the things which I originally understood Douglas to be getting at, and is evident in some of my earlier papers (e.g. Atkinson, 1971)..

12. Douglas, 1967, pp. 284–319. The types of meanings are: 'Suicide as a Means of Transforming the Soul from this World to the Other World' (pp. 284–304), 'Suicidal Actions as a Means of Achieving Fellow-Feeling' (pp. 304–10), 'Suicidal Actions as a Means of Getting Revenge' (pp. 310–19).

NOTES TO CHAPTER 5

1. As was noted in Chapter 3, Scotland has different legal provisions for the registration of sudden death, and the official statistics are collected and published separately from those for England and Wales. The attention in this book is exclusively directed to this latter system, as the attempt to examine and possibly compare two seems premature when no detailed studies of single systems for registering sudden deaths have been conducted (c.f. the critique presented in Chapter 3.4 above).

2. The origins of this remain obscure, but probably relate to the apparent reason why suicide was defined as a felony in the first place. This occurred because the property of convicted felons used to be transferred to the Crown, so that suicide could be resorted to before trial in order to prevent the crown from obtaining the property. By making suicide a felony, the Crown was effectively able to put a stop to such avoidance strategies and hence it seems possible that these failed attempted murderers could also be posthumously penalized by defining their deaths as suicides. That the origins of 'felo de se' had to do with property rights rather than religion or any claims that there was a consensus as to the criminal nature of suicide would no doubt be of special interest to anyone interested in conducting a Marxian analysis of how changes in the law come about.

3. The 1961 *Suicide Act* does include a definition of suicide which is close to the one we deduced above: 'Felo de se or suicide is, where a man of the age of discretion, and compos mentis, voluntarily kills himself by stabbing, poison or any other way, and was a felony at common law. . . . This section abrogates that rule of law.' (*Halsbury's Statutes of England*, 3rd Edition; London: Butterworth, 1969, Vol. 8, p. 519). Whether that abrogation includes the legal definition or not is a problem which is not explicitly answered.

4. See, for example, the table on pp. 386–7 of the 'Broderick Report': *Report of the Committee on Death Certification and Coroners* (London: H.M.S.O., 1971 (Cmnd. 4810)).

5. At the time this question was asked, I had not made my interest in the problem known to him. The dialogue reported here is a reconstruction written immediately following the encounter.

6. This widely used rider was 'borrowed' by coroners from the *Infanticide Act* of 1938, which includes it in the definition of infanticide: 'Where a woman by any wilful act or omission causes the death of her child, being a child under the age of 12 months, but at the time of the act or omission *the balance of her mind was disturbed* by reason of her not having fully recovered from the effect of giving birth to the child or by reason of the effect of lactation consequent upon the birth of the child . . .' (*Halsbury's Statutes*, 2nd Edition, London: Butterworths, 1948, Vol. 5, p. 1120 – my emphasis). The attraction of the phraseology for coroners seems to be that it is distinct from a direct legal pronouncement of insanity or ascription of mental illness. Thus it may be used to lessen any possible imputation of responsibility for what happened on the part of significant others of the deceased, without simultaneously branding the deceased as mad (to which the significant others might object with equal force). Coroners appear to vary in their use of it. Some, like the one interviewed here, add it in almost every case while others discriminate between types of cases for which they regard it as suitable and those for which it is not suitable. One coroner, who was exclusively trained in law, told me that he never uses it precisely because it is legally unnecessary. He also had a 'lay' interest in psychiatry which had led him to the view that it was a 'fairly meaningless phrase anyway'.

7. As was noted in Chapter 3.4, suicidologists do make claims about the differential efficiency of coroners. Seiden (1967, p. 4), for example, argues that the San Francisco coroner's office is particularly efficient in its registration procedures: 'There is a distinctive attribute which differentiates San

Francisco from almost any other municipality. This attribute is the extremely high, essentially universal autopsy rate.'

8. These descriptions were from a coroner's officer, a pathologist and a clerk in the police records office respectively. A Superintendent of the local police force also made many complementary remarks about him. In passing it is interesting to note what such persons regard as evidence of a 'bad' coroner. The 'X town' one referred to was regarded as 'a terror' by the speaker because he only came to town two days a week and insisted on holding inquests on those days. The reason why that was a 'nuisance' was that those were the days that two local breweries delivered beer to the pubs in the town, and publicans, it emerged, were the coroner's officer's main source of recruitment for inquest juries ('They're the only men free to come during the day, and women get too upset at inquests.'). Hence the coroner's town visiting habits posed severe practical problems for his officer, which led to the latter's view of him as a 'bad coroner'.

9. This discussion relies heavily on *Medico-Legal Investigation of Deaths in the Community* (report prepared by the Private Practice Committee of the British Medical Association), London: B.M.A., 1964.

10. Unlike the other quotations from respondents to this point in the chapter, this one is from a tape-recorded interview which was transcribed verbatim. It was conducted for a BBC/Open University radio programme on the sociology of suicide.

11. Detailed accounts of these are to be found in Havard (1960), the *Broderick Report* (1971) and *Deaths in the Community* (B.M.A., 1964).

12. The proportion of all deaths reported to coroners has increased steadily from 11.2% in 1928 to 21.4% in 1959 (B.M.A., 1964, p. 8).

13. The conclusions of the B.M.A.'s (1964) special committee were very critical of current procedures and such pressures seem to have been partly instrumental in the setting up of the Broderick Committee on Death Certification and Coroners. That investigation, however, only recommended very minor changes in the present system, such as making post-mortems a more routine procedure and giving coroners greater discretion as to when to hold an inquest (see *Broderick Report*, 1971, pp. 346–350). The coroner's officer with whom I did participant observation, however, considered that the proposed changes would make little or no difference to the work of his coroner's jurisdiction. Post-mortems were routine there, and the coroner believed inquests to be important ways of publicly removing doubt, irrespective of how 'clear' the post-mortem conclusions were.

14. These, together with special provisions for cases where embalming is proposed, are intended to prevent the premature destruction of or interference with the body prior to the completion of investigations. Burials, of course, provide for the possibility of exhumation should that become necessary. Again, these issues are given extensive treatment in Harvard (1960), B.M.A. (1964) and the *Broderick Report* (1971).

15. These figures may suggest that my earlier conclusion (Atkinson, 1971, pp. 173–4) that 'at the majority of inquests . . . it is almost a two horse race' between suicides and accidents is something of an exaggeration. The proportion of inquests resulting in verdicts of either accident or suicide, however, is sufficiently high to give that statement some justification,

though I do plead 'poetic licence' in that authors were invited to write in a quasi-journalistic style for the book (Cohen, 1971) in which the earlier paper appeared.

16. Lawyers sometimes do appear at inquests and may question witnesses. This is most likely to happen in cases where legal proceedings are pending following a road accident, where some kind of negligence is suspected or where insurance interests are involved. They are allowed to question witnesses, and anything said on oath by a witness at an inquest may be noted down and used by lawyers at another court. Because of this, police witnesses to road accidents, for example, are noticeably loathe to commit themselves definitely in replying to lawyers at inquests lest they jeopardize the chances of a successful prosecution in another court. I am grateful to the coroner's officer with whom I did participant observation for explaining this situation to me. In his view the lawyer's presence was typically 'a nuisance', as it usually meant that inquests lasted much longer than was necessary.

17. I have seen a coroner's officer talking to obviously distressed relatives for up to an hour after the end of an inquest. He told me that he regarded this consoling of the bereaved as a very important part of his work.

18. A full list of the jurisdictions together with certain statistical information on each is contained in Appendix 3 of the *Broderick Report*, 1971, pp. 375–381.

19. I am grateful to Douglas Benson for drawing this feature of studies of official statistics derived from the police to my attention.

20. I say here that the official procedures can always be made to seem inadequate because so long as the police do not devote equal attention to all matters reported to them, it will indeed always be possible to propose that more attention be given to some particular type of offence. Much of the sociological interest in 'white-collar crime' seems to involve this kind of recommendation, and, if the police diverted more resources in that direction from say burglary, then presumably it would be open to some other sociologist to come along and propose a further redirection of resources back to burglary.

21. That is, the analysis reported on in the next chapter had already begun to take shape on the basis of preliminary talks with coroners.

NOTES TO CHAPTER 6

1. This part of the research was not started until 1972, and that late start means that only intermittent references to it are made in the present study. For further details of the problems of obtaining the necessary access, see Appendix II in Atkinson (1972).

2. J. M. Atkinson, 'Societal Reactions to Suicide: The Role of Coroners' Definitions', in S. Cohen (Ed.), 1971, pp. 165–181. The difficulties of writing the research after parts had been published, which were referred to in the introduction, were particularly acute in this present chapter. The published version would not, in its entirety, have 'fitted' given some of the arguments presented in earlier chapters, yet some of the discussion and findings seemed worth repeating at this point in the book. It was also the case that the previously published version dealt with preliminary conclusions based on relatively little evidence. In preparing this chapter, therefore, I

have kept parts of the original evidence and discussion, which are mainly presented in quotes and have added more empirical evidence in support of the original arguments.
3. This interpretation depends, of course, on reading 'ticker' as 'heart' and hence the statement as one about the writer's deteriorating heart condition.
4. This is dealt with in more detail later in the chapter.
5. As with all other extracts and examples given in the book, names, addresses, place-names, dates and any other feature which could lead to the identification of persons referred to have been changed.
6. This information was given to me by the Coroner's Officer with whom I was doing participant observation.
7. Perhaps the best documented examination of the way questioning the obvious typically leads, to angry and tense situations are Garfinkel's celebrated 'experiments'. See his *Studies in Ethnomethodology*, 1967, pp. 41–4.
8. That these conclusions were arrived at on the basis of much less extensive research than that reported on in this chapter may of course be taken as a sign that it was published prematurely. With that view I am inclined to agree, as the published version had originally been written as a preliminary working paper on 'pilot' investigations. It was presented in the then relatively informal atmosphere of the National Deviancy Symposium at the University of York in January, 1970. Afterwards, I was asked by the editor of the book in which it appeared if I would make it available for the book, and the attractions of the offer outweighed my doubts about the 'preliminary' nature of the empirical work on which the analysis was based.

NOTES TO CHAPTER 7

1. See L. T. Wilkins, *Social Policy, Action and Research*, Englewood Cliffs, New Jersey: Prentice Hall, 1964. Examples of the application of the Deviance Amplification Model to particular types of deviance are S. Cohen, 'Mods, Rockers and the rest: Community Reactions to Juvenile Delinquency', *Howard Journal*, 1967, *12*, pp. 121–130, and J. Young, *The Drugtakers*, London: MacGibbon and Kee, 1971.
2. This section is based on an earlier paper (Atkinson, 1970b). I am indebted to Alistair Blunt for assistance in coding the data, and to Olivia Ross who discussed some of the same data in an undergraduate dissertation.
3. There is wide variation in the extent of coroners' use of post-mortems in their investigations. The special sub-committee of the British Medical Association reported that the proportion of coroners' cases on which post-mortems were conducted ranged from 32% to 95%. See *Deaths in the Community*, London: British Medical Association, 1964, pp. 24–25.
4. A detailed list of these is to be found in Appendix II to Atkinson (1972).
5. In Edinburgh, the suicide rate for women has now just overtaken that for men. Personal communication from Dr Norman Kreitman, 1971.
6. See for example the discussions presented in the session 'Suicide in Adolescents and Youth', in N. L. Farberow (Ed.), 1968, pp. 356–395.
7. In the original paper on which this section is based, for example, an 'accident-suicide ratio' was computed for different modes of dying, and it was argued that these provided a way of constructing a rank order of modes of

death with typical suicides at one end, typical accidents at the other and more 'equivocal' modes in between. My increasing scepticism of such quantitative procedures subsequently led me to see this and other parts of the original analysis as providing the analysis with a spurious appearance of 'objectivity'.

8. See for example W. W. Sharrock's discussion of 'The Problem of Order' in P. Worsley et al., 1970. Comparing conflict and consensus theories of order, Sharrock shows how both attend to similar data and use similar methods so that the difference between them is essentially an *interpretive* one which cannot simply be resolved by reference to any clear warranting procedures.

9. That study was directed to Burnley newspapers, the interest being stimulated by Stengel and Cook's claim (1961) that there were special reasons for a high suicide rate in that town.

10. There was no special reason why 'sampling' was stopped when the collection reached 100 other than that it seemed 'enough' to provide a basis for analysis. In retrospect, a more detailed study of fewer stories might have yielded a more interesting analysis. I am indebted to Cathy Gash for assistance in collecting these reports.

11. Although sociologists and philosophers debate about what constitutes an explanation with reference, for example, to distinctions between motives, reasons and causes, I would argue that the findings of this present research show that at a common sense level of discourse, such things are invoked as providing some sort of adequate explanation of suicide. In Garfinkel's terms, suicide is very much an 'accountable' matter for which grounds have to be found which render it 'rationally accountable for all practical purposes'. In the analysis which follows, then, I am suggesting that, in doing that, the newspaper reports offer or imply 'explanations' of a 'for all practical purposes' kind which posit relationships very similar to those found in the literature of suicidology.

12. The place names and other identifying features have been changed to protect anonymity in both the headlines and the subsequent story extracts. This may seem a strange practice given the public nature of newspaper reports and the low probability of any of the persons involved seeing this study. So long as there is even that small possibility, however, I see no reason why persons should have to suffer further publicity being given to past trauma. Nor do the changes affect the analysis presented here in any substantial way.

13. In one post-mortem study of consecutive suicides (Stewart, 1960) it was found that only one third of the sample were 'healthy'.

14. Barraclough (1970, pp. 7–8) reports that half his sample of 100 suicides had seen a doctor within one week of their deaths and that 83% had seen a doctor within three months of their last medical contact.

15. Academic psychiatry's abiding concern for the relationship between mental illness and specific sorts of mental illness is epitomized in the following remarks by Peter Sainsbury (1968, pp. 6–7):

> Let us now return from the study of population and rates, and proceed to the other, and to the psychiatrist more interesting, approach to the problem of suicide and affective illness: the study of cases. These may be coroners' cases, or attempted suicides, or depressed patients who are

followed up. The questions we can expect clinical data from these sources to answer are: (a) to what extent are suicides suffering from psychiatric disorders and what proportion of them have a recognizable depressive illness? (b) what is the risk of a depressed patient committing suicide? and (c) what clinical or environmental characteristics of depressives are associated with a risk of suicide?

16. Stengel (1964, p. 52), for example, has noted that 'Towards the end of a period of depressive illness, when the depressive mood still persists, but when initiative is returning, the risk of suicide is particularly high.'

17. That is to say, a sort of an answer has here been provided to the research problem of how some deaths get categorized as suicides in the sense that we can say that officials and others do this by analysing the event of the death and the biographical circumstances of the deceased by reference to common sense theories about suicide. If such a generalized conclusion were deemed adequate, then it would be unclear as to whether the issue was worth pursuing further and thus the research would indeed appear to be at an end.

NOTES TO CHAPTER 8

1. I owe a very great debt to D. R. Watson for convincing me that Garfinkel and his colleagues were not merely interactionists who wrote in a rather obscure and incomprehensible way. Had it not been for his almost daily lunch-time debates with the professional 'theorists' and 'philosophers' at Lancaster, I might never have been convinced.

2. In both this and the subsequent section the problem of summarizing the central ideas of Garfinkel and Sacks (in particular) is much more severe than is normally the case in such enterprises in sociology. A major reason for this is that neither has divorced programmatic statements from detailed reference to empirical materials in any extended form. Thus it is extremely difficult to do justice to their case without reproducing the (very extensive) data contained in their studies.

3. This strong emphasis on doing empirical work, which is so central to ethnomethodology, was one of its main attractions for me. Thus the research reported in the thesis was originally stimulated by an interest in 'improving' data and, as the research proceeded, a continual problem was the lack of clear direction as to how central methodological issues could be solved.

4. Though this discussion of correspondence theory was greatly influenced by unpublished papers by Garfinkel, the formulation used here is to be regularly found in published ethnomethodological writings.

5. In ethnomethodological terms, a member is one with a command of the natural language (see H. Garfinkel and H. Sacks, 1970, p. 342).

6. See especially H. Garfinkel (1967a, pp. 24–34) on the problem of literal description. The concern is also prominent in the previous cited studies by Sacks. An early and much neglected paper by him on description is 'Sociological Description' (1963). The most recent and probably the clearest of all his analyses of how recognizable descriptions get done is 'On the Analysability of Stories by Children' (1972a).

7. Remark by Garfinkel in reply to a question about his interest in Parsons at

a lecture in the Department of Sociology, University of Manchester, 1973. It may also be noted that a considerable corpus of unpublished work by Garfinkel is directly concerned with Parsons' approach to the problem of order including his 'The Perception of Other: a Study in Social Order' (1952), and the 'Parsons' Primer' unpublished draft of a manuscript based on notes from Garfinkel's course 'Sociology 251', University of California at Los Angeles, 1959 (Spring).

8. An alternative way of coping with commonsense theorizing, which has not been elaborated in this thesis, is to claim that it is a manifestation of some 'ideological' stance. In general it may be noted that this way of repairing indexical expressions involves sociologists in an unquestioning use of the documentary method (see Garfinkel, 1967a, pp. 40–65). Thus utterances are recorded by the sociologist, who then makes the claim that they 'stand for', are 'manifestations of' some general underlying pattern (i.e. this or that 'ideology'). That the issue has not been dealt with in any detail in the present context reflects a further feature of the inadequacy of such an approach, namely that the ability to make 'ideological' inferences from selected utterances is easier with respect to some subject matters than others. Thus with respect to suicide as a topic, the imposition of some plausible interpretation by reference to ideology would require great imagination on the part of the person doing it. It is also not at all clear to me how such an argument might be shown to be relevant to the task of categorizing deaths as suicide.

9. This view of their work is implicit in their frequent inclusion in 'Interactionist' textbooks and Readers. It is not unusual to find Cicourel's book is listed under the heading 'Interactionist Studies' in guides to further reading (e.g. L. Taylor, 1971). The tendency to see such studies as 'the same as' interactionists is also very evident in Denzin (1971). The mistake is also one to which I subscribed throughout much of the work reported in this thesis.

10. Given the way Sacks formulated the problem and the date at which the paper was published, it may be regarded as somewhat surprising that it was apparently overlooked by Douglas (1967). It may also be regarded as an important omission from my earlier search through the literature.

11. I am indebted to D. R. Watson for this clarification of the notion of reflexivity with reference to the idea of 'monitoring' descriptions.

12. No attempt is made here to elaborate or summarize these analyses for, as was noted earlier (see Note 2 above) there are severe problems in doing so in any adequate way without copying out the entire analysis. Thus, the various rules of application of M.C.D.'s are presented by Sacks with direct reference to empirical materials, without which their sense would not be readily apparent.

Select Bibliography

ACHILLE-DELMAS, F. (1932) *Psychologie Pathologique du Suicide*. Paris: Alcan.

ANDERSON, N. (1923) *The Hobo*. Chicago: Chicago University Press.

ATKINSON, J. M. (1968) 'On the Sociology of Suicide', *Sociological Review*. 16: 83–92.

ATKINSON, J. M. (1969) 'Suicide and the Student', *Universities Quarterly*. 23: 213–224.

ATKINSON, J. M. (1970a) 'Old Age and Suicide'. Paper presented at the Annual Conference of the Samaritans, Exeter.

ATKINSON, J. M. (1970b) The Registration of Sudden Deaths: A Preliminary Analysis of 140 Verdicts of Suicide and Accidental Death. Paper presented at the *B.S.A. Medical Sociology Conference*, Blackpool.

ATKINSON, J. M. (1971) Societal Reactions to Suicide: The Role of Coroners' Definitions. In COHEN (Ed.) 1971: 165–91.

ATKINSON, J. M. (1972) Suicide and the Social Organisation of Sudden Death. Ph.D. Dissertation, University of Essex, Department of Sociology.

ATKINSON, J. M. (1973) Status Integration, Suicide and Pseudo-Science. *Sociology* 4: 251–264.

ATKINSON, J. M. (1974) Versions of Deviance. *Sociological Review* 22: 616–625.

BAGLEY, C. (1970) Causes and Prevention of Repeated Attempted Suicide. In Fox (ed.), 1970: 96–101.

BAGLEY, C. (1972) Authoritarianism, Status Integration and Suicide. *Sociology* 6: 395–404.

BARRACLOUGH, B., NELSON, B., SAINSBURY, P. (1967) The Diagnostic Classification and Psychiatric Treatment of 25 Suicides. In Farberow, N. L. 1967: 61–66.

BARRACLOUGH, B. (1970) Suicide in Old Age. Mimeo, M.R.C. Clinical Psychiatry Research Unit, Graylingwell Hospital, Chichester, Sussex.

BATCHELOR, I. R. C., NAPIER, M. B. (1953) Attempted Suicide in Old Age. *British Medical Journal* 1953(2): 1186–1190.

BECKER, H. S. (1963) *Outsiders: Studies in the Sociology of Deviance*. New York: The Free Press.

BECKER, H. S. (Ed.). (1964) *The Other Side*. New York: The Free Press.

BERGER, P., LUCKMANN, T. (1966) *The Social Construction of Reality*. Garden City: Doubleday, 1966.

BLALOCK, H. M. (1964) *Causal Inferences in Non-Experimental Research*. Chapel Hill, North Carolina: University of North Carolina Press.

BLALOCK, H. M., BLALOCK, A. B. (Eds.). (1968) *Methodology in Social Research*. New York: McGraw Hill.

BLUM, A. F., McHUGH, P. (1971) The Social Ascription of Motives. *American Sociological Review* 36: 98–109.

BLUMER, H. (1969) *Symbolic Interactionism.* Englewood Cliffs, New Jersey: Prentice Hall.

BOWDEN, R. (1968) 'A New Look at Correlation Analysis'. In Blalock and Blalock, 1968: 199–235.

BOX, S. (1971) *Deviance, Reality and Society.* London: Holt, Rinehart and Winston.

BREED, W. (1963) Occupational Mobility and Suicide among White Males. *American Sociological Review* 28: 179–188.

BRITISH MEDICAL ASSOCIATION. (1964) *Medico-Legal Investigation of Deaths in the Community* (report prepared by the Private Practice Committee of the B.M.A.) London: B.M.A.

Broderick Report. (1971) *Report of the Committee on Death Certification and Coroners.* London: Her Majesty's Stationery Office. (Cmnd. 4810).

CARSON, W. G., WILES, P., (Eds.). (1971) Crime and *Deliquency in Britain.* London: Martin Robertson.

CAVAN, R. S. (1928) *Suicide.* Chicago: Chicago University Press.

CHAPMAN, D. (1968) *Sociology and the Stereotype of the Criminal,* London: Tavistock.

CICOUREL, A. V., KITSUSE, J. I. (1963) *The Educational Decision Makers.* Indianapolis: Bobbs Merrill.

CICOUREL, A. V. (1964) *Method and Measurement in Sociology.* New York: The Free Press.

CICOUREL, A. V. (1968) *The Social Organisation of Juvenile Justice.* New York: John Wiley and Son.

CLINARD, M. B., (Ed.). (1964) *Anomie and Deviant Behaviour.* New York: The Free Press.

COHEN, A. K. (1966) *Deviance and Control,* Englewood Cliffs, New Jersey: Prentice Hall.

COHEN, J. (1961) A Study of Suicide Pacts. *Medico-Legal Journal.* 29: 144–151.

COHEN, S. (1967) Mods, Rockers and the Rest: Community Reactions to Juvenile Delinquency. *Howard Journal* 12: 121–130.

COHEN, S., (Ed.). (1971) Images of Deviance. Harmondsworth, Middlesex: Penguin.

COHEN, S. (1972) *Folk Devils and Moral Panics.* London: MacGibbon and Kee (St Albans, Herts: Paladin, 1973).

COLEMAN, J. S. (1964) *Introduction to Mathematical Sociology.* New York: The Free Press.

COULSON, M., RIDDELL, D. (1970) *Approaching Sociology.* London: Routledge and Kegan Paul.

COULTER, J. (1973) What's wrong with the New Criminology? *Sociological Review.* 22: 119–135.

CRESSEY, D. R. (1951) Criminological Research and the Definition of Crimes. *American Journal of Sociology.* 61: 546–551.

DALGAARD, J. (1962) Om International Sammenligning af Selvmordsfrekvenser (Critical Remarks on International Comparisions of Suicide Rates.) *Sociologiske Meddelelser.* 7: 53–60.

DELONG, W. B., ROBBINS, E. (1961) The Communication of Suicidal Intent prior to Psychiatric Hospitalization. *American Journal of Psychiatry*, 117: 695–705.

DENZIN, N. (1971) Symbolic Interactionism and Ethnomethodology. In Douglas (Ed.) 1971: 259–284.

DE FLEURY, M. (1924) *L'Angoisse Humaine*. Paris: Editions de France.

DOREIAN, P., STOCKMAN, N. (1969) A Critique of the Multidimensional Approach to Stratification. *Sociological Review*, 17: 47–65.

DOUGLAS, J. D. (1965) *The Sociological Study of Suicide*. Ph.D. Dissertation, Princeton University, Department of Sociology.

DOUGLAS, J. D. (1966). The Sociological Analysis of the Social Meanings of Suicide *European Journal of Sociology*, 7: 249–298.

DOUGLAS, J. D. (1967) *The Social Meanings of Suicide*. Princeton, New Jersey: Princeton University Press.

DOUGLAS, J. D., (Ed.). (1970a) *Deviance and Respectability*. New York: Basic Books.

DOUGLAS, J. D., (Ed.). (1970b) *Observations of Deviance*. New York: Random House.

DOUGLAS, J. D., (Ed.). (1971) *Understanding Everyday Life*. London: Routledge and Kegan Paul.

DURKHEIM, E. (1897) *Le Suicide*. Paris Alcan. (English translation cited as Durkheim, 1952).

DURKHEIM, E. (1938) *The Rules of Sociological Method*. New York: The Free Press.

DURKHEIM, E. (1952) *Suicide*. English translation by J. A. Spaulding and G. Simpson with an introduction by G. Simpson. London: Routledge and Kegan Paul.

DURKHEIM, E. (1954) *The Division of Labour in Society*. New York: The Free Press.

DURKHEIM, E. (1954) *The Elementary Forms of the Religious Life*. New York: The Free Press.

EMMET, D., MACINTYRE, A. (Eds.). (1970) *Sociological Theory and Philosophical Analysis*. London: Macmillan.

ESQUIROL, E. (1838) *Des Maladies Mentales*. Paris.

FARBEROW, N. L. (Ed.). (1967) *Proceedings of the Fourth International Conference for Suicide Prevention*. Los Angeles: Delmar Publishing Company.

FARBEROW, N. L., SHNEIDMAN, E. S. (Eds.). (1957) *Clues to Suicide*. New York: McGraw Hill.

FARBEROW, N. L., SHNEIDMAN, E. S. (Eds.). (1961) *The Cry for Help*. New York: McGraw Hill.

FIRTH, R. (1961) Suicide and Risk-Taking in Tikopia Society. *Psychiatry*. 24: 1–17.

FORD, R., MOSELEY, A. L. (1963) Motor Vehicular Suicides. *Journal of Criminal Law, Criminology and Police Science*. 54: 257–259.

FOX, R. (Ed.). (1970) *Proceedings of the 5th International Conference for Suicide Prevention*. Vienna: International Association for Suicide Prevention.

GALTUNG, J. (1969) On the Structure of Creativity. Mimeo, University of Essex, Department of Sociology.

GARDNER, E. A., BAHN, A. K., MACK, M. (1954) Suicide and Psychiatric Care in the Aging. *Archives of General Psychiatry*. 10: 547–553.

GARFINKEL, H. (1952). The Perception of the Other: A Study in Social Order. Unpublished doctoral dissertation, Harvard University.

GARFINKEL, H. (1967a) *Studies in Ethnomethodology*. Englewood Cliffs, New Jersey: Prentice Hall.

GARFINKEL, H. (1967b) Practical Sociological Reasoning. Some Features in the Work of the Los Angeles Suicide Prevention Center. In Shneidman, 1967: 171–187.

GARFINKEL, H., SACKS, H. (1970) On Formal Structures of Practical Actions. In McKinney and Tiryakian (Eds.) 1970.

GERTH, H. H., MILLS, C. W. (1953) *Character and Social Structure*. New York: The Free Press.

GIBBS, J. P. (1966) *Suicide*. In Merton and Nisbet, 1966: 281–321 (for a slightly revised version see Gibbs, 1971).

GIBBS, J. P. (Ed.). (1968) *Suicide*. New York: Harper and Row.

GIBBS, J. P. (1971) Suicide. In Merton and Nisbet (Eds.).

GIBBS, J. P., MARTIN, W. T. (1964) *Status Integration and Suicide*. Eugene, Oregon: Oregon University Press.

GIDDENS, A. (1965) The Suicide Problem in French Sociology. *British Journal of Sociology*. 16: 276–295.

GIDDENS, A. (1966) A Typology of Suicide. *European Journal of Sociology*. 7: 276–295.

GIDDENS, A. (Ed.). (1971) *The Sociology of Suicide*. London: Frank Cass.

GOFFMAN, E. (1961) *Asylums*. New York: Anchor.

GOLDTHORPE, J. (1973) A Revolution in Sociology? *Sociology*. 7: 449–462.

GORDON, C., GERGE, K. J. (Eds.). (1968) *The Self in Social Interaction: Vol. 1: Classic and Contemporary Perspectives*. New York: John Wiley.

GOULDNER, A. W. (1968) The Sociologist as Partisan: Sociology and the Welfare State. *American Sociologist*. 3: 103–116.

GOULDNER, A. W. (1970) *The Coming Crisis in Western Sociology*. New York: Basic Books.

GUMPERTZ, J., HYMES, D. (Eds.). (1972) *Directions in Socio-Linguistics: The Ethnography of Communication*. New York: Holt, Rhinehart and Winston.

HALBWACHS, M. (1930) *Les Causes du Suicide*. Paris: Alcan.

HALSBURY'S Statutes of England (2nd Ed.), 1948. (3rd Ed.), 1969. London: Butterworth.

HAVARD, J. D. J. (1960) *The Detection of Secret Homicide*. London: Macmillan.

HENDIN, H. (1956) Suicide in Denmark. *Psychiatric Quarterly*. 30: 267–282.

HENDIN, H. (1962) Suicide in Sweden. *Psychiatric Quarterly*. 35: 1–28.

HENDIN, H. (1964) *Suicide and Scandinavia*. New York: Grune and Stratton.

HENRY, A. F., SHORT, J. F. (1954) *Suicide and Homicide*. New York: The Free Press.

HENSLIN, J. (1970) Guilt and Guilt Neutralization: Response and Adjustment to Suicide. In Douglas, J. D. (Ed.) 1970.

HINKLE, R. C. (1960) Durkheim in American Sociology. In Wolff 1960: 267–295.

HIRSHI, T., SELVIN, H. (1967) *Delinquency Research: An Appraisal of Analytic Methods*. New York: The Free Press.

HOOD, R., SPARKS, R. (1971) *Key Issues in Criminology*. London: Weidenfeld & Nicolson.

HUGHES, H. S. (1967) *Consciousness and Society: The Reorientation of European Social Thoughts 1890–1930.* London: MacGibbon and Kee.

INKELES, A. (1959) Personality and Social Structure. In Merton, Broom and Cottrell, 1959.

JACOBS, J. (1967) A Phenomenological Study of Suicide Notes. Social Problems. 15: 60–72.

JERVIS, SIR J. (1957) *The Office and Duties of Coroners.* (9th Ed.) Edited by Purchase, W. B. and Wollaston, H. W. London: Sweet and Maxwell.

KESSEL, W. I. N. (1965) Self Poisoning. *British Medical Journal.* (2): 1265–1270; 1336–1340.

KITSUSE, J. I., CICOUREL, A. V. (1963) A Note on the Uses of Official Statistics. *Social Problems.* 11: 131–139.

KOBLER, A. L., STOTLAND, E. (1964) *The End of Hope.* New York: The Free Press.

KRUIJT, C. S. (1965) Suicide: A Sociological and Statistical Investigation. *Sociologica Nederlandica.* 3:

KUHN, T. (1962) *The Structure of Scientific Revolutions.* Chicago: Chicago University Press.

LABOWITZ, S. (1968) Variation in Suicide Rates. In Gibbs, 1968: 57–73.

LAING, R. D. (1967) *The Politics of Experience and the Bird of Paradise.* Harmondsworth, Middlesex: Penguin.

LAZARSFELD, P. F. (1959) *Problems in Methodology.* In Merton, Broom and Cottrell, 1959: 33–78.

LEMERT, E. (1951) *Social Pathology.* New York: McGraw Hill.

LEMERT, E. (1967) *Human Deviance, Social Problems and Social Control.* Englewood Cliffs, New Jersey: Prentice Hall.

LINDESMITH, A. R., STRAUSS, A. (1949) *Social Psychology.* New York: The Dryden Press.

LUKES, S. M. (1970) *Methodological Individualism Reconsidered.* In Emmet and MacIntyre, 1970.

McCARTHY, P. D., WALSH, D. (1966) Suicide in Dublin. *British Medical Journal.* (1): 1393–1396.

McCLINTOCK, F. H., GIBSON, E. (1961) *Robbery in London.* London: MacMillan.

MacINTYRE, A. (1967) The Idea of a Social Science. *Proceedings of the Aristotelian Society.* 1967: 95–132.

McKINNEY, J. C., TIRYAKIAN, E. (Eds.). (1970) *Theoretical Sociology: Perspectives and Developments.* New York: Appleton-Century-Crofts.

MANIS, J. G., MELTZER, B. N. (Eds.), 1967. *Symbolic Interaction: A Reader in Social Psychology.* Boston: Allyn and Bacon.

MARIS, R. W. (1969) *Social Forces in Urban Suicide.* Homewood, Illinois: The Dorsey Press.

MARTIN, W. T. (1968) Survey of Theories and Research Findings. In GIBBS, 1968: 74–96.

MASARYK, T. G. (1881) *Der Selbstmord als sociale Massenerscheinung der modernen Civilisation.* Vienna. English language eds., Masaryk, 1970.

MASARYK, T. G. (1970) *Suicide and the Meaning of Civilization* (translated by W. B. Weist and R. G. Batson with an introduction by A. Giddens). Chicago: Chicago University Press.

MATZA, D. (1964) *Delinquency and Drift*. New York: John Wiley.
MATZA, D. (1969) *Becoming Deviant*. Englewood Cliffs, New Jersey: Prentice Hall.
MEAD, G. H. (1934) *Mind, Self and Society*. Chicago: Chicago University Press.
MEAD, G. H. (1964). *Selected Writings*. Indianapolis: Bobbs-Merrill.
MENNINGER, K. (1938) *Man Against Himself*. New York: Harcourt, Brace and Company.
MERTON, R. K. (1938) Social Structure and Anomie. *American Sociological Review*. 3: 672–682.
MERTON, R. K. (1956). New Perspectives for Research on Juvenile Delinquency. In Witmer and Kotinsky, 1956.
MERTON, R. K., BROOM, L., COTTRELL, L. S. (Eds.). (1959) *Sociology Today*. New York: Basic Books.
MERTON, R. K., NISBET, R. A. (Eds.). (1966, 1971) *Contemporary Social Problems*, (2nd Ed. 1966). New York: Harcourt, Brace and World. (3rd Ed. 1971; New York: Harcourt, Brace and Jovanovich.)
MOTTO, J. A. (1969) Newspaper Influence on Suicide – A Controlled Study. In R. Fox (Ed.), 1970.
NEWMAN, D. J. (1956) Pleading Guilty for Considerations: A Study of Bargain Justice. *Journal of Criminal Law, Criminology and Police Science*. 46: 780–790.
PARK, R. E., et al. (1925) *The City*. Chicago: Chicago University Press.
PARSONS, T. (1964) *Social Structure and Personality*. New York: The Free Press.
PIERCE, A. (1960) Durkheim and Functionalism. In Wolff, 1960.
POLSKY, N. (1967) *Hustlers, Beats and Others*. Chicago: Aldine Publishing Company.
POLSKY, N. (1971) *Hustlers, Beats and Others*. Harmondsworth, Middlesex: Penguin.
POPPER, K. R. (1945) *The Open Society and its Enemies*. London: Routledge.
PORTERFIELD, A. L. (1968) The Problem of Suicide. In Gibbs, 1968: 31–57.
PROKUPEK, J. (1968) Certification of Suicides in Czechoslovakia. In FARBEROW (Ed.), 1968.
QUINNEY, R. (1970) *The Social Reality of Crime*. Boston: Little Brown Company.
REX, J. A. (1961) *Key Problems in Sociological Theory*. London: Routledge and Kegan Paul.
ROBBINS, E., et al. (1959) The Communication of Suicide Intent A Study of 134 Consecutive cases of Successful Suicides. *American Journal of Psychiatry*. 115: 724–733.
ROSE, A. M. (Ed.). (1962) *Human Behaviour and Social Processes*. London: Routledge and Kegan Paul.
ROST, H. (1927) *Bibliographie des Selbstmords*. Augsburg: Haas and Grabherr.
RUBINGTON, E., WEINBERG, M. S. (Eds.). (1968) *Deviance: The Interactionist Perspective*. London: Collier Macmillan.
RUDFELD, K. (1962) Sprang han eller feldt han. In bidgag til belysning af graenseomradet mellan selvmord og ulikka. *Sociologiske Meddelelser*. 7: 3–24.
RUSHING, W. A. (1968) Individual Behaviour and Suicide. In Gibbs, 1968. 96–121.

RUSHING, W. A. (Ed.). (1969) *Deviant Behaviour and Social Process.* Chicago: Rand McNally.

SACKS, H. (1963) *Sociological Description. Berkeley Journal of Sociology.* 8: 1–16.

SACKS, H. (1966). The Search for Help: No One to Turn To. Unpublished doctoral dissertation, University of California at Berkeley, Department of Sociology.

SACKS, H. (1972(a)) On the Analysability of Stories by Children. In Gumpertz and Hymes (Eds.), 1972: 329–345.

SACKS, H. (1972(b)) An Initial Investigation of the Usability of Conversational Data for Doing Sociology. In Sudnow (Ed.), 1972: 31–74.

SAINSBURY, P. (1955) *Suicide in London.* London: Oxford University Press.

SAINSBURY, P. (1968) Suicide and Depression. *Recent Developments in Affective Disorders: Special Publication No. 2.* London: Royal Medico–Psychological Association.

SAINSBURY, P., BARRACLOUGH, B. M. (1968) Difference between Suicide Rates. *Nature.* 220: 1252.

SAINSBURY, P., BARRACLOUGH, B. M. (1970) National Suicide Statistics. In Fox (Ed.), 1970: 176–179.

SCHEGLOFF, E. (1972) Notes on a Conversational Practice: Formulating Place. In Sudnow (Ed.), 1972: 75–119.

SCHMID, C. F. (1928) *Suicides in Seattle 1914–1925: An Ecological and Behavioristic Study.* Seattle: University of Washington Press.

SCHMID, C. F. (1933) Suicide in Minneapolis, Minnesota: 1928–1932. *American Journal of Sociology.* 34:

SCHUTZ, A. (1968) On Multiple Realities. In Gordon and Gergen, 1968.

SCHUTZ, A. (1962) *Collected Papers I: The Problem of Social Reality* (Edited by M. Natanson). The Hague: Martinus Nijhoff.

SEIDEN, R. H. (1967) Suicide Capital. A Study of the San Francisco Suicide Rate. *Bulletin of Suicidology* (December 1967).

SELVIN, H. (1954) Durkheim's Suicide and Problems of Empirical Research. *American Journal of Sociology.* 63: 607–619.

SELVIN, H. (1957) A Critique of Tests of Significance in Survey Research. *American Sociological Review.* 22: 519–527.

SHARROCK, W. W. (1970) The Problem of Order. In P. Worsley et al. 1970.

SHAW, C. R. (1930) *The Jack Roller.* Chicago: Chicago University Press.

SHNEIDMAN, E. S., FARBEROW, N. L. (1957) Genuine and Simulated Suicide Notes. In Farberow and Shneidman (Eds.) 1957.

SHNEIDMAN, E. S. (Ed.). (1967) *Essays in Self Destruction.* New York: Science House Inc.

SIMPSON, G. (1952) Editor's Introduction. In E. Durkheim, 1952.

SKOLNICK, J. (1966) *Justice without Trial.* New York: John Wiley.

STENGEL, E. (1964) *Suicide and Attempted Suicide.* Harmondsworth, Middlesex: Penguin, 1964.

STENGEL, E., COOK, N. G. (1961) Contrasting Suicide Rates in Industrial Communities. *Journal of Mental Science.* 107: 1011–1019.

STENGEL, E., COOK, N. G., KREEGER, I. S. (1958) *Attempted Suicide: Its Social Significance and Effects.* London: Oxford University Press.

STENGEL, E., FARBEROW, N. L. (1967) Certification of Suicide around the World. In Farberow (Ed.) 1967: 8–15.

STEWART, I. (1960) Suicide: The Influence of Organic Disease. *Lancet*, 1960 (2), p. 919.

STINCHCOMBE, A. (1968) *Constructing Social Theories*. New York: Harcourt, Brace and World.

STOTLAND, E., KOBLER, A. L. (1965) *The Life and Death of a Mental Hospital*. New York: The Free Press.

SUDNOW, D. (1965) Normal Crimes: Sociological Features of the Penal Code in a Public Defender Office. *Social Problems*. 12: 255–276.

SUDNOW, D. (Ed.). (1972) *Studies in Social Interaction*. New York: The Free Press.

TANNENBAUM, F. (1938) *Crime and the Community*. New York: Columbia University Press.

TAPPAN, P. W. (1947) Who is the Criminal? *American Sociological Review*. 12: 96–103.

TAYLOR, I. (1971) Soccer Consciousness and Soccer Hooliganism. In Cohen, S. (Ed.) 1971.

TAYLOR, I., WALTON, P., YOUNG, J. (1973) *The New Criminology: For a Social Theory of Deviance*. London: Routledge and Kegan Paul.

TAYLOR, L. (1971) *Deviance and Society*. London: Nelson.

WALSH, D., McCARTHY, P. D. (1967) Suicide in Dublin's Elderly. *Acta Psychiatrica Scandanavica*. 41: 227–235.

WAYNE, I. (1969) *Suicide Statistics in the United States: An Exploration of Some Factors Affecting the Quality of Data*. Washington, D.C.; Bureau of Social Science Inc.

WEINBERG, M. S. (1968a) Becoming a Nudist. In Rubington and Weinberg (Eds.): 240–251.

WEINBERG, M. S. (1968b) Sexual Modesty and the Nudist Camp. In Rubington and Weinberg (Eds.): 271–9.

WEISS, H. P. (1964) Durkheim, Denmark and Suicide: A Sociological Interpretation of Statistical Data. *Acta Sociologica*. 7: 264–278.

WEST, D. J. (1965) *Murder followed by Suicide*. London: Heineman.

WHYTE, W. F. (1943) *Street Corner Society*. Chicago: Chicago University Press.

WILES, P. Criminal Statistics and Sociological Explanations of Crime. In CARSON, and WILES, 1971: 174–192.

WILKINS, J. (1967) Suicidal Behaviour. *American Sociological Review*. 32: 286–298.

WILKINS, J., GOFFMAN, I. (1966) Accomplishing Suicide. Paper presented at the Annual Meeting of the American Sociological Association, Miami.

WILKINS, L. T. (1964) *Social Policy, Action and Research*. London: Tavistock.

WILLETT, T. C. (1964) *Criminal on the Road*. London: Macmillan.

WINCH, P. (1958) *The Idea of a Social Science*. London: Routledge and Kegan Paul.

WOLFF, K. H. (Ed.). (1960) *Emile Durkheim, 1858–1917*. Columbus, Ohio: Ohio State University Press.

WOLFGANG, M. E. (1969) A Sociological Analysis of Criminal Homicide. In Rushing (Ed.): 233–240.

WORSLEY, P. et al. (1970) *Introducing Sociology*. Harmondsworth, Middlesex: Penguin.

WORSLEY, P. (1974) The State of Theory and the Status of Theory. *Sociology.* 8: 1–17.

YOUNG, J. (1971(a)) *The Drugtakers: The Social Meanings of Drug Use.* London: MacGibbon and Kee.

YOUNG, J. (1971(b)) The Role of the Police as Amplifiers of Deviancy, Negotiators of Reality and Translators of Fantasy. In Cohen (Ed.) 1971: 27–61.

ZILBOORG, G. (1936) Suicide among Civilized and Primitive Races. *American Journal of Psychiatry.* 92: 1347–1369.

ZIMMERMAN, D., POLLNER, M. (1971) The Everyday World as a Phenomenon. In Douglas (Ed.), 1971: 80–103.

Index